With so much love
and faith in
miracles

Judy Skutch

DOUBLE VISION

TAMARA COHEN &
JUDITH SKUTCH

CELESTIALARTS • BERKELEY, CALIFORNIA

Celestial Arts
P.O. Box 7327
Berkeley, CA 94707

First printing, September 1985

Cover and interior design by Ken Scott
Typography by Ann Flanagan
Cover photo by Kathleen Karp

Made in the United States of America

Library of Congress Cataloging in Publication Data
ISBN: 0-89087-411-5

1 2 3 4 5 6 - 88 87 86 85 84

DEDICATION

We lovingly dedicate this book to the one other person
who has equally shared and participated in our lives.
>   the brother,
>   the son,
>   the constant friend,
>   Jonathan David Cohen

To learn that giving and receiving are the same has special usefulness, because it can be tried so easily and seen as true. And when this special case has proved it always works, in every circumstance where it is tried, the thought behind it can be generalized to other areas of doubt and double vision. And from there it will extend and finally arrive at the one Thought which underlies them all.

A Course in Miracles

CONTENTS

A PREFACE PRAYER

There is a parable that impresses us for its wisdom as well as its humor. A pious Jewish man was on his way to worship on the holiest day of the Hebrew calendar. Before he got to synagogue, however, he received word that his wife had suddenly taken ill, and he had to return immediately to his dwelling. Unable to leave his spouse, the religious man began to pray in the privacy of his home. But, when he tried to recite the specific prayers befitting the High Holy Day, the man sadly realized that without the synagogue's prayer book he could not recall the incantations. So, as his wife slept, the old man began to sing the Hebrew alphabet with all of his heart and soul. As the Jewish day of worship drew to a close, he concluded his recital with a prayer: "Dear God, I am a pious man with a piteous memory. I respectfully recite for You all the letters of the alphabet, knowing that You, in Your infinite wisdom, will reassemble the letters into the proper prayers. Amen."

It seems to us that the message of this parable underlies our book. We've recited our recollections with the heartfelt passion of the pious man. We leave it to the reader to "reassemble the letters into the proper prayers." Knowing we have inevitably colored our own perceptions, we invite you to put on your own shades while sharing our double vision. Amen.

TC

TAMARA
COHEN

JS

JUDITH
SKUTCH

1
A LABOR OF LOVE

The delivery-room clock had a single hand, pointed at
twelve. There was a bustle of activity at my feet. Nurses received
my baby and the doctor cut the umbilicus. A short, high wail, then
my new infant was placed on my chest. "Congratulations, Judy,
you made it. It's the witching hour and you have a little witch!"
Suddenly I recalled my obstetrician's lament when I phoned him
much earlier in the evening: "I've had late-night deliveries all
week and I'm exhausted. If you can't produce this baby by midnight, I'm afraid my assistant will have to take over." That was an
admonition I didn't appreciate, but now my irritation was gone.
I had a girl, just what I hoped for as my secondborn. Won't her
father and brother be pleased! A girl, and I must have delivered
on time, because my doctor was there. I glanced once again at the
clock. Two hands were now visible, separated from their praying
position; it was a few seconds after midnight. The witching hour.
And I had a little witch. Little did I know.

A few hours later I was awakened gently from a deep and
forgetful sleep. "Do you want to hold your little girl?" I held out
my arms to my new daughter and the nurse left us alone. I checked
carefully what was *not* there to make certain this was the girl I
longed for. And then I looked down at her, peacefully breathing
by my heart, for the first time.

In that instant I felt a shock of recognition so strong I nearly
dropped my child. It reverberated through my body in jolts and I

trembled violently. Tears poured down my cheeks as I sobbed aloud "Thank God, you're here. At last you're here." I did not know, intellectually, what I meant. I experienced only awareness of profound relief, as if a sigh long held were just released. An unrecognized tension gave way to a mighty joy. I felt propelled into an ecstasy I could not measure, and wave after wave of gratitude engulfed me. "You're finally here," I repeated, as if to a much-missed friend.

How would *you* feel, knowing that the first descriptive term uttered at your delivery into the world was *witch*? Since I was born in 1959 on the stroke of midnight between Groundhog's Day and February third, I prefer to refer to myself as a groundhog. My only comment about the entire event is that it was a good thing I didn't see my shadow and return to the womb or, according to the doctor's threat, he might not have assisted in my post-midnight re-delivery. Although, had I been a Born Again, my mother's experience of my deliverance might've been all the *more* religious.

Suffice it to say, I was only born once, whereupon I was immediately called a witch, and spring came early that year.

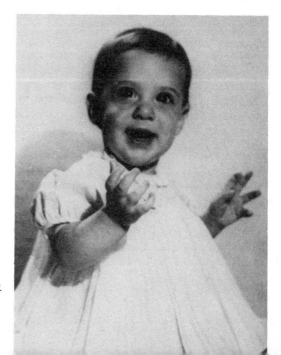

Tammy as infant.

2
LIGHT YEARS AWAY FROM HOME

Js

Judy's childhood home in Brooklyn.

In 1934, three years old, I was sitting next to an open window in our family's house in Brooklyn. Seeing a friend I wanted to greet, I accidentally pushed the screen out of the frame and fell onto the pavement eight feet below. My thought on the way down was "I want to go home!" and when I crashed unhurt that's what I was saying. My mother tried to reassure me that I *was* home. But, although I knew that I was at my *house,* it no longer felt like *home.* The home I was yearning for was one safe from harm. This world couldn't be home, because it was too dangerous.

When I was about six years old and living in that large corner house in an upper-middle-class neighborhood, often instead of practicing the piano I slid between the living room curtain and the window and practiced my secret activity. I waited in happy anticipation until pedestrians passed, and then "zapped" them with fingers of light from my solar plexus. As they walked by I'd get this tickly, tingly, excited feeling in the center of my body, and I would stretch out five finger rays of light and grab the people, holding them in this light of love until they disappeared. As I "touched" them, I felt so much love within me that it seemed as thought I were floating. When the person walked out of my immediate range, I let go my hold and eagerly awaited my next catch. I didn't like people coming in opposite directions, because I'd get all scrambled in finger knots.

Judy's grandmother Anna Solomon.

Judy and mother 1934.

I remember performing this ritual often, as it brought me so much peace. One day, while I was zapping people, the curtain was torn away and my mother cried, "There you are! You're supposed to be practicing the piano! What are you doing?" I was so upset at being found out that I burst into tears. I went back to the piano bench but I never again thought of playing the piano as fun.

I was taught in Hebrew school to kiss my index finger when touching the name of God or the Torah. From doing this, I felt that my finger was sensitized. I remember touching the light switches at night with my "holy" finger in order to alleviate my fear of the dark. I would touch everything that I wanted kept safe with my holy finger. So in retrospect it was natural to use the image of fingers to reach out, hold people with love, and then let them go. But when I was "caught," it felt like my fingers clenched into a fist and tightened my insides. It took me years to re-open that fist and remember what it was that I had so innocently held in the palm of my hand as a child.

There's an old wives' tale that psychic traits skip a generation. In my case, they skipped two. My maternal grandmother, Anna Solomon, with whom we lived throughout my childhood, had a happy habit of knowing things in advance. It was considered a positive personality trait and taken lightly, with humor. "Grandma is just being a witch" her family would observe when she mentioned that an out-of-touch relative was going to call that day. And it would happen. Once I remember her telling us offhandedly that a woman she hadn't seen or heard from in years was going to visit her. No one was surprised when it happened.

A remarkably versatile woman who had been self-liberated years before the women's movement, Grandma was my model. She was able to balance a thriving business with raising a large family. She was available for business advice, counseling and constant nourishing—being, in addition, a superb cook. I don't know what sourced her energy, but she seemed tireless and whirled through all her roles from daybreak until everyone had gone to sleep. Her touch was healing for me through childhood and I was aware that she absolutely adored me. She had been first to hold me at my birth, and she was always first to receive my confidences and hear my problems. The precognitive trait my grandmother exhibited was so much a part of her multi-faceted personality that, throughout my childhood, no one seemed to be amazed. And neither was I.

One night, while sharing a bedroom, she awakened me from a deep sleep with an urgent question. She had dreamt that her lifelong friend Simon was cold and that he had no extra cover on his bed. His window was open and the night had turned chilly. We discussed calling him to tell him to close the window so he wouldn't catch cold. Finally Grandma decided just to nudge him mentally in his sleep. We went back to bed ourselves and forgot the incident. The next evening Simon joined us for dinner. During the main course he casually remarked "Thanks, Annie, for awakening me last night. It got so cold and I wasn't prepared. It was you who made me close the window, wasn't it?"

My home life during those early years was lit by an ever-widening circle of love. Our house was constantly filled with relatives and visitors. Both my father, Samuel Rothstein, and my mother, Bobbie, came from large families and our home was the center of their comings and goings. I was the only child in a houseful of adults until the birth of my sister Carol when I was nine years old. I led the existence of an only child. An only *lonely* child, since I attended an experimental "learning environment for gifted children" in a grade school a long drive from my neighborhood. We were served an enriched educational program that left me feasting on facts but fasting for friends. Immediately after school I was whisked off to Hebrew school four afternoons a week, where I studied until evening, going home again for dinner and homework until bedtime. This schedule, which also included music and dance lessons, plus synagogue on Saturday and Sunday School on Sunday, left no time to develop friendships. *Play* is not a word I remember from my childhood. My father, who had been born in Russia-Poland and emigrated to the United States with his family when he was two, had been raised as an Orthodox Jew and imbued with a reverence for learning. By the time I "met" him he was a practicing attorney and already a lay leader of organized world Jewry. His many organizational commitments kept him busy during office hours and well beyond. I was proud of him, but regretted his absences from home.

Judy's parents Sam and Bobbie Rothstein.

My favorite room was the living room, where people gathered to talk about wonderful things. I could not contribute much, but their enthusiasm was contagious. For me, the room was dominated by bookshelves exhibiting a range of subjects from classical works to modern novels to Hebrew lore and law. My father always caressed his books when he showed them to me. "Books are your friends," he told me, "Treat them gently." It is no wonder that an undersized, somewhat friendless little girl should follow his advice.

At the age of thirteen I had a spontaneous transcendent or mystical experience that touched me so deeply that I incorporated it into the very essence of my awareness of self. Without understanding what the experience meant, because my intellect couldn't cope with the power of it, I knew it was Truth.

The incident occurred when I had dental surgery. Not knowing I was to be given nitrous oxide, I found myself strapped

5

*Judy and younger
sister Carol 1943.*

in a chair with an attendant on either side. When the mask was put over my face I naturally started to fight the sensation of losing consciousness; suddenly I was terribly afraid of losing myself. The emotional pain was intense, and the physical sensation was one of tremendous force, as if a pulling were occurring inside my head. I felt suspended in consciousness along a line of black dots. Somehow, I knew that I had to progress higher and, when the outline of dots surrounded me by becoming a triangle, I knew my consciousness had to be forced through the apex of it. This I equated with death. The internal struggle was immense, but I couldn't fight it. Finally, in one shearing stab of pain, I felt myself catapulted through the barrier of pain and into total peace.

There was no perception, just a feeling of beautiful, distilled, absolute light. I was not a body; I was seeing without eyes. I had an awareness of a total reality that far transcends the senses. An overwhelming feeling of well-being encompassed me, and in that place we call *knowing* I was one with the universe—with all living souls and with God. In this state of knowing, the peace, the joy and fulfillment were beyond belief. I vividly remember the thought "At last I'm home," and when that occurred to me there was an echoing voice from within and all around me saying "Now you know, now you know, now you know." I didn't know *what* I knew, but it seemed I knew All.

After the surgery I tried to tell my mother about this beautiful, incomprehensible awareness of what life really is. She listened with a smile, saying she was pleased that I had had such a nice dream. I recognized then that it would be impossible for me to translate or explain in words the absolute quality of my new knowledge.

Not able to talk about the episode, and having no guidance to search for literature on what I had experienced, I repressed the incident. So successfully did I repress it, that even in college I was not interested in courses that could have helped me to understand the experience. Yet, somewhere deep in my consciousness, I never lost touch with the vague and mystical reality that one's true home is in the realm of total knowledge, and not in the world of form.

My college curriculum was rich in the humanities, and it soon became apparent that what I most loved to do was read. Therefore, I chose English literature as my major and psychology as a minor. I had no sense of career or mission, because I knew I was preparing for motherhood. Although studies came easily to me, I was neither a scholar nor a deep thinker. I quickly realized that my true agenda was *men*. My values at the time were those of my family, and I was in total agreement that I must find a suitable mate. The field was wide open and the sun was always shining as I made hay.

It wasn't until graduation in 1952 that I met the perfect partner. Howard Cohen was a Harvard lawyer possessing a Phi Beta Kappa key, an Editor-of-*Law-Review* standing, and a new corporate job. He was the next-best choice to a doctor, for a Jewish girl from Brooklyn. We were married within weeks of meeting, and moved to New York City. Children were on my mind. The firstborn was to be a son and would be named Jonathan David. He was to be brilliant, handsome—a parent's dream. He appeared on schedule in 1955 exactly as ordered. The following year the three of us sought out the suburbs and settled in Crestwood, an easy commute from New York City. It was time to plan the daughter.

Judy and
Howard Cohen 1952

Jonathan Cohen
1957.

3
FWEND

Looking back, it now seems that my ongoing dialogue with newborn Tammy was strange indeed. From the beginning I talked to Tammy as an equal. My favorite time of day was the four a.m. feeding. I'd automatically awaken seconds before she began to stir, pick her up, settle with a bottle in a comfortable rocking chair, and begin my monologue—all about the day's events and my feelings. My miniature therapist just gurgled and sucked and finally nestled into sleep. The calming influence of her receptivity was very welcome. I knew I was pouring out my soul to a sentient being, albeit an infant.

It should not have been such a surprise when, at the age of two and still trapped in a playpen, my tiny daughter began to answer my thoughts.

I was standing in the kitchen, musing about the imminent return from kindergarten of Jonathan and his best friend. It was my turn to make the children's lunch. Tammy was absorbed in her playpen with her stuffed animals. "I wonder what I should give them to eat," I thought. "Not tuna fish, Mommy, I hates it," came a baby voice from the living room. I whirled around, startled, knowing I had not spoken aloud. "Why did you say that?" I asked her through the open doorway. "I didn't talk to you." "Yes, Mommy, you did. I heard you."

A few days later it happened again, this time with witnesses. I was more relieved that I had not been talking to myself than concerned that my baby girl was responding to my unarticulated thoughts. After all, mothers were supposed to be closely linked to their children, weren't they? So often I'd heard tales of friends "hearing" their baby's cry in the night before it happened. I experienced this enough myself to know it was "natural." But then there were the other things.

One evening after I had put her to bed, I passed Tammy's room and heard her talking to someone. I listened outside, wondering whether her brother had decided to amuse himself by keeping her awake, as he too was supposed to be bedded for the night. I was used to Tammy's nightly song to herself about the day's events; it lulled her to sleep. But this seemed different. There was a dialogue, but with whom?

I opened the door quietly. She was alone, but having a full-fledged conversation to which I could hear no one's response. Yet she cocked her head as if she were listening to a reply.

"Hi, honey. It's late. You should be sleeping. Who are you talking to?"

She jumped as if I'd suddenly interrupted an intense exchange. "Oh, it's you, Mommy. You skeert me. I'm talking to my fwend."

"Oh, do you have a little invisible friend? An elf, perhaps?" I suddenly remembered my younger sister Carol, at the age of five or so, creating an imaginary friend named Elizabeth who was her constant companion and could not be ignored. We had to be very careful where we sat, as invariably she would moan "Look out, you just sat on Elizabeth!"

Now Tammy responded indignantly "No. Mommy, my fwend is *not* an elf, my fwend is much bigger."

"Big as you are?" I joked.

"No, bigger."

"That sounds like a giant. Is your friend a giant?"

"My fwend is so big, my fwend is bigger than this whole world."

"Can I see your friend?"

"No one can *see* my fwend. My fwend is everywhere. But you can talk to my fwend, Mommy, and my fwend always answers. I tell my fwend everything and my fwend tells me what to do."

I was stunned. Speechless. I kissed her goodnight again, and sidled out of the room, closing the door quietly. And that was that.

Tammy's "reals" started to occur at about the time she could speak coherently. She would awaken me in the middle of the night by calling from her bed, sometimes crying as if from a nightmare. She'd describe the dream to me, and when I assured her that it wasn't real, she would insist the situation *had* happened and was a "real."

I quickly found that those times were truly different from the fantasies of sleep, as there often would be repercussions within the next day or two. An example of this genre of precognition, which turned out to be quite precise, occurred when she was barely three. I heard Tammy crying in her room and rushed in to her. She seemed neither sick nor frightened, just kept repeating "Mommy is so sad. Mommy is so sad. The letter makes Mommy cry." I assured her I had no letter making me cry, and that she should forget the dream. I held her awhile and she surrendered to sleep.

The next day we were playing in the living room when the mail was delivered. I thumbed through the letters and removed my personal mail. Opening the first one, I began to read and immediately burst into tears. The letter was deeply disturbing in regard to a personal relationship that had gone sour. I felt desolate. There was a tug at my blue jeans. My small daughter was counseling me not to be sad. "See, Mommy, I told you, you cry at letter. Let me kiss and make you feel better."

Tammy and Jon
in France.

4

WHEN I WAS LITTLER

As I am a mere five-feet nothing. I find it appropriate to refer to my childhood as "when I was littler than I am now." When I was *much* littler than I am now, the world was one big magic show. I can remember feeling that everything was my friend: rocks, people, pillows, toes. Like most children, when I learned to describe things, I was quite graphic. My mother says when I first saw a beach I was overjoyed that it was the biggest sandbox I'd ever seen. When the silvered moon was lying horizontally in the sky, I was excited to see that the sky was "smiling." "Oh Mommy, look, big bubble bath!" was my response to a heavy snowfall. And I particularly remember my family's laughter when I called to them from my first exploration of the ocean "I see a gefilte fish swimming."

I even had a special fondness for my feces, which I liked to liberate from my diapers and artistically display in drawings on the wall—a trick I undoubtedly learned from my brother Jonathan. Although most of these ordinary, early escapades are hearsay to me, some memories of my early toddlerhood (between the years of two and four) remain.

> *I know I'm a little girl. My mommy told me so.*
> *Besides I know I'm a girl cause I don't have a wee-er*
> *like Jon does. One day I got so mad at Jon I bit his*

wee-er. It was the only place I could reach. Daddy got so mad he hit me. Gramma got so mad at Daddy she wanted to hit him. Mommy saved us. Jonny was really mad at me until the next day at school when it made him famous in Show and Tell.

Today I'm in my crib taking my nap. I can't sleep cause Mommy doesn't feel right. She has a big headache. It hurst me when Mommy has a headache. I need out of crib. I can crawl out cause I'm brave. I'm a monkey, my Daddy told me so. Sometimes I jump off the fidgedater into Daddy's arms. Jonny won't do it even though he's bigger than me. He's a chicken. Sometimes I'm a pussycat.

I can hear Mommy downstairs in the kitchen. I gotta get asspain cause her head hurts so I don't nap. I sneak into the bathroom. I'm quiet but I have to smile. I hold my breff. I step on the potty. Now I grab the top of sink and pull me up. I stand on the pink sink and open mirror. I see my bottle of baby asspain. I grab it. I close mirror.

Daddy likes me to put everything back in place. Jonny and I get little sticky stars every night when we do good in the day. I gotta get my cup off sink fore I jump down. My feet get a little wet in sink but I won't catch cold cause I'm wearing feety pajamas. Uh, oh. I jump off sink and lots of water spills. I might not get a little sticky star. I wipe the water with my feety pajamas. I take water and asspain all the way downstairs to Mommy. Boy is she surprised!

"What are you doing out of your crib?"

"Mommy has headache." I hand her the medicine.

"How did you know?"

"I know."

I always know when Mommy has headache. I always know what she's feeling. I know because I know. I made Mommy feel better. Yay for me!

I think Mommy is cuckoo. She asks questions but when I answer them she gets surprised cause she says she didn't ask me anything out loud. She says she was just thinking it. I hear her ask me. Sometimes no one else hears her ask but I always do.

I think maybe I believe Mommy about not asking questions out loud. My best friend Cindy and I got into a big fight. We weren't talking to each other but I was thinking about how I always share everything with her and she doesn't with me. It's not really true but I was

Cindy and Tammy.

mad and I wanted to think it anyways. I didn't tell her but all of a sudden she said "I do too share my things with you." "I didn't say that." "You did too." "I did not!" No one else heard me either. But now sometimes I believe Mommy. She's got a real loud voice when she thinks. I guess I do too sometimes.

Know what? I find things real good. I'm the best finder in the family and everyone knows it. My Daddy once lost a tie pin and everyone but me looked all over for it. Then I went outside and stuck my hand under all those leaves under the car and felt Daddy's tie pin. "Yay, I found it!" Mommy and Daddy asked me how I found it but that's not fair. I found it because Daddy wanted it.

Something very funny strange happened to me. It never happened before. I was playing with my slinky toy and having so much fun that I wrapped it all around my leg. I went in to Mommy. When Mommy asked me what happened I told her that Jonny wrapped it all around me. Mommy went to yell at Jonny but he said he didn't do it and she believed him. She came back to me and asked me again what happened. I finally admitted the truth and she put me in my room and punished me for having blamed Jonny. I was leaning against my door and crying. All of a sudden I knew something. A loud voice way inside me said "I am three years old and this is the first time I ever lied. I have to remember this."

I have always remembered that instant as though it happened this morning. That was the first time in my life I remember feeling conscious of being alive. It was so important for me to know that was the first time I'd ever lied. It was as though I'd taken my initial bite from the apple and I was never to forget it.

Js

Part of me felt peaceful and comfortable with Tammy's apparent abilities. Certainly I was conversant with the idea of extrasensory perception (ESP). There was no doubt that my little girl possessed an unusual attunement to all living things. Her telepathic communiques appeared so natural that I came to think of this ability as an additional personality trait. I was thus not surprised that these abilities also included clairvoyance (distant viewing). One morning I went into her walk-in closet to choose her dress. The position of the closet made it impossible for her to see me from her bed, yet as I reached for a little red frock she complained "Please, not that one, Mommy, I don't like red."

It began to dawn on me that I couldn't put anything over on Tammy, and I would always have to deal with this child in a direct and honest manner. This conclusion was verified as my marriage to her father began to falter and I spent many hours in unhappy reflection on the turn of events. I tried to keep myself busy and cheerful during the day, but at night, when Tammy and Jonathan were asleep, I wept silently into my pillow. Often Tammy would awaken in her room far down the hall and, when I went to comfort her she would tell me that she couldn't sleep because she "heard Mommy crying."

When I was four years old my parents packed up all of their belongings, along with my brother and myself, and moved us to Paris, France. My father was to open the Paris office of his law firm. This was my parents' last attempt at saving their marriage. It was a flop, and eventually their marriage ended in divorce. In any case, my memories of France consist of frequent nose bleeds, nightmares about a French fox chasing me through the streets of Paris, frostbite on ski slopes, trying to communicate with my French nursery-school classmates using sign language, and playing with Yves St. Laurent's cat in the garden of our apartment. These recollections of my year in France are vague and rather distorted. I remember hearing about John Kennedy's death and for the longest time I had the notion that he died in a swimming pool. Just a few years ago I heard a repeat of a newscast saying that President Kennedy died in a pool of blood. Vague memories of France are drowning in my mind. Vivid memories of a move to Brooklyn are swimming to the shore.

Brooklyn. My parent's separation. Living with Grandpa. Grandma, Nana, Mom and me. A strong matriarchy. Losing my first teeth, painting and playing Scrabble with Nana, eating Grandma's cakes, going to synagogue with Grandpa, and going to a Hebrew parochial school from kindergarten through the end of second grade. Having Mom to myself—every child's dream. Jon and Dad were in France for another year without us. The separation that I didn't understand. An abundance of love that I knew. Grandma's house...

I am six years old. I am the littlest girl in my class.
I'm also the youngest. But it doesn't matter because I'm

married. His name is Mark Finkelstein. We had the wedding in Hebrew class.

Mark is a nice little boy. He always gives me his grape juice at lunch. I like him. I like everybody. I have so many people to God Bless at night that it takes me a very long time to get to dream.

I miss Daddy and Jonny but boy, do I love living at Gramma's! I've learned so many things to tell Daddy and Jonny. Like, guess what? I learned to swim! I tried and tried and one day all of a sudden I wasn't drowning anymore. I'm not very good yet but my counselor says that I'm a real tadpole. And I got an all-around camper award because they said I smile a lot.

And I know that there's a tooth fairy because I lost my tooth and didn't tell anyone. I was checking to see if the tooth fairy knew anyway. All night long I had to keep holding my breath and squeezing my hands so I wouldn't tell anyone about my tooth. Anyways, wouldn't you know the next morning I got a quarter under my pillow. That tooth fairy left me money for my teeth and then she wouldn't even take my teeth very far away. I found a little bottle with my teeth in it in Mommy's big dresser drawer. I wonder if maybe one day the tooth fairy will want me to pay her back. I figure that she is saving my teeth for me when I'm old like Nana and need to put them in and out all the time.

I love Nana. Nana is very old. She's Gramma's Mommy. She's Mommy's Grandma. Nana lived with the dinosaurs when she was little. She teaches me all the time how to play with paints and how to make trees. I always paint trees and bunnies. Me and Nana also always play Scrabble together. I always win. I always win everyone in Scrabble because I know how to pick the good letters. Whenever I need a letter I just reach in the box and get it. It's not cheating because I never look at the letter before I take it—I can just tell which letter to pick. I'm good at that. Nana teaches me big words to spell. I know how to spell mishuguna. *Nana says that* mishuguna *means "crazy" in Yiddish.*

Gramma is fat and she makes me laugh. We bake cakes together and we sneak candy and ice cream so Grampa won't yell at Gramma for eating them. One time Gramma and I were sneaking candy and when we heard Grampa coming Gramma hid the sweets in her big bosom. She's funny. She bounces up and down so hard when she laughs that when I'm in bed with her

I have to hold on to something or the bouncing would throw me on the floor.

Gramma has won an award from Weight Watchers for having lost the most collected weight of any of their members. I think in the past bunch of years she's lost over a thousand pounds, cause when she loses twenty she keeps finding thirty more. I think she hides them in the goody cabinet. Her heart is so big that whenever robbers come in and take a whole bunch of stuff from the house, she goes out and replaces everything just so when the robbers return they won't go away empty-handed. They do keep returning. When we have parties, Gramma makes five cakes for fifteen people. Grampa complains.

Lots of times everyone picks on Grampa cause he's fussy. He hardly talks about anything besides Jewish things. After Grampa dies if he could tell us one thing about an afterlife he would only tell us which rabbis he met there. I made him so proud of me when I told him I was called the top Jew in my class. Whenever anyone picks on Grampa I crawl in his lap. Mommy, Gramma and Nana laugh.

Mommy and I love each other more than anything in the whole world. Mommy tells me that it's OK to know what people are thinking even if they don't tell you. We play a game together that always works. It's magic. On special days when I come home from school Mommy takes out the wishing duck. I can wish for anything I want. I close my eyes and put the little plastic duck in my hand and open my other hand for the wish present. One day all I wanted was a piece of bubble gum. I almost never eat gum but that day I wanted a piece to split with my husband. When I came home from school Mommy let me use the wishing duck and—yay!—I got the gum. Mommy says that whenever I wish to share something with someone else it'll come true. Jonny told me that the wishing duck isn't real and that Mommy goes and gets the presents. When I told Mommy that I thought Jonny might be right, the wishing duck game ended. If I got to have one last wish on the duck it would be never to have doubted the magic wishing duck.

Looking back on those years I lived with my grandparents, Grammy says she often felt great sadness for me. She says that I used to come home from school and go upstairs to play for hours all by myself. Although she knew I had several friends at school, she thought of me as a lonely child. The irony of my grandmother's perception is that I remember running home from school and loving to go upstairs and play. I never realized that I was all alone. I used to tell myself funny stories, and I would often sit in front of the mirror, having a running dialogue with myself as a chipmunk, alternating with my "normal" self. More often I would play with and chatter to my "fwend," who was in every object in the room. But most of all, my "fwend" was inside me, and together we made up one big giggle.

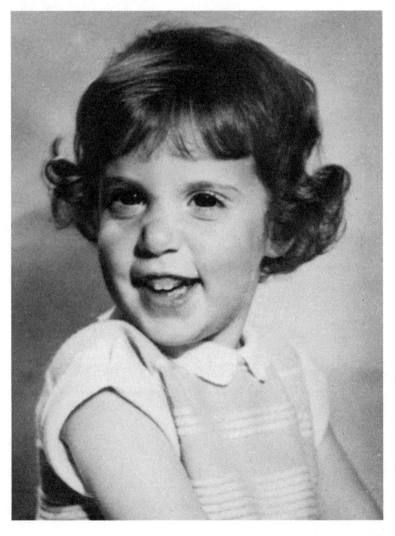

Tammy's big giggle.

Four generations

5

SIMON SAYS

Js

Once again I was sharing a bedroom with my grandmother
in my childhood home in Brooklyn. With no money, no career
training, and two small children, it seemed a womb-like refuge as
I began to reconstruct my life. This particular night, my grandmother had a dream that disturbed her so much she had to awaken
me. He dearest friend Simon was in excellent health in his eighty-
fifth year, but she had envisioned him dead. She told me that in
the dream she saw him walking home from work and falling on
the sidewalk in a backward flip that resulted in a concussion. She
related the story with much agitation. The dream continued with
his admittance to a local hospital, where he died three days later.
The dilemma was whether or not to warn him. We discussed it for
hours and finally decided to ignore the dream. A few days later it
came to pass.

After the funeral, memories of this beloved person crowded
the conversations of my mother and grandmother and I was privileged to come to know, through their recollections, a remarkable
man. At first I was consumed by regret and frustration that I had
never been taken into the confidence of the three of them regarding the secret part of Simon's life. Now I interrogated my mother
and grandmother, begging them to dredge up every detail. I put
the pieces together in a magical mosaic to recreate the combined
version of what they had witnessed. And then I was flooded with

gratitude for the picture they had created, which fit perfectly into the body of literature I had just started studying.

When he was a young man with a very young family, Simon was mysteriously approached by a professional acquaintance and invited to meet a teacher of higher wisdom, a "Master" who, it seems, had singled Simon out through unknown means for his specific training. When introduced to this enlightened being, Simon was shown demonstrations of a startling and mind-boggling variety which challenged every fundamental belief he had in a physical reality. Somehow there was no question in his mind of the veracity of the teacher or the credibility of the other students in the group. Simon joined them in pure faith and with little speculation of what lay ahead. The discipline was rigorous and involved a great deal of time and total commitment. Simon was shown a different world functioning behind the one he thought he knew so well. The curriculum included a set of books he called "The Great Works." They were Eastern in thought, with a metaphysical basis. His training proved to him a universal order in which there is no death, one wherein the human being is engaged through consecutive lives in a process of learning toward higher soul evolution.

After three years of intensive training with his teacher, Simon realized he had to make an unhappy choice. He felt he needed to pursue a financially lucrative career to support his wife and three small children. He announced that he was going to discontinue his studies. His fellow associates and Master were dismayed, as he was coming along so well and much effort had been invested in teaching him. He later said he had always regretted having to stop at that point. I was never able to elicit from either my mother or grandmother exactly what the outcome of this training was supposed to be. My mother guessed that he was to reach a certain level of knowledge and then train others.

Simon's subsequent life became one of marked professional and financial success. He was revered by all who knew him as a sage and generous man who gave to others of himself and his fortune. He was a model to us of perfect philanthropy as he donated anonymously and with heart. There was no request too large or small for him to honor and all who knew him benefited.

Simon told both my mother and grandmother that he had witnessed things they would be unlikely to accept because they had no grounding for such a belief to rest upon. He did claim to have watched the essence of a man leave his body upon physical death, and remarked with great joy what a beautiful and inspiring sight it was. He reminded my mother after the death of his only daughter—her best friend—that the spirit lives on, and showed her through his peaceful acceptance of his deep loss that he truly believed this to be so.

One of the inexplicable processes Simon had been trained to perform was a singular one-mindedness that allowed him to transcend the intellectual barriers of the rational mind. Repeatedly he performed the task for my mother and grandmother that illustrated an uncanny psychic concentration. He would tell my mother to go to her bookcase and choose any book from the shelf. While sitting in another room, unaware of her choice, and armed with a pad and pen, he would have my mother open her book to a page at random and concentrate on the page. He would then write words in vertical columns until he had covered a sheet of paper. He would then call my mother in and compare his writing to the page she had chosen. Much to her astonishment she would find an exact replica. My grandmother said Simon tried in vain to teach the two of them to do this, and finally gave up in frustration when his lessons didn't "take."

My only close contact with Simon as a child occurred when I was barely in my teens and he decided to take me and his grandson to Washington, D.C. He loved our country's capital and showed us the beautiful city for three days with infectious enthusiasm.

Although I had always felt Simon to be a replacement for the grandfather I never knew who had died four years before my birth, I never really appreciated him while alive as intimately as I came to know him through the beautiful stories lovingly told by my mother and grandmother. I felt he had bequeathed me a precious gift for my difficult sojourn in Brooklyn while undergoing a painful divorce. Because of Simon, Tammy's unusual experiences found a perfect breeding ground in the nourishing environment provided in my parent's home, and it became obvious to me that I need explain nothing to my already accepting maternal line.

One afternoon we were visiting our former neighbors in Crestwood. The parents of my children's friends were well aware of the unique connection between our daughters and of Tammy's psychic experiences. I was given a book by the children's father: *Edgar Cayce, The Sleeping Prophet,* by Jess Stearn.

"You might be interested in this," I was told. "It may explain a lot that has been happening to Tammy." With great eagerness I devoured this book, which was to be the trigger for a massive self-study campaign I launched into the subject of ESP. It was wonderful and exhilarating the way volumes seemed to find me! At libraries, in bookstores, through gifts from other interested friends—I was bombarded into psychic literacy. Finally I was finding a niche for my intellectual curiosity about psychic functioning, or *psi*.

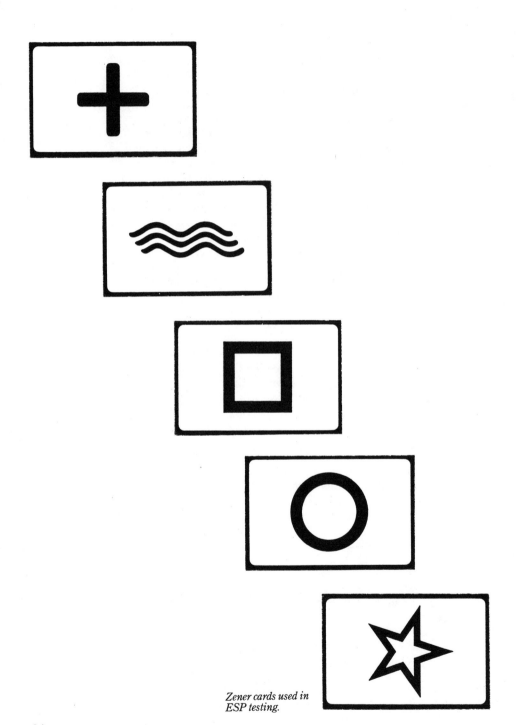

*Zener cards used in
ESP testing.*

6

EYE WITNESS

The last year I lived with my grandparents in Brooklyn I was seven years old. My brother and father had just returned from Paris and my parents were undergoing a bitter divorce. I was extremely well-sheltered from the hostility between my parents, but my brother was caught in the middle of a fight over his custody. It was clear to my parents that I was to remain with my mother, but my father thought it best that he raise Jon. My mother disagreed.

> *I'm seven years old. See? Seven fingers for seven years. I'm still the littlest girl in my class. Everyone always pats me on the head. My hair is very skinny. I like to laugh a lot but not the other night. The other night was very very bad. Jonny and Daddy came back from France. One night everyone got mad. Daddy came here to get Jonny from us but nobody would let him go. We heard Daddy on the staircase yelling. Me, Gramma and Jonny were in Gramma's room. We were hiding Jonny. Gramma leaned on the door so nobody could open it. Jonny was crying very loud. I was crying just as loud cause nobody was fighting over me. Why not? Doesn't anybody want me? Doesn't Daddy love me too?*

My mother and father agreed on joint custody of Jon and me; both parents would share equally in our upbringing. We would have two residences, near enough to be convenient. After the divorce, Jon, Mom and I moved to Manhattan. Shortly thereafter my mother married Bob Skutch, a man I adore. My father insisted my mother take me to a psychiatrist to see how I had been affected by (as he called it) her "ill-fated re-marriage." Apparently I told the doctor I was thrilled about having two new siblings, Bob's daughter and son from a previous marriage, who visited us on alternate weekends. When asked how I felt about Bob, I enthusiastically replied that I loved him because I could crawl on his lap and cuddle with him—something not encouraged by my father. The doctor told my parents I had adjusted just fine.

But there was an adverse outcome. For, in my blossoming relationship with Bob, I distanced my father. I resented him for seeming to care more about my brother, and this feeling of rejection caused me constantly to seek my father's approval, which was often withheld. Despite my mother's continual emphasis on my uniqueness, I never felt I could live up to both parent's awe of my brother's genius. Perhaps this feeling of intellectual inferiority acted as a catalyst to heighten my only substitute for intellect: intuition.

When I was in third grade I began having dreams that came true; sometimes they were situational, but more often they revealed a specific location that I would later happen upon. By fourth grade, due to my extreme shyness, I began to rely on sending classmates telepathic messages to come over and talk with me. My mother taught me that nothing is impossible, so I never knew I was doing something "out of the ordinary." In fact, it came quite naturally out of my desperation for social contact. It wasn't until fifth grade that I became a bit shaken by my own "active imagination."

Mommy and I were in the car and I wanted to know about insurance: "Mommy, if a big truck crashed into us, who would have to pay for the mess?" Mommy said it depended on whose fault it was. "Well, what if a big blue truck driven by a man who didn't speak English hit us and it wasn't our fault, would we have to pay anything?" A few minutes later a big blue truck hit us from behind. The driver was making a right turn from the wrong lane and didn't see our car. BANG! My head crashed against the window. I was crying, but I wasn't really hurt. Neither was Mommy. The driver got out of his truck, speaking Italian. Later, Mommy took me to a neurologist to X-ray my head. I couldn't stop crying. The doctor said that I was fine and asked the reason for my tears. "It was all my fault! I made it happen!" I yelled. Mommy explained to the doctor that we had been talking about the accident before it happened. The next thing I knew, the doctor brought me into his office and blindfolded me. Then he asked me to tell him what card he was looking at. I had my choice of a triangle, a swiggly line, a cross, a circle or a square. He told me that the cards were called Zener cards. After we went through twenty-five of the cards, he did the same thing with colors. Then he told me I had a special talent to sometimes see things before they happen, and that it's OK. He said that I don't make them happen, I just see them first—like seeing a preview to a movie. I love Coming Attractions of movies; sometimes I like them better than the main film. Anyway, this doctor convinced me that it wasn't my fault and I was glad. I didn't want to pay for our car to be repaired!

Mommy got a deck of Zener cards and now I play with them all the time. First I write on a piece of paper the order of shapes in the deck. Then I look at the cards and check my list to see how right I am. Mommy sometimes tests me with the cards, and she says I'm very good at knowing what card she's looking at.

Nana knows how to play psychic games real good too. We always play the game Guess a Color. In this game one   thinks of a color and the other one guesses what color it is. We're really good at it. I think these psychic games are lots of fun.

The neurologist who examined Tammy after the car accident explained to me in private that I had a little girl with a well-developed sixth sense. He told me he had studied medicine at Duke University, where he had been influenced by Dr. J. B. Rhine, who in his early work used statistics to validate psychic phenomena. Since I was already familiar with Doctors Louisa and J. B. Rhine through their books, we launched into the first conversation I ever had with a professional about this subject. The neurologist showed me how to use the Zener Deck and explained the laws of chance regarding card guessing. He encouraged me to explore this with my daughter, while keeping an open and supportive mind. "The more you learn about this very natural function, the better it will be for Tammy,'' he advised. I needed no prompting.

In 1967 New York City was still one of the only meccas for pilgrims on this path. I was introduced to the American Society for Psychical Research (A.S.P.R.) founded by the legendary Dr. William James. I made constant trips to its library and started to meet individuals moving in the same direction. One afternoon, as I was collecting my quota of literature, the librarian whispered with awe, ''Do you know who that is on the other side of the room?'' It was David Kahn, long-time friend and associate of Edgar Cayce. It was Edgar Cayce, the much-researched psychic diagnostician who through his amazing abilities helped so many people, was my ''entry point'' into validating the whole field of psi. I had read everything in print about this famous humanitarian and greatly regretted that he died long before my interest flowered. But here was the person closest to him. I overcame my shyness and introduced myself, expressing sincere interest. He was charming and cooperative, recommending I contact the pioneers of parapsychology. And so I did, joining the Association for Research and Enlightenment (A.R.E.), which is based in Virginia Beach and dedicated to perpetuating Edgar Cayce's legacy.

Edgar Cayce.

The A.R.E. sponsored an excellent lecture series in New York City, and there I met those who were to become my early mentors and close friends. Dr. Lawrence LaShan introduced me to the subject of psychic healing, which he had been researching for years. His stature as a psychologist added a glow of acceptability to the subject and I knew he was someone I could learn from and respect. Dr. Raynor Johnson, an author whose philosophy I had come to admire in his book *The Imprisoned Splendour,* was a physicist from Australia whose credentials were impeccable. His powerful conviction regarding our spiritual reality started to fill the void I had been experiencing.

At the A.S.P.R. I was introduced to Dr. Stanley Krippner and his intriguing work at the Maimonides Hospital Dream Laboratory in Brooklyn. Under the aegis of Dr. Montague Ullman and a staff including Charles Honorton, fascinating investigations in the area of alternate states of consciousness were pursued. Stan Krippner directed a gaggle of bright young people who volunteered their time, both as subjects and assistants. So eager were students to apprentice to the charismatic Stanley, that we dubbed him The Pied Piper of Parapsychology.

Some friends who were attorneys had obtained the patent on a device they called the "sleep machine." Through tiny electrodes an insomniac was administered a very low current of electricity, which seemed to have the effect of a calming soporific. I wondered if my new friend might find this Russian device useful in inducing altered states of consciousness in the Dream Lab at Maimonides, so I phoned Stan and offered to donate one of the machines for investigation. When I arrived at the laboratory with the equipment, Stanley decided to be the first guinea pig. He asked me to hook him up while I explained how the device worked. As he lay on a bed with the electrodes in place on his scalp, I mentioned that during the process some people felt a vague tingling on their heads, often followed by the sensation of flashing lights and colors behind their eyes. Stanley began to murmur "Oh yes, I am starting to feel some slight tingling and now the flashes are beginning to appear. Oh my, what beautiful colors!" I was mortified, but had to interject "Dr. Krippner, I haven't yet plugged in the machine." Without losing face Stanley retorted "Far out! That just goes to show you how suggestible some people are." At that moment I became his number one fan.

Courageous and open-minded, this insightful man represented exactly what I needed for my post-graduate course in the psychology of psi. At his urging I re-entered academia at the New School for Social Research in downtown Manhattan. Teaching a popular course there, Experimental Parapsychology, was Dr. Bob Brier. Never before had I felt such excitement in learning. Disappointed that I couldn't attend the class daily, I compensated by repeating it three times!

Dr. Brier encouraged me to gather data on Tammy's performance in card guessing. Using the Zener Deck, we began to keep records of her guesses. In a deck of twenty-five cards possessing five different symbols, chance was computed at the level of five. Any score consistently above or below five would indicate that something other than chance was at work. Tammy liked to score high. She took great delight in beating her previous record, and when I brought the results of our trials into the classroom for computation, we were continually surprised. The game became a highlight of the day.

One evening as I was dressing to go out, Tammy reminded me I had promised to play the game with her. She fussed and fumed. Finally, in exasperation and with one foot out the door, I got the Zener Deck. The atmosphere was filled with hositility. We went through one trial after another with Tammy missing all her guesses. She had five scores of zero. Realizing what the odds were against that happening, I was virtually speechless. Tammy wore a secret little smile as she snapped "There, Mommy, I knew I couldn't guess anything when I was angry!" Later, when our feelings were healed, I explained to her that she had performed psychically even though she guessed incorrectly. *Psi missing* is also an important indicator of psychic functioning because it is against the laws of chance. Our new game became High-Low, at will.

My husband Bob, a financial advisor at the time, considered himself an agnostic with a mind for numbers. He never asked himself the age-old philosophical questions: "Who am I? Where did I come from? What am I doing here?" It became impossible for him to ignore Tammy's uncanny success with all games of chance. He began his own adventure into reading about psi. During this period he developed an unsightly growth on the outer rim of his ear. A dermatologist who charged a considerable fee for the office visit suggested minor surgery. I had recently read in my Edgar Cayce material of a treatment for this condition (geriatric keritosis). The suggestion, given by Edgar Cayce in a trance, was to apply a dab of camphor oil to the ear at night and a dab of castor oil to the ear in the morning. We decided to experiment before choosing surgery. Bob visited his personal physician, a family friend, and told him what we were about to do. Surprisingly, our doctor did not scoff; he encouraged us, first making measurements of the affected area. At a follow-up visit six weeks later, Bob exhibited an unmarred surface where the keritosis had lived. Our friend advised us to recover our fee from the dermatologist and buy more books about Edgar Cayce! Bob was converted.

The Mulberry Street Fair, a yearly occasion in Little Italy in Manhattan, seemed a good place to take the youngsters. Neither Jon nor Tammy had ever experienced such a rich ethnic mix. They ran from booth to booth, sampling exotic delicacies, and then we handed each a quarter with instructions to choose any game of chance. Jon tried throwing balls at a row of wooden ducks at a penny per shot. He did quite well and won a prize. Tammy slowly checked out the games until she saw a prize she wanted. It was at the roulette wheel, a quarter a spin. Jonathan told her she'd never be able to win at roulette because the odds were greatly against her. Tammy didn't know what odds were— she only knew she wanted the wallet.

The booth had attracted no customers. People knew better. Tammy scarcely could see above the counter where the wheel rested. We watched as she explained to the stout, disinterested woman that she wanted the wallet as her prize. The woman shrugged and told her to pick a number on either red or black. Tammy picked her lucky number, twenty-two, on red. The operator took her quarter and languidly spun the wheel. When it started to slow down Tammy became very excited and her brother muttered to himself "Little Dumbbell." We held our breath. The wheel clicked slowly to a stop. Twenty-two on red. With an incredulous stare the woman handed Tammy the wallet. Jonathan was furious. "Well, now you have nothing to put into it, as you spent your twenty-five cents," was all he could think to say. We continued as a family, walking through the crowd. Suddenly Tammy dove through some legs and came up with a shiny new quarter. "See, Jon, now I do have something to put in my new wallet."

In late 1968 Bob and I had the strong impetus to find a larger residence. Bob's children Laura and Andrew, who were now very much a part of our family, visited us often, and the four active youngsters needed more space. A large, airy, solid apartment building perches on Central Park West at Eighty-first Street overlooking the park (which acts as an enormous backyard for New York City's children) and facing the Museum of Natural History. Since we were beginning to get a premonition of our own history in the making, this welcoming space seemed perfect for family and guests. Already our circle was expanding to include many new, like-minded friends, and they became legion. Eventually our home in the sky was to evolve into a popular salon of the burgeoning consciousness community. I was beginning to be far more involved than I would ever have dreamed.

It was a good thing I was studying parapsychology or I never would have known how to handle the unusual pattern developing in our home. Tammy would rush through the front

Beresford Apartment house in New York City.

The Skutch Family 1968.

31

door with something to tell me about school. On a scale of one to ten I guess her problems were eight or nine to her, but to me they were rather insignificant and all had simple solutions. But, while relaying the day's recent trauma Tammy would become fairly agitated, and the light bulbs would begin to explode. At first it started with a flicker that might indicate a loose connection. I would try to adjust the bulb, to no avail. Then the flicker became a burnout, and as the weeks wore on the shattering began. A nice, gentle progression of poltergeist phenomena! I had read all about these outbursts of pre-adolescent energy. (The theory of the day held that the poltergeist phenomenon might be caused not by a noisy ghost, but by a strong projection of adolescent energy.) We decided to buy bulbs wholesale until the phase was over.

Then Tammy had another trauma. She burst in the door after school one day, tearfully fretting "Oh Mommy, I lost it! I lost my ESP."

"Where did you lose it, darling, in the street, in the sewer?"

"Don't joke Mommy, I tried guessing license plates and it just didn't work."

I knew that guessing the numbers on the plates of cars about to come into view was one of her favorite games with her friends on the walk home from school. She was pretty good at it, and some of her friends were beginning to guess successfully too.

"Did anything happen that made you lose it?"

She proceeded to tell me an incident that transpired at lunch time in the school cafeteria. Tammy was in line with her tray, waiting for the cashier to total her lunch bill. She had chosen a brownie for dessert and another one was stuck to her choice. As she explained it, they were inseparable. The cashier didn't notice and charged her for one. Tammy didn't tell. I thought about this and had to suppress a smile at the solution.

"Do you want your ESP back?"

"Sure. It's fun."

"Well, then, why don't you tell the cashier the truth tomorrow and pay an extra dime for today's mistake," I suggested.

"Oh Mommy, I'd be so embarrassed!"

"Well then, don't."

The next day Tammy strolled in after school. I was busy and had forgotten the incident. Tammy snuggled up and said happily "I got it back today Mom," I had to think a moment before responding.

"What happened?"

"Well, I wasn't going to because I was afraid, but then I remembered it would only take a second, so I told the cashier what I had done and gave her another ten cents for yesterday's extra brownie. You know what she said, Mommy? She said I was such as honest girl I should keep the dime. And I said 'Oh, no, I can't do that!' And I wouldn't take it back. Then on the way home Janet and I played license plates and I got one completely correct!"

The telephone never stopped ringing. The family was aware that not all the calls were for me. A pre-teen girl with an incredible array of friends had begun to monopolize the talking time. In self-defense, we got Tammy her own telephone, with the understanding that any costs over the carrying charge she had to pay. She was already babysitting with children in our apartment building to supplement her allowance. When Bob opened the next phone bill he was sure Ma Bell had made a mistake. Tammy's private number showed an amount due of $86.43. We asked for an explanation. Tammy was appalled by the amount, but it had been her best friend's birthday and the girl now lived in Brussels. Bob wanted to know how soon Tammy could reimburse him. She quickly rose to the challenge, saying that she would win the money that night through a popular call-in radio program in which the first person to name the tune played over the airwaves would receive $100. Always the mathematician, Jonathan tried to compute the odds and discourage his sister. She was not swayed. Shutting herself in her bedroom so she could concentrate, she waited until the program was aired. Bob, Jon, and I tuned in to the station to monitor the experiment. The announcer played many tunes until correct answers were phoned in, and we thought she had missed her chance. But then we all heard the disc jockey taking Tammy's call and acknowledging that she had indeed just named the tune and won a hundred dollars. Jonathan yelled "It's not fair" and slammed his bedroom door. Tammy emerged with a grin and promised to pay her phone bill. I was curious as to what she would do with the surplus. Becoming serious, she explained "I'm gonna give it to charity so someone else can share in my present."

Tammy came home from school with glazed eyes, a bad headache and a scratchy throat. Her temperature registered over 102. When I called the pediatrician, he assured me Tammy's symptoms were consistent with the latest viral epidemic, and recommended aspirin, fluids and bed rest. Tammy began to wail.

"I *must* go to school tomorrow. We're having a history test."

"You can take a makeup test, Tammy. You know that they don't expect you to go to school when you're sick."

"But I want to take the test with my class."

"I'm sorry, but as long as you have a fever, you must stay in bed. Only when your temperature is normal two days in a row can you return to school."

Tammy didn't like that at all. But she was not ready to concede defeat.

"Mommy, if I have no more fever *right now,* may I go to school tomorrow?"

"If you had no fever, you would not be sick now."

"Well, would you take my temperature again?"

I looked at her closely. Her eyes seemed clear. The flush had left her cheeks and her skin felt cool. I shook the thermometer vigorously and popped it back in her mouth. It now read 98.6 degrees. I did it again. Same result. The next day Tammy went to school, took the test, and got an "A."

A week later, during a bedtime discussion, Tammy asked me if I was interested in how she got well so quickly.

"Promise you won't be mad," she pleaded. I promised.

"Well, I was watching *King of Kings* on television before I got sick, so I decided to pray to Jesus."

"Why should I be angry?"

"Because we're Jewish."

"Well, so was he," I reminded her. But I wanted to know more. "What made you think that praying to Jesus would make you better?"

"Because they said he was a healer."

There was nothing more to say.

Everyone else had left for school or office one day after our usual chaotic morning routine. Riding down to the apartment lobby, I felt that I had forgotten something. Reaching the main floor, I pressed the up button to retrace my steps. In my apartment I searched vaguely, walking aimlessly from room to room until I reached the kitchen. Robot-like, I moved toward the refrigerator and, feeling quite foolish, opened it. There on the second shelf was Tammy's forgotten lunch. With relief, I rescued it. On the way to my office I asked the taxi driver to drop me for a moment at Tammy's school. The receptionist smiled.

"Tammy told me to thank you when you brought her lunch,'" she said.

"Mmm, of course," And I was on my way.

Bob and I were traveling through the south of France in the summer of 1969. We had made the mistake of joining another couple on this trip without knowing them too well. In fact, Tammy had warned me about the husband, whom she had dubbed "Fat Frederick." She still had not forgiven him for plopping into her much-prized inflated chair. The sound it made as it was violated was horrendous, and the explosion that followed was devastating. Another reason he was not her favorite person was his attitude about his wealth. He constantly referred to his only child, not by her name, but as "the heiress." We should have known better.

Motoring through the countryside should have been a pleasant experience. The scenery was magnificent and the little out-of-the-way museums tucked into tiny towns made us feel like treasure hunters who had discovered bounty. Fat Frederick complained all the time. He didn't like art, the roads were in bad repair, and he was always hungry. His wife Doris, a meek long-suffering mate, did not quite compensate for his vulgarity. I was beginning to regret the whole vacation when one day I noticed a signpost pointing towards St. Paul de Vence. I had just finished reading the autobiography of Mrs. Eileen Garrett, *Adventures in the Supernatural,* by one of the most respected sensitives in the world. She had become yet another role model for me in my quest for teachers in unchartered territory.

Eileen Garrett.

As actress, business woman, researcher, writer and philanthropist, Mrs. Garrett demonstrated such a zest for living that I knew I had to meet her. In New York City she had established the Parapsychology Foundation, the goal of which was to further scientific research into the paranormal and encourage a forum of like ideas in all disciplines. I had been told that Mrs. Garrett spent part of her time administering the foundation, but most of the time she was living and writing in the south of France. Le Piol in St. Paul de Vence was the setting for yearly conferences sponsored by Mrs. Garrett. "Oh," I mused, "if only I could visit Le Piol and soak up the atmosphere during a great lunch, perhaps the taste of Fat Frederick would be replaced by fine food." For Le Piol, under Mrs. Garrett's ownership, had become a superb restaurant and an inn well worth the trip. But how to convince the others? When I started to reveal my devout interest in psychic phenomena to our traveling companions, Doris was noncommittal but Fat Frederick scoffed. I had to do something quickly, as we were soon to pass the spot. I reached for the *Guide Michelin* and, sure enough, there was Le Piol, and with two stars at that. Fat Frederick was mollified.

We were charmed by Le Piol's ambiance and delighted by its food, and even Fat Frederick had to admit that this sudden flash I had was a boon to his belly. But my appetite was only whetted. To be this close and not get more information about Mrs. Garrett was unthinkable. The manager appeared and, to my inquiry about Mrs. Garrett, informed me that she was an absentee owner as she had been quite ill and was now very old. I wondered out loud where she was living and he pointed down the hill. "She resides there very quietly, Madame, with her companion at 'La Ferme.'" He indicated I should not visit her unannounced. I thanked him and decided to telephone.

This was a once-in-a-lifetime chance and I was going to try for it. Her housekeeper regretted that I could not speak with Mrs. Garrett, who was resting. In fractured French, I explained my mission. My fervor was communicated and it was agreed that I could visit for a very short while. I was ecstatic.

Fat Frederick was computing the bill. He challenged everything and I wanted to vanish. His voice rose decibels higher as he insisted he was being cheated. I suggested that he and Doris relax while Bob and I scooted down the hill to be introduced to Mrs. Garrett. He said nothing doing, he would join us.

At a lovely restored farm house, resplendent with flowers, the four of us were ushered into a lush garden where Eileen Garrett was resting. I quickly introduced us all, hoping that our two friends would be aware of my desire to be alone with the famous woman. After the amenities, Mrs. Garrett gave a chortle of delight and proceeded to address herself to Fat Frederick.

"My goodness," she grinned, "you really are a sly one. You huff and you puff and you make lots of noise, but underneath hides a huge heart. Why don't you let the world see you as you really are? Such a waste my dear, such a waste."

I was so astonished, rage was wiped out of my mind. Just the thought of Fat Frederick having a heart at all was amazing. I continued to listen as Mrs. Garrett gave a full-fledged psychic reading to Fat Frederick the Scoffer. She must have touched upon many deeply repressed memories, for Frederick seemed startled and speechless, but nodded agreement over and over as she spoke. And then it was finished and the queen summoned her subject. "Now come here and kiss me, you wicked big thing." With utter meekness and humility Frederick obeyed.

Mrs. Garrett must have been aware of my disappointment at the time taken away from us. She graciously asked if I had a question for her. I explained my enthusiasm for her work and sketched the reason why I was on this search. She seemed most interested when I mentioned Tammy as the trigger for my studies and wanted to know as much about her as I could tell. We passed another hour in conversation and she had strong advice.

"I want to work with your daughter," she said, "and perhaps I can help her through understanding the mistakes that were made in my early training. I never should have been trained as a trance medium. People just didn't understand things in those days. But now we are so much more scientifically aware. There is much benefit to be derived from a meeting with your little girl."

I asked her what my role would be in all of this and very tersely she commented, "You are to be her mother and nothing more. That is your function." And then she added, "If I were you, I would begin regularly recording in a journal everything of a paranormal nature which occurs in reference to your daughter. Be especially careful to include evidence from witnesses whenever possible. This was never done for me and I much regret it.''

We parted, and I knew I had been given a very special treat. Mrs. Garrett said she planned to try to make another visit to the United States in October and would contact me then. Fat Frederick was very quiet in the car. We all knew he was digesting more than his meal. I suddenly realized I loved him.

October came and I had heard that Mrs. Garrett was indeed anticipated in New York at the Parapsychology Foundation office. I told Tammy about her and she seemed mildly interested. A few weeks later, during our family dinner, a good friend called to tell me she had just read in the evening newspaper that Eileen Garrett had died. I felt cheated, and mentioned this fact at the table. As soon as she heard of the death of Mrs. Garrett, Tammy jumped up from the table and ran crying into her room. I could not believe Mrs. Garrett's death would affect her that much, and went to find out the reason for her sobs. She had locked her door and would not speak. An hour later Tammy emerged dry-eyed and recovered. She said simply, with a smile, "It's OK, Mom. She said she'd be with me anyway."

Dad and Marge—
the odd couple.

7

SIGHT EFFECTS

*Daddy didn't believe in ESP until we played
Scrabble together. I picked all the letters he wanted
from the closed bag without looking. He was so surprised! It was easy for me, cause Nana and I have been
doing it for years. It was so much fun to surprise
Daddy, even if he did have to explain it scientifically.*

*Daddy's remarried now, to Margie. I think Daddy's
a lot happier. Margie has a daughter named Terry and
a son named John. Now we have two Jons in the family,
but Daddy still calls the bathroom "the john."*

*Daddy and Margie are quite the odd couple. Daddy's
a neat fanatic who even uses spot-remover on his blue
jeans. Margie is usually the one who makes the spot
on his jeans. Daddy loves to save money as much as
Margie loves to spend it. Daddy's completely rational
and intellectual, while Margie is intuitive and often
irrational. After Margie took an assertiveness course,
Daddy asked her to pass the salt at dinner. She asserted
herself by refusing! This kind of reaction so dumb-
founds my dad that it overloads his brain, and all that's
left is laughter. I think she's great for him. Daddy has
a bad sinus condition and hates smoke. Margie is a
chain smoker, forced to puff away outside the apart-*

ment near the incinerator. Daddy sleeps with an eye mask and a little whirring device called The White Noise Machine. Margie snores, walks and talks in her sleep. While Margie washes her hair with things such as beer, eggs and mayonnaise, Daddy only washes his hair on Labor Day and Memorial Day—and even then he only uses soap. He insists that the stewing natural oils keep his hair from prematurely balding. Together they make a funny duo.

My father's family began to play a greater influence in my life as I got older. The lessons of pain and love that I learned with them were most important in my dealings with the outside world. I learned how to look past teasing and criticism at my father's house. I vividly remember several times in sixth grade when very reluctantly I went to my father's apartment only to return home in a fit of tears. It was all due to a new game we had to play at my father's called "go around the dinner table and point out the faults of each person."

I didn't want to go, but I went to Daddy's house tonight. I don't feel very comfortable there. His apartment on Fifth Avenue is like a museum. None of us kids are allowed to sit anywhere other than our rooms without permission. And we get fined a nickel if we leave the lights on after we've left a room. I don't mind those things nearly so much as I hate to play that stupid game we always have to play. First Jon is ridiculed for talking a lot and being too serious. Then Margie is ribbed for being so illogical. John is roasted for always breaking things. Terry's laugh is mocked, as well as any new boyfriend that she may have. Then Daddy gets to me. He is always the leader in this game. He starts to mimic me by saying "Oh Daddy, I love you!" He keeps saying this in a high, shrill voice, and then he says that I try to manipulate him by telling him that I love him. I just bite my lip very hard, hold my hands together tightly, and curl up my toes. I pretend to laugh. Daddy says I'm too sensitive. Maybe I am, but I still think he's mean. It's so hard for me to tell him that I love him. I don't know why. Maybe it's because I don't think I really mean it. All I know is he makes me cry. He says this teasing game builds character and makes us stronger. I hate it! I go home with headaches. Mommy makes me feel better; she tells me that Daddy is a good man who loves me very much but doesn't

*know how to show it. She suggests I should look past
these games and see Daddy seeking to love me. I try but
sometimes it's very hard.*

The most interesting part of my entire experience with my
father's game to build character is that it worked. As soon as I
was able to resist being bothered by teasing, I was truly able to
laugh at myself. It forced me to go deep within to experience my
old constant "fwend," my real sense of self, a loving feeling of
security.

Despite my growing ability to laugh at my father's ribbings,
I was developing a reluctance to share personal things with him.
One of the topics I found myself protecting from him was my
psychic experience. An honored teacher has said that there is no
arguing an experience: an experience is an experience. In this
vein, I never felt like putting my own valid experiences on the
battlefield with my father—even if they involved him.

In sixth grade I was going to be vacationing with my father's
side of the family. We were going to Greece and Israel in celebration of my step-grandparents' fiftieth wedding anniversary. A
couple of weeks before we left, I had a disturbing dream. I dreamt
that I saw a group of soldiers presenting someone with a wheelchair. The wheelchair was for a maternal figure but I couldn't
distinguish who she was. I awoke petrified. By this time I had
learned to trust my early morning dreams as "reals." I knew they
were precognitive. I was afraid that perhaps, while I was on vacation with my father, my mother was going to get hurt. She assured
me that she'd take good care of herself. I recorded the dream on
paper. In the event that the dream came true, my mother would
send the record of the experience to Dr. Ian Stevenson at the
University of Virginia, who was collecting data on precognition.
It was all a game to me, except for my momentary apprehension.

By the time I left for the vacation, the dream was out of my
mind. About a week into our trip, my step-grandmother fell ill.
We went to the airport to fly from Greece to Israel. Because of
my step-grandmother's poor health, at the airport a group of
guards brought her a wheelchair and accompanied her onto the
plane. I remembered my dream and was very relieved that it was
nothing more serious. I did not disclose the experience to my
father. After all, what would've been the point?

That same year, I began to engage more than usual in what
I called "message receiving and sending." I had developed a
great technique with my friend Janet. I could consistently pick up
the telephone before it rang, only to find her on the other end.
We thought it was a great trick. And whenever I couldn't reach
my mother, I would send her a mental message to telephone me.

I'd sit alone and form a mental picture of my mother calling me. About three minutes later, the phone would ring. Before waiting to hear who was on the other end, I would say, "Hi, Mom!" Her response grew to be "What do you want?" It became a joke between us and a surprise to anyone newly acquainted with us. There were also times when my mother would think of calling me as I was sending her a mental message, but she would then rationalize that I wouldn't be home yet. It was these times when I fervently reprimanded my mother for letting her logic "go to her head" in the place of her intuition.

Towards the end of sixth grade, my mother's interest in the field of parapsychology became ever   more pronounced. With my consent, she offered me as a subject for testing at the Maimonides Dream Laboratory in Brooklyn. I enjoyed the outings to Brooklyn with my mother, I loved the attention I got from the scientists, and I considered the tests as games.

I've really enjoyed the psychic experiments I played with this year. A nice man named Dr. Stanley Krippner is the head of all the games that I do there. What I'm supposed to do in these tests is to find out what picture is inside a doubly sealed vanilla envelope, without opening the envelope and looking inside. I couldn't even if I wanted to. I'm given one vanilla envelope when I'm in a soundproof room. I get the second envelope when I'm in a room with colored lights flashing at me and different songs playing in each of my ears through a set of headphones. I get a third envelope when I'm sitting with my eyes closed in front of a bright flashing strobe light. Then I'm given a fourth envelope when I'm hooked up to an electric box called the Sleep Machine. The machine is supposed to help me see pictures on my eyelids when my eyes are closed. It makes my eyes tingle a lot. Once the scientists were fiddling with the machine when I was hooked up to it and they accidentally gave me a big shock. They were scared at first, but I was fine.

Each time I have to hold the special envelope and say what pictures I see in my mind. I get to hold the envelope but I'm not allowed to open it. After each envelope I have to fill in a bunch of forms about how I was feeling when I was doing the experiment. Whenever I describe the picture inside the envelope exactly right without having seen it before, everyone gets all excited. Stanley said he is writing about some of my experiments in his next book. I like it when everyone gets excited so I try to be right a lot. I'm not really sure how I do it—I just see the picture in my head. It's really no big deal. I can't understand why everyone makes such a fuss over the whole thing but I feel good when they do.

Mommy says that I'm really psychic but it sounds so dumb to me. I'm not different from anyone else except that I am pretty small. I do like to play these games because they're like Bewitched *on television. It's fun. Everyone can do all these things if they try but first they have to stop making such a fuss over them.*

Lots of times after the experiments in Brooklyn, Mom and I go over to Grandma and Grandpa's house. A funny thing has been happening and I'm not really sure about it. Everyone has always lovingly called Nana a witch cause she's good at psychic games too. But lately it's as though everyone likes to play this game of testing Nana. They often make Nana try to guess the number they're thinking. Of course, Nana can't get it right all the time, and it seems to me they get a little disappointed. So Nana and I have made up this game where they tell me the number, and then I tap her leg under the table the amount of times that the number is. Nana's always been great at math. She can add up twenty numbers in her head faster than most people can do it on paper. But I have to admit that it does get confusing when the number is something like seventeen, because besides losing count of all the leg taps, I'm afraid I'm giving her black-and-blue marks. Especially in these cases, the two of us always end up bursting into giggles when everyone else is surprised by her accuracy. Sometimes I feel a little bit funny about it, but Nana tells me it's all a game, and that's what people who need constant proof are always going to be up against. She said that what's important is that we know what's real for us, and if they want to play with unfair rules, we might as well have fun with the game. But when we play with each other, we are always sincere, and she's my best Scrabble partner because we play with the same advantage, so I don't feel like I'm cheating.

It was not until the end of sixth grade that my first dose of awareness hit me. I previously had not been conscious that any of my 'fun games' or precognitive dreams and telepathy were out of the ordinary until a certain occurrence took place.

Tonight, Bob, Mommy and I were just about to go to see a French movie called Claire's Knee. *Just before we left the house, we got a call from Nana saying that my Uncle Mark (Nana's son) hurt his leg in Brooklyn and had to go to the hospital. Grandma and Grandpa had come in to the city to go to the ballet or opera or something. They couldn't be reached, but Mommy said that it was very important that they know about Uncle Mark and that they get back to Brooklyn immediately. Mommy told me to go into my room and send Grandma a message to call Nana in Brooklyn. So I went into my bathroom and did what I always do to send a message. I came out when I had sent the message. Then we went to the movie.*

At the theatre Mommy called and found that Grandma had called Nana right after I sent the message. Grandma said that she had been waiting in the car while Grandpa went up to his office. All of a sudden she had a strong impression that maybe she should call Nana. So she went to Grandpa's office and called. I was glad that everything was all right, because Mommy stopped worrying and we got to see the movie. But I was more excited that I surprised Mommy and Bob with my comprehension of the French movie. I felt smart and I was proud.

I didn't give the message-sending a second thought; I had to do it, so I did. But what followed later that night was my first inkling that I might be different from my friends and family. My mother often told me stories about people who could see colored fields of energy around living and non-living matter. She called these colors of energy *auras*. I had always wished I could see auras like the unusual people of whom my mother spoke so highly. But I never quite understood what it was that my mother had been telling me about, until . . .

After we got home from the movie tonight, Mommy talked on the phone with Grandma for a long time. I got into my softest nightgown and jumped into bed. I started to sing my song about everything that happened during the day—just like I do every night. I sang for a long time about each part of my day waiting for Mommy to kiss me goodnight. Mommy came in and told me that Uncle Mark was all right. Then she asked me something she never asked me before: "Tammy, how did you send Grandma that message?"

"Just like I always do."

"But how is that?"

"I just do it."

"No. I want you to really think about how you do it, and tell me."

"OK, it's easy. Like tonight you mean?"

"That's fine, what did you do tonight?"

"Well, I looked in the mirror and stared at myself till my eyes got all fuzzy.

"I watched myself disappear. Then when I started seeing colors, I pictured Grandma calling Nana. In my head, I kept repeating the words Grandma call home. *I didn't think of anything else but that. After I said it a few times I blinked and saw myself in the mirror again and that was all."*

Mommy looked at me sort of funny and asked, "What colors did you see?"

"Y' know, all those colors you see around something after you've been staring at it for a long time."

"Do you mean auras?"

"No, not auras—just colors."

"That's what an aura is."

"You mean I can see auras?"

"It seems that way."

"Well can't you? It's so easy."

"No, I don't think I've ever seen auras. I can't even stare at something long enough for it to blur. It hurts my eyes too much."

"Oh."

Something hit me deep inside when I said "Oh." I vividly remember suddenly feeling a little nervous. There was a mysterious sense of being different. All of a sudden I wasn't so sure that I wanted to be like all the "exceptional people" about whom my mother told me stories. I didn't want to be different. I wanted to be just like everybody else.

At that moment a tiny little door closed deep within me and a little laughing person inside me heard a "click" in the depths of my soul. I had locked the door and hidden the key somewhere in my subconscious. It was going to take me a very long time to remember where I had put that key. From that day on, I could no longer see the vivid colors around objects at the blurring of an eye. I developed a new method of sending messages. If I wanted my mother to call, I would close my eyes and clearly image her. I would visualize her picking up a phone and calling me. I would mentally hear the phone ring, and see myself answering it. Behind the visualization, my mind would repeat the mantra "Mom, call home" but I would go through the process for about five minutes. The entire procedure had become more complicated but I was grateful that I no longer saw "unusual" colors.

Years later, when I felt ready to re-open my door to aura sight, I found I had misplaced my own key. It became an arduous effort to blur my eyes to the point when colors subtly crept through my peripheral of vision. Yet, it was as though the colors I later taught myself to see were only the light that filtered through the keyhole of the door I had shut. Locking that door was my first step out of the naivete of my childhood.

8

Mediums Rare

My adored grandmother was dying at the age of ninety.
Trying to cope with my fear of losing her, and wanting to share
something meaningful in her last months, I began to read to her
various books dealing with continuing life experience: *The
Tibetan Book of the Dead,* the Edgar Cayce material, reincarnation
literature, anything I could get my hands on. I asked her whether
she believed that self-awareness might survive physical death and
she answered "I don't know—I never really thought about it
before. But if it's humanly possible to get back, I'll surely get
back to *you!*"

When I told her about a new experiment involving the conscious survival of bodily death that Dr. Ian Stevenson had
devised, she asked to participate in the test. Since Dr. Stevenson
was looking for volunteer subjects, he was delighted.

The test subject was to choose a six-letter word that had
great emotional significance. No one was to be told the word.
The subject translated the word into six numbers through a
simple code: A was 1, B was 2, and so on. This translated number
was then used to set a combination lock. Dr. Stevenson's hypothesis was that a word having a strong emotional meaning to a person could better be "remembered" through the trauma of death
than could plain numbers. He proposed that the family of the subject try to guess the secret combination while the person was still

alive, to eliminate the possibility of telepathy. My grandmother gave us a marvelous time as we played a game of hot or cold guesses about her word. We were often convulsed by giggles as we thought up significant English or Yiddish words she could have chosen, but she said we never even came close! Thus we all spent many loving hours walking with my grandmother towards death.

The newly set lock was mailed to Dr. Stevenson at the University of Virginia. After filing it away, he asked a number of clairvoyants to try to perceive the word—or the numerical combination—while the subject was still alive. They all failed, and the test was put on hold until my grandmother died. Dr. Stevenson's theory was that if the word were not picked up while the subject was alive, but it *was* revealed after death, the chances were greater of its having been transmitted by a consciousness that had survived bodily death.

My grandmother was getting progressively weaker. I felt powerless as I sat by her bedside and watched her drift in and out of a coma. Once, sitting next to her as she slept, I was yearning for her to stay. Suddenly she opened her eyes and asked me "Am I still here?" I assured her she was, but she seemed troubled. "I should have gone long ago," she said. "I keep seeing hands held out to me." I asked her whether she saw particular people in the vision. "No, I only know they are waiting to welcome me."

I began to feel that my selfish desire was holding her back. On my next visit I again sat by her bed with her hand in mine. We were alone in the room and I silently versed a prayer: "All right darling, I let you go in love. Be at peace." The next morning she died.

I called Ian Stevenson in Virginia, and he said the clairvoyants would begin their work immediately.

Two days later I was sorting some of my grandmother's belongings when an extraordinary thing happened. What seemed to be an external voice said authoritatively "Go see Ena Twigg." There was no one in the room, yet the voice was powerfully commanding. I vaguely remembered that Ena Twigg was the medium involved in solving the mystery of Bishop James Pike's disappearance and death in the Israeli desert.

I immediately contacted Dr. Stevenson, who said Mrs. Twigg lived in London and urged me to act upon the command. Since my husband and I had plans to go to Europe a few days later, it was simple to change our itinerary to include London. But first I telephoned Mrs. Twigg.

I did not identify myself by name, merely told her I was calling from the United States and that I would like to have a reading in four days when I arrived in London. Mrs. Twigg was not inclined to cooperate, saying "You Americans are all so impatient. I can't possibly make an appointment on such short notice." I told her we would be arriving Friday and would pray that she'd change her mind. Mrs. Twigg offered no hope of a meeting, but said I could call her from the airport and she would check her schedule.

Mrs. Twigg did see us that Friday, laughingly explaining that "my misty people had given me the dickens for being so impolite on the telephone." Inviting us into her small living room for tea, she asked why we had come. We said we didn't know for sure, but we had been guided to come. "It's no matter," she said. "If something's to come of it, fine. If not, we'll have a nice visit." And for the next half hour we mostly listened to her describe how overwhelmed she'd been with mail and requests since "the Bishop Pike business."

We had finished our tea and did not really know what to do next, when Mrs. Twigg suddenly was startled by the light she saw around the ring my grandmother gave me just before she died. Neither Bob nor I could see the light. But Mrs. Twigg became very excited, and asked me to hand her the ring. As she held it she said "This is from someone recently passed over. Not a mother. Beyond a mother. A grandmother." Thus began a reading that changed both our lives. Mrs. Twigg gave us not only names and facts, but also compelling phrases that painted a perfect picture of my grandmother.

Ian Stevenson had carefully prepared me for a session with a medium. He warned me not to lose my objectivity, and to respond unemotionally to any questions with only a yes or no. Above all, I was not to coach the medium. At first, despite all the facts we were being given, I felt in full control. Bob was managing the tape recorder and seemed somewhat distant from the proceedings. Then the mood began to shift. Ena Twigg reminded me so much of a perky little bird, with her head cocked to one side "listening" to the flow of conversation from the "other side." I felt her attentiveness to be sincere and natural. It was broad daylight. The room was well-lit and comfortable—an ordinary middle-class suburban setting. As I started to relax, and to accept the situation less as a researcher and more as a participant, I began to marvel at the wonder of it all. I heard Ena chattering to what I thought of by now as the spirit of my grandmother. I had stepped into the action.

Suddenly Ena was talking directly to me, relaying what she "heard" from my grandmother. "Your grandmother wants you to know that she told you if it was at all humanly possible she would get back to you. She's laughing now, and she says she may not be human but she's here anyway!" I felt riveted to my seat. "Your grandmother says that she is really glad to have read so many books with you, as they prepared her for this experience. She tells me that it was hard to get ready to leave because she felt the pull of your need so strongly. Until you leaned over her bed and said, 'All right, darling, I let you go in love. Be at peace.' After that it was so easy. It was like a hand withdrawing from a well-fitted glove." I heard myself gasp out loud and realized I had blown my cool. No matter. I had been reached.

After more information recalling shared events and family occasions, Ena Twigg turned to Bob. "They tell me that you have not been practicing your function. You do know you are a natural healer, don't you? Why aren't you acting like one? You must do your work!" I glanced at Bob. I was sure he scarcely understood what that meant and neither did I, but I could see there had been an impact. He too had been reached.

At one point in the middle of a sentence Ena suddenly stopped and with some difficulty tried to say a word. It had nothing to do with anything she had just been saying: "Wuh, wah . . . walker . . . walker . . . your grandmother is saying walker. Does that mean anything to you?" I answered that I wasn't sure, but inside myself I felt a burst of excitement, because I personally had bought her an aluminum walker toward the end of her life since I was keenly aware of her fierce independence and knew the humiliation she felt when she had to ask for help. The mechanical assistance she received from the walker had given her back her dignity, and she had called for the walker by name every time she'd wanted to move. I strongly felt that "walker" could be the word to open the lock. But there was no time to dwell on that, even if it was the reason I had come. So much more was happening.

Ena Twigg.

Now Ena was instructing the two of us. "I am being told to tell you that you are to start a not-for-profit foundation as soon as you get home." I asked "For what purpose?" She shrugged "I don't have the faintest idea, they're not telling *me* to do it." By this time I was well into the dialogue. "Well, ask them for *me* and tell me what they say." Of course I hadn't the slightest idea who the "they" were and I still don't. "They said use it for whatever you choose, and in time you will know what it's for." Bob and I exchanged glances and nodded our assent.

We had been visiting with Ena for more than three hours. I could tell she was tiring, and somehow knew we were coming to the end of the sitting. She indicated my grandmother was beginning to fade and then started to chirp about a man my grandmother was bringing into the session. "Isn't that lovely! She's leading a retiring, elderly man by the hand. She wants him to talk to you. He is bald except for a fringe of white hair all around his head. He's so shy. Wait a minute. He's coming forward." And then a very strange thing happened for which I was totally unprepared. I searched my mind to try to surmise who this could be. Perhaps the grandfather I never knew, who died before I was born. Perhaps an old teacher or a favorite uncle. Ena's face and gestures reflected a dramatic change as she looked piercingly at me. With a deep, gentle, masculine voice filled with love she exclaimed "Went to Washington with you, my dear." I began to sob out loud. So many years had passed since I as a young teenager was taken to our nation's capitol by Simon, my grandmother's closest friend. I had almost forgotten that powerful incident. There could be no better way for this treasured figure to identify himself.

"And now," Ena continued, "your grandmother is bringing you a gift. She's holding in her hands a lovely, simple, golden crown. Do you know what that means?" I assured her I did not. "Well, you are to hold out your hands anyway and receive the gift, as it is a very precious one for you. She says someday you will understand." I did as requested.

So ended an intense encounter which was to have a dramatic effect on our lives. Immediately on our return to New York City, still in the mood of the emotional session with Mrs. Twigg, we started a not-for-profit foundation, though it seemed to make no sense. There were already a number of excellent organizations in the field of parapsychology, yet the urging through Ena Twigg was so insistent, and our driving need for evidence that would lead to an acceptance of the continuum of life was so strong, that we did just that. We named it the Foundation for ParaSensory Investigation.

Of course I had cabled the word *walker* to Dr. Ian Stevenson from London. It didn't open my grandmother's combination lock. I could have been disappointed had I not felt that something so much more important had happened. The transcript of the taped interview with Ena Twigg yielded more verifiable information than I thought possible. Names of relatives I had never heard of checked out with my family's older generation. Still-living great aunts remembered well the Uncle Joseph my grandmother described who visited the United States from Germany when she was a child in the late 1800s. Ena Twigg had even mentioned that he was a diamond cutter. I researched the references as best I could and turned over my findings, along with the transcript, to my teachers, who helped me determine the percentage of accuracy. It was gratifying to learn that the statistics supported the veracity of the experience. I must admit I found many excuses why the lock did not yield to *walker,* the most persuasive being that my grandmother's eyesight was failing and her hands painfully arthritic when she set the lock. She had actually apologized for probably setting it wrong. I could have asked Ian Stevenson to have it opened in a way that would have revealed the combination, but it no longer seemed so important. My personal attitude had shifted from suspended disbelief to complete acceptance of the possibility of life after death. Still the door was not yet closed on my search.

It was midnight and I was reading in bed. Twelve-year-old Tammy, who had been asleep, broke the silence with loud crying, and I rushed into her room to investigate. I held her as she sobbed, waiting for her to calm down. "Mommy, I saw Nana," she wailed.

"But darling, you loved Nana, why is that so terrible?"

"Because she's dead and I saw her for *real*." I thought about this for a moment.

"Well, did she look all right? What was happening in the dream to scare you?"

Tammy was much more relaxed as she answered "Yes, she looked wonderful and we were playing Scrabble and I was winning. And oh, Mommy, she had a message for you. Nana said 'Tell Mommy, Sugar Plum.'"

"That's the name she called me when I was a tiny girl. I haven't heard that in years! Did anyone ever tell you that?"

"I really don't think so, Mommy, but I can't remember."

"No matter, darling, it's enough for me to hear it again. It makes me so happy. But why should this dream upset you so much?"

"Because she's truly dead, Mommy, and I spoke to her and I am *not*. That scares me, and I'm afraid to go to sleep because I don't want it to happen again."

"Since Nana loved you so much, you know she would never do anything to hurt you. Why don't you just ask her to keep invisible and not frighten you again until you are ready to call her back?" Tammy felt this was an excellent solution. And so to bed.

The ensuing year is etched on my mind as The Year of the Mediums. Dr. Stevenson encouraged me to continue to visit sensitives whenever possible. I began to accumulate hundreds of pages of transcripts. Although my introduction to these procedures had been quite an eye-opener, I was able to divorce emotion from many of the sittings. The quality of the sessions was varied, and yet each one produced another piece of the puzzle of survival. At the A.S.P.R. I was told about a woman named Caroline Chapman. The scientist who recommended her described her as the "dean of American mediums." He said he could arrange to have me visit her. She had been involved in some of their research projects and he felt her to be highly accurate. "She's a very old woman now and sees few clients. I will try to book you for an hour at her convenience and will not tell her your identity or your mission. It is very important that we keep all personal information out of this."

I was assigned an appointment three months from that date.

On July 16, 1972 my mother called to report that three paintings created by my grandmother in her artist years had mysteriously fallen to the floor. "Isn't that interesting that it happens to be Grandma's birthday today?" I could hear the smile in her voice We were of like mind. I asked her to check how secure the hangings had been and she reported that there seemed to be no reason why three of my grandmother's paintings had suddenly jumped clear of their positions while many other works of art stayed put. I had no answer, but there certainly was precedent. For about a month after my grandmother's death we had an unusual spate of tempermental technology. Dishwashers, air conditioners and lighting fixtures acted abnormally. We often heard the whirr of a washing machine when no one had turned it on. Light bulbs had shattered spontaneously. The rational part of us called in repairmen. The wondering part greeted Grandma.

My father alerted me that his synagogue was planning the dedication of a commemorative plaque to my grandmother on one of the Jewish holidays. The whole family was to gather there on the morning of October 12 to honor her. Command performance. But that was my long-awaited date with Caroline Chapman. It also happened to be the mutual wedding date of my parents and Bob and me. There was no way that I was going to cancel the hard-to-come-by appointment with the medium even for dedication ceremonies on behalf of my grandmother. My father found it hard to understand the conflict. Periodically I had reminded him that Moses talked to the burning bush, that Joseph had precognitive dreams, and that Ezekiel had seen visions. But this was going too far. I consulted my live-in oracle, Tammy. She was abrupt and precise. "Mother, I'll cover for you at the synagogue with Gramps. I'll sit next to him and read all the prayers with him in Hebrew. He likes that. You go and visit Nana with Caroline Chapman. And maybe Nana can be in two places at once."

Precisely at ten, I appeared at Caroline Chapman's apartment on East 34th Street in New York City. A slim, elegant, gracious Southern lady in her late eighties greeted me and welcomed the unseen (by me) apparition accompanying me. She was quick and to the point. "Oh, I see such a lovely young woman with you. She's so beautiful. She's about eighteen years old. She says you have a picture of her wearing this dress and holding her dance card, which was filled with the names of her beaux. She's really not young, you know, she just wanted you to see her this way now. It was such a lovely age. She's your grandmother." Once again I was dumbfounded. I did have a sepia-toned photograph of my grandmother just as she was described. Mrs. Chapman continued "She's brought along a gentleman who she says is her father. You named your son after him. His name is Johann. He is calling her Anna." Mrs. Chapman pronounced Anna with a distinctive German accent, which impressed me since I knew my grandmother's much-loved father had been Austrian. But this was just the beginning.

"First of all," Mrs. Chapman conveyed, "your grandmother wants you to know that you made the right decision to come here today. She says that she can indeed be in two places at once because time and space are different concepts to her now and she need not obey physical laws." Then she added "And tell Tammy that you know the memorial service is starting later than scheduled. It won't begin until 11:30 a.m." From then on I was as attentive as I had ever been in my life.

Mrs. Chapman, who knew nothing about me in advance, including my name, proceeded to emit a strangling sound from her throat. She clutched her neck as she tried to spit out a word. I wondered if this could be the key to open the lock. Instead all I heard was "J-J-J-Judy...JUDY!" "Your name is Judy," she stuttered. "She wanted to call you that herself. She certainly is a strong personality. I have never done voice mediumship before and it was quite uncomfortable." I assured her she was correct in her appraisal of my dead grandmother's character. "Your grandmother wants me to tell you to say Happy Anniversary to Bobbie and Sam. Aren't they your parents?" I assented. "And oh, dear, how nice! It seems it's yours and Bob's anniversary too. How good to be married on the same date as your parents." There was more powerfully moving communication, yet still no secret word. I remembered thinking "At this point I plain don't care." As if in response to my thought, Caroline Chapman revealed "Your grandmother is getting quite impatient with this year of searching. Don't you know by now that her presence exists and there is no death? She says forget more proof, you have proof enough. On with the work!" I could not dispute that, and I felt the deep relief of closure.

9

THE LIVING END

Every child experiences some form of death. Whether it be that of a bug stepped on or the death of leaves in autumn, a child somehow assimilates death within the framework of life. But it is not until the child recognizes death as a concept in itself that she begins to create her own meaning of life.

When I was three years old I had a pet parakeet named Patty. I spent hours trying to teach Patty how to talk and sing. Coming home from a family trip to Boston, I was not allowed to go to Patty's cage. I can't remember how my mother told me Patty was dead. I just knew that Patty had also gone on a trip, but she wasn't coming back.

When I lived in Brooklyn, my mother bought me a kitten for my sixth birthday. I named her Bitsy. We were inseparable, until Bitsy developed ringworm. One day I returned from school to find Bitsy missing. My mother let me know she had something of great importance to tell me. "Bitsy has gone to the country where she'll be able to run around and play." After a brief pause, my mother drew in a deep breath and contradicted "No, I was going to tell you that, but I have to tell you the truth. Bitsy had to be put to sleep because she was very sick." I cried because I realized I wouldn't see my kitten again. I remember being relieved that Bitsy was put to sleep. "Sleeping is okay," I thought, "at least she isn't dead." For the longest time I thought that Bitsy was going to wake up in the country some day. Despite my mother's disclosure of Bitsy's death, I still manipulated her explanation to fit my own comprehension.

Not until I was seven-and-a-half years old did it occur to me that *I* could die.

My friend Cindy and I had a propensity for getting into mischief. She was chubby, with short, dark, curly hair. I was scrawny, with light, thin, straight hair. The combination of the two of us was chaos.

One average day, Cindy and I decided to surprise her mother and clean out the garage. In doing so, we managed to wedge a metal bucket between the ground and the now-jammed electric garage door.

"Boy, are we ever gonna get it!" We threw down the dustpan and brooms and ran upstairs to the farthest room in the house. We squooshed our two bodies into the big black easy chair in the farthest corner of the farthest room in the house. The chair was equipped with a foot rest and I vividly remember staring down at our Keds sneakers.

"Do ya think our mommies are gonna kill us, Tam?"

"Yep, for sure," I answered as I grabbed Cindy's pudgy hand and affixed it to my scrawny palm. "Know what? I'm gonna leave my favorite red sneakers to Jon."

"I guess I'll leave one of mine to Marty, and the other to Lenny," Cindy replied, referring to her two brothers.

The waiting became unbearable. I absolutely knew that we were going to die and I wanted to get it over with. We sat quietly, listening for our mothers' voices or footsteps. We heard footsteps, then voices. But the sounds were not soft and maternal; they were loud and fraternal. Our ten-year-old brothers ran into the house, slamming the door. There was a stampede up the stairs, passing our room for the bathroom. Suddenly there was a double take, as three heads popped into our doorway.

"What're you girls doin' in here?"

"Waiting to die."

"Huh?"

"Mommy's gonna kill us," said Cindy.

"Great! How come?" asked my brother, eagerly.

We explained our predicament as our brothers fidgeted and laughed.

"Maybe we can fix it," said Marty.

Cindy and I looked at each other in amazement. The thought of being saved had never occurred to us. A miracle might just have entered our lives.

"Could you really?"

"For a small fee," said Jon.

"What?" asked Cindy and I.

"You guys have to be our servants for the day."

"Yeah, yeah," chimed Marty and Lenny.

Cindy and I looked at each other. Our eyes conveyed the same emotion. "Maybe we'd rather die." Our choices weren't so good. If we lived, we knew our brothers would always hold this over our heads and threaten to tell at any moment.

"Okay," I said, "but only if you swear never to tell."

The boys thought it over for a second and swore to us they'd never tell, then ran downstairs to fix the garage door before our mothers found out.

I don't know how they fixed it, but they did. Cindy and I hugged each other because we were going to live. I don't remember being servants for the day to our brothers. I guess we forget the most stressful memories.

That was my first experience with the realization that I could die. I didn't think about what death was, but I knew it was something big and bad that would take me away from my family and cover me with dirt. But for the rest of that day everything seemed a little more special.

My next experience with death was that of my father's father. My relationship with Poppy Lou was never very intimate, but I did love to see him. He'd seat me on his lap and tell me the newest rendition of a story involving a fire and firetrucks. Whenever he got to the part where the firemen were putting out the huge blaze with the powerful hoses, Poppy Lou would pucker his lips in imitation of the fire hoses and spray saliva all over me. We'd burst into hysterical laughter, my grandmother would remark how childish he was, and I'd beg him to tell me the story again. I always thought he looked like a fire hose. He was very thin and bald. When water sprayed from his mouth, I knew that I would call him immediately if ever my house was on fire.

Just before I was eight years old, my father told me that Poppy Lou was very sick. Jon told me that he was going to die. We went to visit him for one last time. He was lying in bed, looking very pale. There was a doctor in the room. My father was holding his hand, telling him that Jon and I had come to visit him. His eyes were glazed and his head was not as shiny as usual. Jon said hello to him and I repeated the greeting in a whisper. His eyes turned to look at Jon and then me. He didn't smile but I knew that he was feeling a smile. I wanted to cheer him up and tell him a fire-hose story. I thought he would like to hear it, but I knew the older relatives in the room would not have liked seeing me spitting all over my dying grandfather. I kept quiet and waited to imitate any of my brother's actions. He took Poppy Lou's hand. I moved next to him and touched my grandfather's thumb. My father signaled to my brother that it was time for us to leave. I went to kiss

Poppy Lou goodbye and felt that his face was pasty.

Soon afterward, I was told that Poppy Lou had gone to heaven. Jon got to miss an afternoon of school when he went to Poppy Lou's funeral. They wouldn't let me go. They said that I was too young. I resented that, and I wanted to miss the afternoon of school. I was told to send Poppy Lou good thoughts. I wondered if he'd have hair in heaven. For the next few weeks, whenever it rained I thought that maybe God had put Poppy Lou in charge of some fire in heaven. That made me happy. I loved Poppy Lou but I didn't miss him.

Montana was our housekeeper before Hattie. Montana used to get drunk a lot. One of the things I remember most about Montana was her attitude about funerals. I always knew when Tana was about to go to a funeral because she'd be in an especially happy mood, humming a certain hymn to herself. One day I asked "Montana, how come you like going to funerals so much? Aren't you sad that someone has died?"

"Are you kiddin', honey? I'd only be sad because I'd miss 'em. They's the lucky ones cause they's going up to heaven. Black funerals ain't like white funerals. We have a party when someone dies. We celebrate and whoop it up real good!"

I knew that Tana was telling me the truth because she always came back from a weekend funeral still drunk on Monday morning, and still merrily singing that hymn. When I was in sixth grade, Montana fell very ill while in our apartment. I was informed there was something wrong with her liver, probably from being an alcoholic. An ambulance came and took Tana. I was told I couldn't visit her because she wouldn't recognize me. I couldn't understand why she wouldn't recognize me when she knew me all my life. Soon she was dead. There was no funeral I wanted to attend more than hers. I wasn't allowed to go because there was going to be an open casket. My mother thought it would be too much for me to handle. The day of her funeral I went into Montana's room and put on one of her wigs. I danced around her room humming as much as I could remember of the hymn she used to sing. I wondered if there was the same heaven for Blacks as there was for Whites, and I wondered whether that same heaven had birds and cats. I thought that one day I would have a great reunion up in the hereafter, and I was looking forward to it.

The funeral of my grandmother's sister, Aunt Charlotte, was the first I ever attended. I didn't know Aunt Charlotte very well because she lived in Florida. Although I saw her only a few times in my life, she was well worth remembering. As did my grandmother and great-grandmother, Aunt Charlotte had a wonderful sense of humor. Like my grandmother, my great-aunt was excessively overweight. Actually Aunt Charlotte took the cake for being one of the fattest women I'd ever seen. Aunt Charlotte died an untimely death. Her funeral was to be in Florida. I asked my mother if I could go along and, since she promised me that I could attend the next family funeral, she did not go back on her word.

My mother and I walked into the funeral parlor to find that Uncle Dave had arranged to leave the casket open. We didn't expect it, as it is not customary in the Jewish faith to display the deceased. My mother told me that it was not necessary for me to look at my aunt's body in the casket. At first, the idea frightened me. But soon curiosity overwhelmed my fear. I took a breath and held it as I sheepishly walked towards the coffin. I allowed the image of Aunt Charlotte's body to creep into the corner of only one of my eyes before I took a full-front, both-eyes view of the corpse.

Once both my eyes focused on the image in front of me, I fearlessly walked as close to the coffin as possible. I studied the body. I looked at the way two red blotches of makeup were smeared on my aunt's cheeks. I noted a hairdo I thought she would not have liked. I wondered if the dress she was wearing was her favorite, or my uncle's. I looked at the polish on her nails, thinking it would have been a good idea to use oil paint rather than nail polish so it would last longer. The more I looked at the body, the more I noticed something was missing. It wasn't that the hair style was different, or that the expression on her face was unusual, or that she was too pale in some places and too red in others. I couldn't put my finger on it, but something was very different about the aunt who lay in that coffin. I quickly glanced around to see if anyone was either looking at me or approaching the casket. The coast was clear. Swiftly, I reached into the coffin and nudged the hand of my aunt. Her skin felt like rubber. I withdrew my hand and heard myself laugh softly. I had found what was missing. It was my Aunt Charlotte.

I didn't feel the death of Aunt Charlotte, perhaps because I had not spent much time with her. But I had a strong sense that her body was just a dwelling for the real person. Her house was still here, lying in a coffin, all three hundred pounds smushed into a tight-fitting box. But Aunt Charlotte was still hanging around somewhere outside that casket and I knew it. I could picture her somewhere, maybe in heaven, playing card games and telling jokes. When my great-uncle grabbed her huge dead body and tried to pull it out of its form-fitting packaging, death suddenly struck me as something too illusory to get upset about.

I began to realize that death was not fearful to me. I feared pain, but I wasn't at all afraid of dying. Although I could comprehend the grief over the death of a loved one, I couldn't understand why anyone would be afraid of her own death. If everything did stop when one died, then what was there to fear? And if things continued in a new and different way, then it seemed like something to look forward to. I was never one to turn my back on a new adventure! But this was one adventure I planned to save for a long time and then treat as a grand finale.

At the end of sixth grade, I noticed that my great-grandmother Nana could hardly get up from her chair anymore. Just before I left to go to summer camp I helped her clean out her desk drawers. As we pulled out every picture, letter and object, Nana told me a story behind each item. A couple of days before I went to camp I had an uncomfortably strange feeling that I didn't like very much. A little voice in the back of my head told me that I wasn't going to be seeing my Nana again. I decided to ignore the voice. And, just to show I didn't believe it, when everyone was in Nana's room watching TV, I watched downstairs by myself. When time came for us to leave, I ran up to give Nana a huge hug and kiss goodbye —for the summer. I assured her I'd help her clean the last desk drawer when I returned from camp.

"If I'm still here!" she chuckled.

I flashed my eyes at her in anger for saying that. "Of course you'll be here," I said in the cheeriest voice I could muster up. But I saw her eyes, and in them I saw that she was feeling what I was feeling, but without sadness. I left her room and began to walk down the flight of steps. I wanted to run back and give her one more hug, but I couldn't. I couldn't attach meaning to what I was feeling. I thought that maybe if I ignored it, then it wouldn't come true.

I called Nana over the summer to wish her a happy ninety-first birthday. On August third, my half-birthday, my mother called. I immediately knew that she wasn't calling to wish me a happy half-birthday. Nana had died. But it didn't seem real. I wasn't depressed and I wasn't happy. I thought I was supposed to cry, but I didn't feel like crying. All day I felt as though she were still with me, holding my hand.

A transformation began to take place, in which all the qualities of my Nana settled within me. I felt her as a much stronger presence dead than alive, and I wasn't sure whether to feel guilty about that. Whenever I needed help in a situation I would call upon Nana, and somehow everything would be resolved. A few months after Nana's death, I found myself confronted by my own belief system about afterlife.

Tonight I had a dream that scared me to death. I dreamt that I was playing Scrabble with Nana. I knew that she was dead, but she was so full of light that she

*radiated life. We were laughing together as we reached
into the Scrabble bag to pick out the letters we wanted.
I spelled the word LOVE to which she jokingly added
an I as a prefix and a U as a suffix, spelling ILOVEU.
I retaliated by suffixing her word with TOO. All was
going well until Nana told me she had a message for
Mom. She withdrew her hand from the Scrabble bag
and laid down the letters SUGARPLUM. Smiling,
she gazed into my eyes and said "Tell your mother,
'Sugarplum.'" The gaze was so intensely loving that
I woke up with a start. Suddenly I found myself afraid
and I began to cry.*

*Mom came running into my room when she heard
cries. When I told her my dream, she excitedly told me
that "Sugarplum" was Nana's pet name for Mom as
a child. Maybe I had known that, somewhere in the
back of my mind, but neither Mom nor I could remember her ever having mentioned it. Then Mom asked me
why I was still crying.*

"Was Nana scary in your dream?"

"No, course she wasn't scary. She was great!"

"Was the dream itself scary?"

"No, it was fun."

"Then why are you so frightened?"

"Because the dream was so real and Nana's dead!"

*"But she didn't want to hurt you. She just wanted to
play with you."*

"I guess it just scared me to see her so real and all."

*"Well, if you're that scared to see her, then ask her
not to visit you again until you're brave enough. I'm
sure she'll understand."*

"Do you think so?"

*"Of course. She'd never want to upset you. She
loves you."*

*I calmed down and said a prayer to Nana. I asked
her to be there for me when I need her, but not to let me
see her for awhile. Part of me feels much better now,
but something still bugs me a little: Why can't I be
consoled like everyone else when I dream about ghosts?
It seems to me that most parents tell their kids that
ghosts are just make-believe. They don't exist. They're
just figments of the imagination. Then the kid gives a
sigh of relief and goes back to sleep. Soon, the child
grows out of being afraid of ghosts. But not me. When
I dream of dead people, Mom consoles me differently.
She doesn't say that there's no such thing as ghosts.*

All she tells me is that they'd never want to hurt me.
How can I relax about that? Ghosts exist, but
they're nice.
     Fine with me, and do whatever you want, but
please don't let me see you. Okay?

Nana's was the first experience I had with death that involved the spirit. I no longer thought of my great-grandmother as having died and gone to heaven. I felt she had a soul that was continuing to live on and was there for me if I needed her. Suddenly I felt that I had a guardian angel. Part of me felt very lucky, in that I was always protected. Another part of me clung to the television for affirmation when "Casper, the Friendly Ghost" came on. All in all, it was becoming increasingly threatening to believe that nothing is impossible.

10

Psi Kicks

J̲S̲

Stanley Krippner called, wanting to know whether Bob and I would host an experiment at our newly purchased weekend house on a lake in Connecticut. It was Christmas 1971 and we realized there was no better way to spend the last week of the year than in pursuing our mutual interest. A group of us met for five days with Larry LeShan to discover if he could teach us clairvoyance. Tammy and Jonathan Cohen and Laura and Andrew Skutch were with their respective other parents and we had a chance to study with a gifted guide. We did indeed achieve some startling results, which taught us all that the human being is capable of extending consciousness beyond the perimeters of the physical body. When Bob asked Larry how this ability could be put to good use (aside from spying), he smiled and explained that this experiment was a part of his investigation of the healing process, in which he was most interested. He had discovered that in all cultures where healing arts were practiced, from Shamanism to faith healing, the individuals involved shift their focus from a physical reality to a nonphysical way of seeing. In this consciously directed state of oneness, remarkable healings seemed to take place. Bob's eyes lit up as he became intrigued with pursuing the study of healing with Larry LeShan. Didn't Ena Twigg indicate that this was what he was supposed to do?

As a follow-up to our session in Connecticut, the group began to meet twice a week at our apartment on Central Park

Dr. Lawrence LeShan.

West to learn various meditative techniques with Dr. LeShan. I was more interested in watching Bob develop these skills than in utilizing them for myself. A gratifying change had come over my husband, and he seemed infused with a new reason for living.

For more than a year Bob studied, enlarging his repertoire of teachers to include some of the most widely known healers in the world. We visited Harry Edwards in England and were awed at the dedicated work done at his large center. In beautiful and peaceful surroundings we witnessed a parade of intelligent people, for whom medical science had no help, seek out Harry Edwards and his caring staff. We visited George Chapman in a remote English village and experienced his trance presence, who claimed to be a well-known deceased surgeon of Scots origin. There were enough medical practitioners utilizing both these men as last resorts for their patients to keep us open-minded and willing to watch.

In trying to recapture one's personal past, there is always the temptation to gloss over major events quickly and get on with the story. Remembering the slow progression of learning that was afforded Bob through so many channels, I find it hard to do justice to the unobtrusive yet powerful plan of the universe. In retrospect the trip from A to Z looks as if Bob took a monumental leap from agnosticism to faith. Yet it was over a period of years that, step by gentle step, the way was prepared for him. Each experience built carefully upon the last; each incident affirmed the rightness of the journey, until Bob found himself sure-footed on the path of healer.

In those early days of practicing the process of attunement to the other person, Bob would often take a seat in our darkened living room and visualize himself in the far part of the room looking back at his body. When he felt he could achieve that state of awareness, he would then meditate upon the names of various people who were ill. He usually had a photograph of the person handy and a description of the ailment. All of them were individuals who had requested this kind of support and were mentally picturing themselves well at the same time. Often there was fine feedback; sometimes there was none. It didn't seem to matter to Bob's effort as he himself felt such a sense of peace and usefulness.

One afternoon I noticed Bob looking into one of our books about Edgar Cayce, which happened to be lying open in our bedroom. He seemed pensive about the part he had just read and mentioned to me "Edgar Cayce says that anyone can do automatic writing. Do you think that means me?" I said I supposed so. Later that evening I watched my husband take a pen and a legal pad into the living room with him. About an hour later he ambled into our bedroom and tossed a page full of meaningless squiggles onto my lap. "Nothing," he remarked. "Nothing at all."

This was the beginning of Bob's persistent, yet relaxed, search for the "inner voice." And it took only a few more evenings of sitting with his yellow pad before he began to "hear." It soon became apparent to me that Bob had a definite knack for listening to the voice within that he began to call his higher self.

Watching the process became for me as powerful an experience as reading the writings themselves. The words that flowed from Bob's pen truly did not reflect either his belief system at the time or his style of writing. There was no doubt in my mind that this man I knew so well had touched a part of himself never before revealed to either of us.

As the writings unfolded, an entire philosophy began to emerge. Each night I looked forward to yet another inspirational insight, and the excitement of every new message was akin to unwrapping a wondrous gift. The early pages were filled with personal advice which could be followed and tested. The results were always positive. Most of all, I noticed evolving a personalized inner-directed "course" for Bob in healing. The material he would write would often give specific directions to be applied with particular people he was to help. One of the earliest recollections I have of this period concerned the son of a friend who had

Bob Skutch
practicing healing.

been severely retarded since birth. He was then twelve years old and attending a special school in Long Island. His parents despaired of his ever learning to be self-sufficient. The reports from his teachers were negative. He was extremely uncooperative. Our friend Connie totally believed that minds were indeed joined. She asked Bob for his meditative support and told her son what Bob would be doing. David seemed interested but the mother wasn't sure he really understood. Three months later Bob was gratified to receive a semblance of a picture of a smiling face with the words underneath "Thanks from David." Connie reported a remarkable shift in her son's attitude as David had opened to learning.

A cousin was grieving about her mother's terminal illness. She was telling Bob that it was painful enough watching her mother die in such discomfort, but what saddened her even more was the fact that she and her mother had never been close. In her words, "We seem more like mortal enemies." We all knew this woman to have led a sheltered and gracious life that her attitude did not reflect. She was complaining and bitter and continually compared herself to those who had even more than she did. My cousin asked Bob if he would sit in quiet near her mother for a while to see if this might bring her mother some peace. Bob replied that he would do so only if the mother would allow him to be there. The mother was suffering too much to resist, and Bob paid the visit. He remarked later that he had for a while forgotten where he was and felt only a state of unity with the dying woman in which the atmosphere was of love and joy. After spending about an hour, he touched her softly and left. A few days later my cousin appeared at our door with wonder in her eyes. She said the doctors were amazed that her mother no longer needed or wanted pain killers and that a personality change had occurred that surprised the whole family. She claimed her mother had made the first real loving gesture towards her she could remember and that the two of them had embraced and wept. The woman did die a few months later but all during this period the metamorphosis continued and those few short months became the happy memories of her family.

A science writer for *Newsweek* magazine, who had been doing investigative reporting on the field of parapsychology became a good friend. Having not seen him in more than a year, I was taken aback when he visited us one morning at what I saw as an unwelcome change. Ordinarily clean-shaven and handsome, he was now growing an unattractive beard which totally hid his face. I dared the negative comment, softened by the observation that I thought him too good-looking to hide underneath all of the scruff. He nodded seriously, saying "I really don't like the beard myself but it is the only way I can cover up what has happened to my face and neck." "What are you talking about?" He explained that he had a severe case of warts which were so unsightly that he grew the disguise. I wondered whether he had tried various alternative practices to remove them, knowing he certainly would have visited numerous dermatologists. He indicated that he had also employed acupuncture, biofeedback, Sufi dancing, macrobiotics, meditation and Yoga. "Oh, but you haven't tried Bob," I said flippantly. He had not known that Bob was practicing faith healing, and asked just when Bob had hung out his shingle. I divulged the whole story, trying to leave out none of the details and laughingly concluded "But, remember, this is off the record. We don't want to see this in print!" He jokingly responded, "Not unless I see proof." We agreed that he would participate in a visualization with Bob that very night. A few mornings later our friend telephoned enthusiastically with the news. "I woke up this morning and couldn't believe my eyes! There were wart tags lying all over the pillow that had fallen off during the night. I shaved off my beard." He was so excited that all I could think of was "Please don't write about it." This was even too much for me.

A few months later our telephone was ringing unceasingly with requests for help in healing. True to his word, our science-reporter friend from *Newsweek* did not write about what happened. What he had done was talk about it in a radio interview. We promptly changed our number.

The deeper we delved into the healing experience the more people we began to meet who made this their life's work. We started to see the need to bring to public awareness the various pockets of research being conducted in medical practices and scientific laboratories. Stanley Krippner had just started experimentation with Kirlian photography, which he had discovered on a trip to Russia. Physicist Dr. William Tiller was doing investigation of the force fields around matter. Oncologist Dr. O. Carl Simonton was exploring the relationship between attitude and cancer. Internist Dr. Norman Shealey was dealing with alternative therapies for pain and the importance of nutrition in healing. Dr. Dolores Krieger, eminent in nursing, was beginning to develop theories about the efficacy of therapeutic touch with the intent to heal. Professor Douglas Dean of the Newark College of Engineering was surveying the field with the hope of identifying and registering authentic healers worldwide. The Reverend Dr. Olga Worrall and Ethel de Loach were volunteering their time to laboratories and universities, studying the healing response. Dr. Joan Halifax was publicizing her doctoral anthropological dissertation on cross-cultural healing practices.

The concept of holistic health was being born and we felt

ourselves right in the middle of it. Our house was filled with bio-feedback equipment, electrical brain analyzers and Kirlian photographic devices. My son Jonathan was scrutinizing most of this equipment and giving us the benefit of his keen discernment. He had designed a darkroom for the proceedings, and also participated in developing protocols for some of the experimentation. We were seething with enthusiasm. Stanley Krippner called together the "First Worldwide Conference on Kirlian Photography, Healing and the Human Aura." Our Foundation for ParaSensory Investigation was the sponsor and the large room at the Engineering Center in New York City could not hold all the attendees. Among the speakers was a brilliant young man who articulated the caution he felt necessary in exploring the "fringes" of science. He brought such a spark of professionalism to the assemblage that I hoped his voice would be well heard. Stan told me that Brendan O'Regan was then directing research for Buckminster Fuller, and I wished we had him on our team. I also had a chance to hear a British physician describe in his lecture his many years' work with the Chinese method of acupuncture and the excellent effects of its use in his practice. This was considerably before James Reston of *The New York Times* had his appendectomy performed in China with this process as the anesthetic.

The success of the first conference generated the second, which was held at Town Hall in New York City, and attracted even more interested folk than the former. As moderator of the day's events, I was acutely aware of the personal relationships developing among all of us participants in an ever-growing support system as we stepped gingerly into advanced thinking. On the large stage of Town Hall I felt great pride as my sixteen-year-old son took the podium to report, with great poise, on the work he had been doing with Kirlian photography. It seemed as if my whole life was beginning to unfold in a rich panoply of people and events. I had no idea where it was all leading. At that point the process was enough. Unbeknownst to me, seated in the audience as a peripheral observer, was a man I was not to meet for another two years. If I had known what a meeting with him would plunge me into, I might have fled the premises. Instead I was bedazzled by the vision of celebrity author Tom Wolfe, resplendent in pure white like a guardian angel, sitting in the auditorium. A harbinger of things to come.

It was obvious that these public forums were filling a need in educating those who were attracted to such ideas. With Stanley Krippner and his bevy of volunteers we planned yet another function. This one was to be even more enterprising than the others and would focus on alternative healing modalities. We would include some of the best faith healers, along with the medical data of their researchers. We would present the work of biologist Sr. Justa Smith, who had demonstrated changes in enzymes in her work with healers. We would invite psychiatrist Dr. Jerome Frank of Johns Hopkins University to talk about his findings with the placebo effect, and ask him to comment on the entire proceedings.

We wanted to attract a well-respected and charismatic moderator for the panel but could not come up with a name. Sometime during the organization of this enterprise I was asked to host a luncheon for a new voyager in our midst. For once Stanley's favorite expression "far out" was the perfect description for our would-be guest of honor, astronaut Captain Edgar D. Mitchell, who had recently walked on the moon during the Apollo 14 Mission. Ed had received notoriety through the newspapers' exploitation of his interest in ESP. On his return flight from the moon he had conducted a series of telepathic experiments with three willing subjects on earth. It had been statistically significant. We were glad to meet Ed and welcome him into the "family."

The instant he arrived I knew I liked him, but I had yet to know him. We lunched along with the other guests and the conversation was stimulating. We exchanged life stories and were glad to feel camaradarie. At one point Ed left the room for a while. Someone leaving wanted to say goodbye and I went to find him, thinking perhaps he was on the telephone. He was not, and I suddenly realized that he had gone to use the bathroom in the far end of our apartment. I usually warned guests that the toilet paper was cleverly camouflaged behind a sliding panel in the wall. Anxiously I summoned Tammy. She usually had some good advice in times of trial, but she just stood there laughing. Finally Ed emerged. Before I could collect my dignity, Tammy blurted out "Mommy thought you were stuck in there because you couldn't find the toilet paper." Aghast, I tried to cover up, but Ed mischievously retorted "Well, young lady, if I could find the moon I could certainly find the toilet paper." I knew *we* had found our moderator.

Astronaut Edgar D. Mitchell 1973.

The conference was called "New Dimensions in Healing." We leased the prestigious Alice Tulley Hall at Lincoln Center to present our speakers for the day. Although we informed many people of the event through direct mail, we could not afford paid advertising in the media. The week before the conference I was very discouraged by a pre-registration figure I felt was much too small. I was worried that the hall would be mostly empty, that the excellent speakers would be dissatisfied, and that I would be terribly embarrassed. Bob handed me the note pad on which he was doing his guided writing the night I was most depressed and I read "Tell Judy that her anxiety is counterproductive to her efforts. Alice Tulley Hall will be filled on Saturday. Every seat will be taken." I grumbled in despair. There were only five days left until the conference, and we had pre-sold only 308 tickets. The auditorium held 1180 seats! I spent the following day just as nervously, and once again Bob took down "Tell Judy that her anxiety is still counterproductive to her efforts. The room will be filled." This was a promise to be taken on faith, and so I tried a lesson in trust. The day before the event, one of our friends, Sally Hammond, who worked for the *New York Post,* telephoned me to tell of her amazement at a "miracle" that had occurred. She had submitted an article as a news item which described the conference in great detail, and her editor had accepted the article and was printing it in that evening's edition. This, she explained, was totally without precedent as articles describing events that were about to take place were never printed because they could be construed as advertising and not news. The shining spring morning of the conference dawned, and we were amazed and heartened to find a seemingly endless line of folk waiting for the box office to open. By 10 a.m. we were sold out, and that enormous hall was filled with a glorious light that cannot be described.

For me, the most important outcome of these endeavors was the relationships they engendered. Many of my new-found friends became as important to me as members of my family, and we grew and learned together. Dr. Edgar Mitchell had decided to found his own institute, one that would be dedicated to introducing the new scientific concepts to the more orthodox existing institutions. He described to me his own profound transformational experience as he looked back at our planet from his space flight and felt the overpowering presence of unity. His ideas touched me philosophically as well as metaphysically and I believed he felt a mission to share this ancient wisdom with the world in his own manner. He invited me to be a founding board member of the group soon to be called the Institute of Noetic Sciences, and eventually based in the San Francisco area. I quickly realized that Bob's and my two-person, non-profit foundation could serve this greater institute by helping funnel funds for research and catalyzing introductions among those with a common interest.

One of the first projects on which we collaborated was the Stanford Research Institute Study of Israeli psychic Uri Geller. Both Ed and I had met Uri through Dr. Andrija Puharich, a physician and inventor who had worked with Eileen Garrett and other sensitives. Dr. Puharich had been stimulated to invite Uri to the United States for research upon seeing him perform on the stage and in nightclubs in Israel. From years of experience working with people who had similar capacities, Andrija was convinced Uri was worth investigating. When we first met Uri he was in his mid-twenties and I was struck immediately by his darkly dynamic visage. His penetrating eyes were very lively in a uniquely handsome face. I sensed a restlessness in him which reminded me of a thoroughbred left too long at the gate. Uri's idiomatic English was flawless and I could see why he would be a major attraction as he performed. In social surroundings his impetuosity was charming, but that did not hold true in the more mundane environment of scientific laboratories. Uri liked action. Constantly. He would have made a superb rock star. He was more than likeable, and our hearts opened to him. We wanted to help. Excitement followed Uri wherever he went. The energy he generated and the tasks he could perform challenged the very essence of one's belief system. After a short while, we had enough "Uri stories" to fill a book. One of our friends was a competent professional magician, and he explained to us many of the means of distraction a magician could use to produce some of the effects created by Uri. We were cautioned to use film and videotape as much as possible, so that we could play back in slow motion and stop-frame action what the eye could not reveal. In designing the experiments we tried to comply with this as much as possible. The Stanford Research Institute investigations of Uri Geller have been described in such complete detail that my recapitulation of the protocols and results is unnecessary. A good description can be found in *Mind Reach* by Harold Puthoff and Russell Targ. Charles Panati, also a physicist, has covered more in the *Geller Papers*. Although I felt the need to be scientifically involved in the validation process of those with paranormal abilities, the outcome of the experiments touched me much less than the personal experiences.

Dr. Andrija Puharich and Uri Geller.

A group of us were trying to raise funds for the series of experiments with Uri Geller at Stanford Research Institute in Menlo Park, California. Dr. Puthoff and Russell Targ had agreed to conduct the work and it was time to sign a contract. One of our group had a beautiful home on the Upper East Side of Manhattan and had agreed to invite some members of the financial community to witness a demonstration of Uri's repertoire. We hoped that the business people would be inspired to donate the needed amount to our Foundation for the investigations. We gathered at my friend's opulent mansion and watched while Uri displayed his telepathic prowess over cocktails. People were entertained by the many direct hits plucked out of their minds by Uri as he correctly guessed names, numbers or cities they were thinking of. Dinner was announced. About twenty of us sat around a large formal dining room table laden with fine china, crystal and heirloom silver. Uri was seated to my right, near the head of the table. On my left sat a prominent banker in the place of honor. There was the buzz of innocuous conversation until the financier addressed Uri in a resonant baritone "Well now, Uri, we've seen some pretty remarkable things this evening and it's all been very interesting. To what do you owe your extraordinary talent?" Uri stopped eating for a moment and quietly replied, "Why it's the power of God, of course." The banker gave a loud laugh and chided, "Come now, my fine fellow. You seem to be a modern Israeli and I doubt whether you are a religious Jew. I have the feeling you've never even been inside a synagogue, isn't that correct?" Uri reacted as if he had been slapped. "One doesn't have to be a religious Jew to believe in the power of God," he said angrily. The guest of honor continued "But what you're telling me is that everything you do comes from God, isn't that so? And it just doesn't seem to ring true in your case," he challenged. Uri took the bait and I watched as he attempted to stifle an emotion akin to rage. He rose fully from his seat, pushed back his chair and with a purposeful stride advanced to the head of the table. "Sir, do you want to see the power of God?" Surprised, the banker stood to face him. "I certainly do," he said. Uri directed him to pick up a heavy sterling silver dinner fork, richly embossed with a family crest. I thought to myself, "Oh, no! Not that beautiful silver." In front of the whole assemblage Uri instructed the doubter to balance the fork loosely between his two raised index fingers. When the banker was gently holding the prongs and the handle so that the fork was horizontally raised about two feet over the table, Uri held his outstretched palm inches above the fork without touching it. He concentrated with all his might until the veins on his neck stood out. Very slowly the bridge of the fork became flexible, then molten, and then it quickly cracked in two and crashed to the plate below.

Everyone gasped. Uri relaxed and faced the astonished banker. "Now you have seen the power of God," he said softly, and returned to his seat. For a few moments no one said a word and then the innocuous conversations resumed. We raised no money there.

For all the times I had been apprehensive about the appropriateness of conducting research with a self-styled psychic showman, this incident laid those doubts to rest. It was not so much the phenomenon we had witnessed, which had inspired my trust; it was rather the transfer of conviction that eased my mind. In that one moment I had viscerally experienced the sincerity of Uri's faith, which kindled my own.

Not everyone reacted to Uri with the same degree of belief. Our group was trying to stimulate interest among a wider body of scientists, so that the investigative program with Uri could be enlarged. Despite the resistance generated at our financial dinner, we were able privately to fund the Stanford Research Institute experiments and channel this into the Institute of Noetic Sciences, which sponsored the program.

On a snowy winter's night twelve of us were seated at our round dining room table on Central Park West. Uri was demonstrating his psychokinetic capacity to a physicist from the Rockefeller Institute in New York. Our latest scientific recruit was also a world-known metallurgist, and had expressed his desire to develop experiments involving metal bars of varying weights and thicknesses. He had already been in touch with other physicists who had observed "the Geller effect" and was curious about their reports of some metals' having changed weight and properties as well as form. More activity than usual occurred and our table was strewn with dismembered cutlery. We had remembered to use only stainless steel for dining, to protect what little we had left of our family silver. At one point the physicist remarked that he noticed the effects had occurred only in Uri's immediate vicinity. Uri explained that he was not able to control the bending and breaking of metal at all times, but that usually he had to have some physical contact with the object in order for it to happen. As he talked, my attention was drawn to the spoon lying next to the physicist's dessert plate. It had started to curl up by itself, eight feet away from Uri, who was seated directly opposite. An involuntary yelp escaped me as I pointed at the physicist's place. He looked down and was totally bewildered. After dinner I questioned our guest as to how he would like to proceed with his investigation of Uri. He looked at me in a straightforward manner and gave his answer. "Now look, Judy, I have had an absolutely delightful evening. I have eaten delicious food, I have enjoyed pleasant company. I have been exposed to a charming and handsome young man full of high spirits with whom I would love to spend a weekend skiing. As two bachelors I know we'd have a marvelous time. But I definitely will not jeopardize my career by bringing him into my laboratory."

"But why?" I wanted to know. "After all, you've seen him perform some of the most astounding physical feats. Don't you want to get to the bottom of this as we do?" He shrugged, "I saw it, but I don't believe it." And that was that.

Meanwhile, Uri was being invited to perform on a plethora of television talk shows. He became newsworthy enough to be discussed in both *Newsweek* and *Time.* Many other periodicals took up the story. The controversy about his genuineness raged; often the scientific evidence was either disbelieved or challenged. Professional magicians began to imitate the effects Uri achieved and, because they had to use distraction in their design, many of them accused Uri as a fraud. When the brouhaha abated, what was left of the tempest were two camps—those who believed and those who didn't. Everyone uncommitted turned attention to other things. For the first time I noticed that whatever people do not understand they find unconvincing. The scientists continued investigating, for the media blitz had flushed out enough good people with strong paranormal abilities to continue the work in quiet. The episodic adventure with Uri Geller had paved the way for a more widespread curiosity about our psychic functioning.

Family portrait.

11
RULES OF THE GAME

With my entrance into junior high school and my thirteenth year of life came a vast array of new emotions and experiences. Coming out of my shell, socially, while creating a shell, privately. Getting at least fifteen phone calls a night while teasing my brother for not having as many friends. Watching myself social-climb as a means of keeping those friends. Learning how to kiss a boy by practicing on my stuffed animals. First boyfriends and first heartbreaks. Watching thirteen-year-old friends lose their virginity and hoping that no one would find mine. Getting my period, thinking I was a "woman," and praying that I'd never grow up. Noticing that I was being noticed. Noticing myself. Feeling so small and unattractive. Hating my outside, loving my inside. Laughing at all sides. Loving all the new games but struggling to find the right set of rules. Confused when thoughts of how I should be conflicted with how I felt comfortable being. All I wanted was to be just like everyone else. Much to my initial frustration, the odds were against me.

Nineteen Seventy-One was a time when all budding New York City private-school teenagers were cynical and had to dislike their parents. For several months of junior high I went along with the pretense that my parents were villains. Then my friends became well-acquainted with my mother and stepfather and I could no longer keep up the tales of their savagery. I found myself the envy of many. There were times I'd come home from school

Tammy at 12—taken by brother Jon.

75

to find one or several of my friends already there, uninvited. My friends would be talking comfortably with Mom or Bob, as though they'd come to see them instead of me. I began to realize it wasn't necessary to *flow* with the crowd in order to *go* with the crowd. And since the crowd was beginning to come to my home, there was nowhere for me to go but "within."

When my mother and Bob established their Foundation for ParaSensory Investigation, my family was sucked into a frenzied whirlwind, never to return to ordinary dinner-table conversations of frog dissections and summer vacations. My mother was transformed from a simple housewife into den mother of an East Coast center for scientists, researchers, psychics and crazies. Along with the psychics came the scientists, skeptically performing tests, and along with the scientists came a number of wealthy people who had donated money to Mom and Bob's research foundation. Not all the psychics were crazy, of course, but most of them were, at the least, eccentric. People who showed up at our place ranged from actor James Earl Jones to astronaut Edgar Mitchell to enlightened guru Swami Baba Muktananda. Dr. Stanley Krippner was there so often we finally christened the back bedroom "Stanley's room." But, of all the transients, one person struck me as an omen of what was potentially in store for me. His name was Uri Geller. As the public eye opened wider on Uri, I honed in on him with my private eye.

Uri Geller with bent silver—from Horizon Magazine.

After watching Uri a lot this year, I believe he's pretty genuine. I've watched him bend silverware deliberately, but it never impressed me nearly so much as when he did it by accident. Like that time when we were eating dinner and all of a sudden Uri's spoon (our family sterling) melted right into the fruit salad! We thought it was pretty funny, but boy, was Uri embarrassed. He must have apologized twenty times throughout the rest of the meal. After he had been with us a few months, much of our sterling and stainless flatware was bent, twisted, broken in half or contorted somehow. No one could bend the stuff with their bare hands, much less make clean breaks in it or have it melt into cold fruit salad. At first it was funny, but after awhile it got to be a pain, having to keep replacing his place setting throughout the meal. On these occasions his usually large ego was instantly humbled, and that's when he impressed me the most. I watched objects occasionally fly across the room when Uri was around. He didn't seem to have any control over these things and they apparently surprised him as much as us. I also watched him perform for guests by bending their keys or rings without touching them, or by sending or receiving messages. Most of the time he seemed to have conscious control of these acts. But throughout it all I noticed that Uri always said there's a power that works through him. He insists it's the power of God, and that he is really not the one doing these things. When I heard people accuse Uri of "cheating," my first reaction was that it was because he said it was something else working through him. I figured it was sort of like me and my math test.

I needed an A in the math test I took in order to get an A in the course for the trimester. The test was difficult. I guess I didn't study hard enough. Luckily there was an extra-credit question. The only problem was that we were learning algebra and the question involved equations that we weren't going to be taught for another year. Even Wiz, the math genius of the class, couldn't figure out the answer. Of course I couldn't do the calculations, but I had to get that A. So I closed my eyes for a few seconds and prayed to Nana. She was always great at math. I figured that since she was dead, she could help me a little.

I pictured my great-grandmother in my mind and I asked her the answer to the extra-credit question. After a few seconds, on my eyelids I saw an equation as though it was written on a blackboard. What could I do but submit the equation as the ánswer to the extra-credit question? I couldn't just ignore it after Nana had gone through all the trouble, could I? So I scribbled down the X's, Y's and squares, mixed them with a few numbers and separated them by an equal sign. Then I handed in the test.

The next day we got our exams back. I was the only person in the entire class who got the extra-credit question correct. There was no grade yet on my test. Instead, there was a note telling me to see the teacher. When I went to Mr. Matthews, he asked me how I possibly could have gotten the answer to the last question without showing any of the work. He couldn't accuse me of cheating because he knew no one else in the class had come up with the correct answer. What could I tell him? That I asked Nana to help me out? I have enough of a feel for math to be able to figure the odds of his believing that. Was it cheating to ask for Nana's help? I couldn't tell him about my technique, so I told the teacher that I guessed the answer. Mr. Matthews was so confused that he gave me the credit and the A.

I couldn't really decide if I had cheated or not, so I carefully looked through the school rule book to see if it was considered cheating to guess on a test. To my knowledge, and to my relief, it wasn't. So I've used the technique on other tests, especially multiple choice. In times of great competition, I find myself using whichever method works best. And I guess that's what Uri does too, but I think I've watched him carry it further.

One day Jon was using Kirlian (high voltage) photography on Uri's fingers. Jon, who is skeptical about anything he can't explain scientifically, experienced sensory overload when Uri bent my brother's heavy silver ring while it was still in Jon's hand. From then on, my brother kept a close eye on Uri. The Kirlian photography session was taking place in the back room that Jon had turned into a dark room. The experiment developed into a test in which Uri was supposed to think of a number or a shape and project that image on onto the film. At one point, Uri was supposed to be projecting a triangle onto the film. Jon said that he noticed a distinctive triangular scratch mark on the film slate. When the picture was developed, sure enough a triangular shape appeared on the film.

The irony of the situation was that, when attempting to scratch the film through the covering slate, Jon said it was highly improbable to produce the image that showed up on the developed film. We tried to produce the same results by scratching the slate as we suspected Uri of doing, but to no avail. So, even though Uri may have attempted to "cheat," it was virtually impossible for him to have done so. What I couldn't understand was why Uri didn't just trust the power that he believed was working through him. No sooner did I ask myself this question than I found myself learning the answer.

This year I had to finish up the series of experiments with Stanley at Maimonides Dream Lab. I wasn't as excited about doing them as I had been in sixth grade, but I only had a couple more rounds to go, so I submitted. One day at the lab I was so tired, I just didn't

*think I was going to be able to get good results for any-
one. I know Mom says it doesn't matter what the results
are, but then why is everyone always so excited when I
get a direct hit, and just "supportive" when I don't?
Anyway, for the first time ever, I felt under pressure to
be "psychic." So when they left me all alone in the
soundproofed room, I took the manila envelope with
the target picture in it, stood on the chair and held the
envelope against the light fixture on the ceiling. The
light wasn't very bright and I had to relax my eye focus
a little, but I started to blurrily make out the picture on
the inside of the envelope. As soon as I saw what it
was, I jumped back into my seat and waited for them
to come get me. My heart was racing and I felt guilty
as hell. I didn't know if I could go through with it, but
I watched myself nonchalantly describing the picture
as though I'd seen it with my inner eye. Of course, it
was considered a direct hit and everyone was thrilled.
Boy, did I feel rotten. But not rotten enough to tell. The
funny thing is that a little later I found out all the
targets were sealed in three different envelopes and
had been tested in front of the highest intensity lights
to make sure you couldn't see through them. So I hadn't
really cheated after all—or maybe I cheated myself. All
I know is that I completely understand Uri now.*

*Kirlian photograph
of Uri Geller's
fingertip.*

79

Many magicians try to discredit Uri. Yet, although several magicians can imitate most of Uri's performances, none of them will accept the challenge to perform with the same accuracy as Uri under the controlled conditions of the scientific laboratory. Still the magicians appear on TV to "expose" Uri. People then doubt the scientists. It's no wonder people are confused as to who to believe. When do you stop doubting, and who's trying to prove what?

Perhaps Uri did sometimes rely on magic tricks when he couldn't always control his powers. I mean, you go ahead and stand in front of a skeptical audience waiting like vultures for you to slip up so they can attack you. Or you appear on the Johnny Carson show with people making jokes about you and the atmosphere skeptical, and see if you can feel comfortable enough to just let whatever happens, happen. I don't say that Uri did use distraction but I don't doubt that at times he didn't. I firmly believe there was something totally inexplicable about many things that occurred when he was around. One of those involved his ability to pick up on other people's absurd thoughts. How could I be skeptical about that, when I can do those things also? That, in fact, was the main problem between Uri and me.

Uri knew how to make himself the center of attention. Everything he did had to be the greatest. And when I, a thirteen-year-old kid, could do some of the things he could do, he didn't seem to like it very much. In fact, there was one night I thought Uri really made a fool of himself.

I was playing with a machine called the Model 100 Aquarian ESP Teaching Machine. It's a machine designed by scientists Hal Puthoff and Russell Targ with David Hurt at Stanford Research Institute. They're friends of Mom's who did a lot of the scientific tests on Uri. The ESP Teaching Machine, as they explain it, is "a feedback system for enhancing ESP ability." In all modes of operation (clairvoyance, precognition, telepathy) the subject has a choice of five pushbuttons. Four of the pushbuttons correspond to the four target photos. The fifth pushbutton is a "pass" switch. This is used when the subject does not have an ESP feeling of the correct target. Pushing the pass button causes the machine to choose another target without changing the number of TRIALS displayed on the front panel. Pushing any of the five buttons causes the target chosen by the machine to light up. If the subject's choice is a correct one, a bell rings and one (1) is added to his HITS score. If any of the four target buttons is pressed, one (1) is added to his TRIALS score. The machine is designed for runs of 25 trials. This machine was my new plaything. Every time I guessed the target that the machine selected, a bell would ring. As a little girl I had been told that every time a bell rings an angel gets his or her wings, so the sound was magical to me, and I tried to make it happen as much as possible.

On this particular night, I was playing with the ESP machine in the kitchen. Mom, as usual, had a whole bunch of people over. Among them were Uri, Dr. Andrija Puharich (the physician who brought Uri to the U.S. for testing) and the inventors of the ESP Teaching Machine, Russell Targ and Hal Putoff. I wasn't paying attention to the guests in the living room because I was having too much fun with the machine. Trying to make the bells ring as much as possible, I got myself in tune with them and began to get hit after hit. With the norm being five hits out of 25, I found myself getting 15 out of 25, then 19, then back to 14, then 20, and finally achieving 24 hits out of 25 trials! I felt like I was giving every angel in heaven a set of wings. My heart was soaring.

The consistent chiming of bells summoned Mom to come and see what all the noise was about. She walked in just as I got the 24/25 score. I smiled and showed her the lit-up sign at the top of the machine that read "Useful in Las Vegas, Psychic Oracle." It was such a joke.

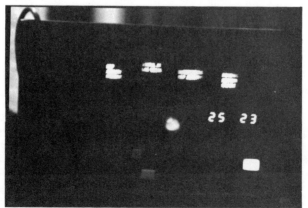

ESP teaching machine—high score.

Mom was excited by my high score. She called Russell and Hal and showed them what I had done. They seemed very excited as well. I shyly backed myself into the corner of the room and wished everyone would go back to the living room. Bob went to get his camera to record my score on the machine. Word was spreading to the other guests and they began to assemble around the machine and make a fuss over the results I'd achieved. Then Uri walked into the kitchen to see what all the commotion was about. My mother pointed out to him what I'd done. I felt myself turning red with embarrassment. Suddenly, like a jealous child, Uri took one look at the machine, shrugged his shoulders, said "Oh, that's nothing" and cancelled my score by pressing the reset button. The machine returned to the 0 HITS, 0 TRIALS reading. Everyone was stunned at his reaction. Part of me was grateful, part of me thought it was hilarious, and part of me knew that, although Uri didn't really mean it, he was right. It was nothing.

Uri Geller served as a mirror for me, reflecting a potential personality type and lifestyle into which I was aware I could develop. Although I grew to care very much for him, I knew I didn't want to emulate either Uri or his lifestyle. Greatly due to this, I developed the propensity for overtly downplaying any of the "psychic" phenomena that managed to occur in my life. Uri showed me that I did not want to be the psychic center of attraction, yet it seemed that the choice was slipping out of my hands.

With Uri's connection to our family, and Mom and Bob's foundation for psychic research, my normal family has attracted some abnormal publicity. For instance, this one guy from New York *magazine came to our apartment asking a bunch of questions about Uri Geller. Mom agreed to be interviewed with the stipulation that I would not be included in the article. But in the published version, the reporter said whatever he wanted anyway. Like he said that I was the president of my seventh-grade class at school. God, we didn't even have a president of the class! Not to mention that he called me "psychic." I was so embarrassed at school after the article came out. You can't imagine the grief I got from my classmates about the presidency bit. I felt so uncomfortable that I just had to laugh it all off in order to deal with it. I was still kind of angry, but not half as angry as Dad was. He wanted to sue the guy. Dad* loves *to sue people—or at least to threaten it. That's why we didn't even tell him about the article in* Horizon *magazine.*

Horizon *magazine did an issue on what was going on in the world of psychic phenomena and research. They decided to include Mom, Bob, Jon and me in the article as a representation of a "psychic family." I thought they made us look like freaks. They took a whole bunch of pictures of us with a wide angle lens. The pictures came out looking like the Alka Seltzer commercials where people look all distorted while they are having a gassy stomach ache. You know, the heads look bigger than the bodies and that sort of thing. I think I minded the pictures more than anyone else in the family. Mom says I'm too critical about these things, but I can't help it if I don't like looking like the Addams Family. I just don't think it's fair of these people to exaggerate the reality of our lives. We're really just a normal family. It's only because we're interested in a new field that people make such a big deal over us. The public will believe anything that's written as long as the information is juicy and gossip-like. If you ask me, I think the public eye is blind.*

Thank God, Mom always refuses the persistent requests of the National Enquirer *and other similar publications. I'm really beginning to hate this whole freak image of the psychic field. Now, because of those stupid articles, people at school are always coming up to me and saying, "You have ESP; read my mind." I can't believe it. That gets me so angry. I can't read anyone's mind like that! Even if I could, who wants to be tested on the spot? Where do people get these ideas? From TV?*

It reminds me of the time some woman tried to sue Uri for her pregnancy. It seems that the woman had her television on as the background to her lovemaking. Apparently, Uri was on the TV, discussing his metal-bending powers with Johnny Carson. Supposedly this woman got pregnant that night because her IUD bent out of shape! People get the strangest notions.

Just as my notoriety at school from the New York *magazine article wore off, a new claim to fame claimed me. A film director, William Friedkin, was making a movie about demonic possession called* The Exorcist. *Friedkin went to Stanley Krippner for background research on psychic phenomena, and asked Stanley if he knew of a young girl who was experienced in this field. Stanley directed him to Mom and me. Mr. Friedken gave me an interview and made me read something. Then he asked Mom if I could be considered to play the part of the possessed girl in his new film. She had the weekend in which to decide.*

Both Mom and Dad read the book over that weekend. They decided that they didn't want their Jewish daughter masturbating with a cross or puking in living color all over the screen. I wasn't sure what was going on, but I trusted my parent's decision. Finally, much to my embarrassment, Mom told Mr. Friedkin that if he ever directs a nice Disney-type film, she'd let me be in it; however, she and my father would not allow me to be in a film about everything negative. I was sort of disappointed that my movie career ended before it started, but I really trust that they know what's right for me. Too bad, though . . . maybe I could've been a movie star. I don't think I want all that attention, but I have to admit it sounds tempting. I doubt the movie will even be popular. No one I knew at school has even heard of The Exorcist. *Who knows what's gonna happen?*

As it happened, *The Exorcist* became a box-office sensation, but I didn't see the movie until four years after it had been released. I must admit that I was at times jealous of actress Linda Blair's instant success. But the jealousy didn't last too long. When the movie was a big hit, some of my friends at school remembered I had been offered a crack at the part. They made a big commotion and, before I knew it, the entire school knew about it. It didn't stop there. Some people from school went to my summer camp, and the entire camp learned about my "almost" fame. For years after that, until I left high school, people I'd never met would ask me if the rumor they'd heard about me and *The Exorcist* was true. I began to see how media-crazed people are. For God's sake, I wasn't even in the film, and there were people treating me no differently than if I had been the star. People will do anything to make themselves feel important. In this case they went so far as to pretend they saw a celebrity by fantasizing me into one.

More and more, I found that I wanted no part of fame, recognition or the word *psychic*—for it also had gotten too much bad publicity.

My outside world was turning into a psychic whirlwind, and psychic forces were at work on my body's entrance into puberty. I began to feel myself caving in. One particular day it came time to push the outside world out.

I was walking down the street to school. My head felt light and very receptive. I was thinking about my social life at school. but every time I passed someone, unfamiliar thoughts crept into my head. These thoughts ranged from "I hope Harry isn't mad at me for being late" and "When is that damned bus gonna come?" to "I wonder if Fran has time for lunch today." I wasn't unused to picking up other people's thoughts, but that particular day I felt they were beginning to clutter my brain. Suddenly, deep inside me, I was fed up. With a tremendous sense of rage, I yelled inside my own head something to the effect of "I don't know Harry, I'm not waiting for a bus, and who the hell is Fran? Everybody GET OUT! NOW!" My soul screamed this last order with such conviction that I felt a physical shift occur in my body. My solar plexis tightened, my mind slammed a door shut, and my insides felt as though they were collectively holding their breath.

From that day on I kept the world outside me. The only repercussion was that I also kept some of myself out. For the next several years, I had an illness of the digestive system in which every five weeks or so I would throw up for ten consecutive hours. Doctors had no clue as to what ailed me or how to cure me, and my father thought I was repressing my sexuality. Unfortunately, that was indeed part of the energy I pushed away, in confusing it with all else that seemed to be invading me at the time. Part of me began to fear growing up, as it meant I would have to re-open this self-imposed block. I yearned to remain a child without the consciousness of what the psychic implied. I cleverly shoved my blocking process into my unconscious.

Yet amidst all that learning of what I didn't want to be, there was one instance that showed me what was truly sacred to me.

At thirteen years old, it came time for me to be initiated into the Jewish religion. It was time for my grandfather to glow with pride for me. It was time for me to sing a passage from the Torah. It was time for me to be Bat Mitzvah'ed.

During my portion of the service, which included my singing of the Haftorah and my speech about what Judaism meant to me, my emotions were pure and my words came from a place deep within me. I spoke about my love for the temple in which I stood; the same temple my great-grandfather helped to build; the very temple my grandfather founded, and where he held the position of president; the temple in which my grandparents' marriage was its first wedding; the temple in which my mother was confirmed; the temple in which a new Torah was donated on behalf of my brother's Bar Mitvah; the temple where my great-grandmother taught and I had learned. How could I feel anything but the purest love, standing on the pulpit where I'd seen my grandfather sit through so many years of holidays? I felt a sense of history, roots. I felt strongly grounded. I felt strongly. I felt strong.

I was aware of the presence of all my relatives, alive and deceased, in that room with me at that moment. The stained-glass windows, the Jewish stars, the altar with the glowing red lights, the candles, the menorahs, the smell of flowers, and the huge crowd of people, all of whom loved me; all that gave me a sense of power that was worlds different from anything I'd ever felt on my climb up the social ladder. I felt an overpowering sense of love. I felt my great-grandmother holding my hand as the rabbi delivered his long-winded, complimentary speech towards me. I felt like a high priestess. I didn't even feel my body. I was so filled with Eternal Love that that Love was all I was. I didn't hear a word of the rabbi's speech. The moment was holy. I wasn't confused. I felt more whole than I'd every consciously felt before. I sang my Haftorah in a voice I didn't recognize; it was crystal clear. I stunned my family, who always teased me about my poor singing voice. I never sang like I did that night. My grandparents cried. My parents cried. My step-parents cried. I glowed. The benediction was delivered. I looked up. It was over. People were stirring. I found my hand reaching out to touch a procession of hands. And with each handshake I was brought back to a connection of love firmly established throughout points of my life leading up to this day.

Gradually I returned to my senses, as my cheeks became blotters for many lips and the scent from their mouths perfumed my neck. Suddenly, it all came back. I was "me" again. I was socially conscious and I was snobby. I re-entered my role as a pampered Jewish princess. But part of me never forgot that place where I was that night—not just with my family, not just in Brooklyn, not just in that temple, but in that place so deep inside me that it evanesced throughout me—it was there that I knew the real me was centered, my real home. And it was only when I was at that place, that I would feel completely comfortable with being the center.

Tammy's Bat Mitzvah

12

THEM THAT CAN'T

Js

Mary Jane called one day to ask for my help with her pet project. She was librarian at an alternative school for high-school dropouts in Westchester County, and many of her students had been expelled from the public schools because of drug use. Volunteers were attempting to interest these bright young people in continuing their education by offering some nontraditional courses. Mary Jane felt some of the students might be interested in ESP, and the guiding group had decided that any subject was valid if it reintroduced the teenagers to reading.

"What do you want me to do?" I asked, "I'm not a teacher."

"You don't have to teach. Just talk to them the way you have to me."

I did not like to refuse my friend but, on the other hand, I lacked the courage to stand before a group of people and speak. Since childhood I had felt tongue-tied in public, and I had avoided all academic courses that might put me on display.

"Please do this," coaxed Mary Jane. "I promise it will take no more than an hour. And only a few show up at any given class."

I rationalized that it couldn't be worse than speaking to my kids' friends, and agreed to give it a try. As the time approached, however, I felt more and more apprehensive. How could I have let myself be coerced into something so terrifying?

On the appointed morning I arrived armed with a dozen

books, a case of slides, a 35mm film, the Zener Deck and assorted games. I was quaking, I felt nauseous, and I wished I had stayed in bed. Mary Jane greeted me at the entrance of the building and conducted me into a sizeable room jammed with people. There were at least fifty youngsters present, along with a healthy sprinkling of interested adults. Even some of the founders of the community program had showed up. I could not believe this was happening to me. I thought of strangling Mary Jane, who beamed happily at her coup. I was in the grip of such panic that I cannot recall much about it. I do remember that, to keep the audience from noticing my legs were trembling, I "casually" perched on a desktop. Before I opened my mouth I silently blamed the spirit of my dead grandmother for making me do this. Somehow, thinking of her at that moment—resurrecting the image of her fearlessness and her ability at leadership—calmed me considerably. I decided to speak to the young people in the conversational tone I used when chatting with my children's friends. It must have worked, because the anticipated hour of class stretched until lunch time and, even then, no one wanted to leave.

I returned home much relieved and grateful that the experience was over. That night Bob received a telephone call. One of the investment analysts from his office (indeed, a vice president of his firm) had been present at my class because he was a sponsor of the program. Recognizing my last name, he'd guessed we were husband and wife. He told Bob the lecture had so interested him that he thought it should be offered in his town as part of an adult education program the following fall. This seemed much more threatening to me that a room full of youngsters, and yet a part of me insisted that I do it. I was beginning to suspect something had been set in motion that was beyond curtailing.

Many of my friends in the parapsychological community offered suggestions as I prepared an entire summer for the course. Luckily, a local psychiatrist was interested in the subject and quite well-informed, and we were assigned to each other as teaching partners. I could not believe how many adults were inquisitive enough about ESP that after a full day's work they were willing to spend their evenings in a classroom. It was the largest seminar of the year, and somehow I muddled through it. The people were open, friendly and supportive; many even had similar happenings to report. We exchanged views and grew. I *almost* came to look forward to those weekly classes.

Before the end of the year one of my "students," an international lawyer, proposed my name as a lecturer for New York University's School of Continuing Education. He was on their Board of Directors and insisted it was about time that the subject be explored there. Once again, I felt the surge of a giant wave lifting me to the next stage. It was hard to resist an invitation to teach in my own backyard, particularly since the buildings adjoined Greenwich Village, where I loved to browse. I called upon my experienced fellows in the field of parapsychology to appear as guest lecturers with me. No one refused, and the first series of twelve-week classes in experimental parapsychology was initiated at New York University. I often marvelled "How did this happen to me?" And then that comic-relief voice within would respond "Them that can, does. Them that can't, teaches."

Judy and Tammy.

13

TORMENTS AND MENTORS

*Mom is getting to be extremely well-known in the field
of parapsychology. She has been traveling a lot lately,
and that kind of bothers me. I'm used to her being around
when I need her. I can still send my mother mental
messages to call me, but it's not the same as her being
here all the time. With Jon in college, I really notice the
gap. I guess I have to respect Mom's desire for an independent career and a life beyond that of mother and
wife. I know I'm old enough to deal with my own problems, but I don't like to admit it. I sort of feel like a
chauvinist. When I love her and think about her needs,
I'm excited for Mom and her developing career; when
I think about myself, I get selfish and never want her
to travel. I have to admit, though, one of the funniest
things that happened had to do with Mom's travel.*

*I didn't remember where Mom was traveling—I just
knew she was to be gone for five days. One of those
days, I came home from school and automatically
turned on the television. The Mike Douglas Show
was airing and, although I rarely watched the show, I
left the TV on as background noise for my studies.
(The louder the background noise, the more able I am
to block it out.) As I was opening my books, I heard*

Mom's voice. I was surprised that she had come home a couple of days early. I called out her name (Mom!) but there was no reply. I could've sworn I'd heard her. Maybe not. Wait, there it was again! I couldn't believe my ears. I was certain I was hearing things. Suddenly her face caught the corner of my eye. I turned around to see Mom talking in her non-stop manner to Mike Douglas. "Hi Mom!" I didn't bother to listen to what she was saying; I've heard it all before. I just kept her on in the background for company.

Once, during that year, I joined Mom on Barbara Walters' show. Mom was being interviewed and I was sitting in the audience. We pre-arranged that, after Mom talked about the ESP Teaching machine, Miss Walters would call me from the audience to come on stage and demonstrate how the machine worked.

Before the show, Mom and I were called to the star's dressing room. As Miss Walters had her makeup applied, Mom briefed her on the mechanics of the ESP Teaching machine. She said that she understood, but it was obvious she was preoccupied by her appearance. On the air, Barbara Walters totally muddled Mom's explanation. Then she called me from the audience to demonstrate the machine. I quickly and nervously pressed the buttons and ended up with a rotten score. At that moment I was completely in sympathy with the skepticism constantly faced by Uri Geller. I held my head high, returned to my seat, and breathed a sigh of relief that the show was going to be broadcast in competition with Macy's Thanksgiving Day Parade. Mom and I watched the show together and laughed at how much fatter we looked on TV.

I guess, no matter where Mom is, we still have our own form of telecommunication. The only problem with this is that it doesn't offer much privacy. When Mom learned how to astral travel, I had a feeling there was gonna be trouble. She proudly told me that, with her body in one place, she now knew how to project her consciousness somewhere else. I haven't been too pleased with her new talent because I don't like the idea of her (astral body or not) popping in on me unexpectedly. So I made her promise she'd never spy on me. I should have known better than to trust her. It's always dumb to believe a mother who claims that she won't check up on her child if she has the chance.

I was lying in bed in my room, feeling tense about an exam at school, so I decided to relax my body through a meditation technique Mom taught me. (She learned it from the same guy who taught her how to astral travel.) I became consciously aware of the flow of my breath as I relaxed each individual muscle in my body.

As the tension disappeared, I noticed a presence in my room. Opening my eyes, I saw the figure of my mother standing near the window. "Go away, get out of here!" I yelled. After a brief moment, she disappeared. I recorded the incident in my journal, and also told a friend.

A couple of days later, my mother berated me on the telephone.

"Your phone's been busy for days! I've been trying non-stop to call you and it's either busy or no one answers!"

I ignored her and got to the point. "Did you come visit me two nights ago?"

"I'm so glad I finally got through to you. How was your exam?"

"Forget it, Mom. Did you spy on me two nights ago at 12:15 a.m. my time?"

"I was afraid you knew. I had to see how you were. I couldn't get through to you and I wanted to make sure you were..."

"You broke your promise! You promised you'd never spy on me!"

"I wasn't spying. I was just relieving my conscience."

She said she had done it at 9:15, California time. She told me what nightgown I was wearing and that I had rearranged the furniture in my room. I warned her, in no uncertain terms, that she must not spy on me. Much to her chagrin, she knew that she could never get away with that again. We finally reached a compromise. I'd give up complaining about her earthly traveling without me, if she'd give up her astral traveling to me.

Even with Mom gone a lot, we still have our fill of psychics, fortune tellers, mystics, healers, and meetings on the coming of extra-terrestrial beings. The doormen in our building have gotten so used to multitudes of people entering and leaving our apartment that they have given up asking identities or buzzing to announce someone's arrival. I must say I can't blame them, but Mom gets annoyed because they just assume every nut off the street is headed for our apartment. Usually they're right, but when someone wanders through our home who doesn't belong, it's a little unnerving.

Even I don't know who does and doesn't belong around here. One day I came home from school and went directly into the kitchen. While getting some food from the fridge, I noticed someone watching me from the kitchen counter. "Hi, I'm Tammy. Who are you?" It seemed like an ordinary enough introduction. But instead of answering me, the guy began to laugh. I was puzzled.

"What's so funny?" I asked.

"I'm sorry. It's just this place. My name is Peter and I already know who you are. I've been living here for four days!"

He thought it was so amusing that I didn't know he was staying in my home. I guess it was *pretty funny. But he didn't eat with us and was out most of the time; I guess he just used our apartment as home base. How was I supposed to keep track of everyone? It's bad enough that I have to kiss everyone hello and goodbye, because I'm never sure who I have or haven't met before! All I can say is, thank God for Hattie—the only constant in the frenetic energy of our home.*

Hattie is our housekeeper. Sort of. She came to us a couple of days after the death of Montana. Hattie walked through our door, announcing that she'd come to take the place of her departed friend. It seemed that Montana used to speak highly of us, so upon her death it became Hattie's conscionable duty to offer us her services.

94   *Hattie and Judy.*

How could we help falling in love with Hattie? She looks like an exaggerated version of the picture of Aunt Jemima on pancake boxes. Hattie is big, fat, and has a tint of blue in her gray hair. She clothes her soft, roly, dark-brown body in a man's white T-shirt and an apron. On her feet she sports rolled-down woolen anklets that serve as both socks and slippers. The cloth around her head is a stocking, a bandanna and a rag. Her eyes protrude from her face, and as they bulge, they sparkle with love. When she smiles, her buck teeth thrust far out of her mouth. In the pockets of her cheeks, Hattie stuffs snuff. I don't know whether it's the snuff that makes her move so slowly or the fact that she has palsy. When people ask Bob if Mom has help managing this big place with all the activities and feeding going on, Bob answers "No, she doesn't have help, she has hindrance."

When Hattie first came to us she didn't know how to cook very well. We had to teach her how to boil water and make salad. But when Hattie learned to make meatballs, we all realized she'd finally found her niche. We have a finicky little Shih-tzu dog named Saki who won't eat hamburger meat unless it's rolled into one-and-a-half-inch meatballs and mixed with cooked rice. We've figured out that, so far, Hattie has made and Saki has eaten over eighteen thousand meatballs. Bob says that if you lined them up they'd stretch around Central Park.

As Hattie can't read, write, or hear very well, she hates answering the phone. Sometimes she lets it ring itself out. Once in a while she gets a whim to pick up the phone and try her luck. On one of these memorable moments I called home from a vacation. I warned the operator to let it ring several times and, sure enough, after ten rings Hattie finally answered the phone.

Hattie: "Hallo?"

Operator: "This is a collect call from Tammy. Will you accept the charges?

Hattie: "Tammy ain't here right now—she's on vacation."

Operator: "No, this is a collect call from Tammy."

Hattie: "Oh, are you one of her friends? Well I ain't sure where she is but her Mama tells me she's havin' a wonderful time. Tell me y'name honey, and I'll try an remember to tell her ya called."

(I'm laughing too hard to be of any assistance to the confused operator.)

Operator: *"You don't seem to understand Miss, that Tammy is calling you now."*

Hattie: *"She is? Well I better hang up, honey, else the line'll be busy."*

Operator: *"She's on this line!"*

Hattie: *"You ain't Tammy!"*

Tammy: *"Hello, Hattie? It's me!"*

Hattie: *"Oooooooweee! Tammy! That you, sugar pie?"*

Tammy: *"Yeah, it's me, Hattie!"*

Hattie: *"There's someone on the phone wantin' to speak to ya."* (Operator laughs.)

Tammy: *"Hattie, is Mom there?"*

Hattie: *"No, honey. She's away for the weekend. When ya comin' home?"*

Tammy: *"Real soon. Tell Mom I'm fine. Gotta go. Love ya. Bye, Hats!"*

Hattie: *"Bye bye!"*

CLICK.

Operator: *"Who in the world was that?"*

Tammy: *"A relative of mine. Sorry—she gets a little confused on the phone. Did that cost anything?"*

Operator: *"Forget it. It was my best call all week!"*

I think Hattie fits so well into our family because she is a bundle of love. Very few things seem too crazy for her, and when they do she just shakes her head, rolls her eyes, and continues making meatballs. Her life's story could compete with Alex Haley's Roots. *The kooks who come to our apartment are mere eccentrics compared to the people she's seen. While Hattie makes meatballs she tells me all kinds of stories. If I'm not around, she mumbles to herself or to Saki. Hattie also has dreams that come true. Lots of times she senses who's good and who's after something. She keeps us warned, and hides me from people I don't care to see. There's no doubt she fits in perfectly around here. As a matter of fact, who doesn't?*

Even Bob is not so much in the background as he likes to pretend. With all the eccentrics coming and going, Bob has not been unaffected. My mild-mannered stepfather plays conventional stockbroker by day, but by night he shifts into: Bob Skutch, Psychic Healer.

Every night around ten, Bob seeks the privacy of the living room. He closes his eyes and draws his mind to a blank. Sometimes he holds in his hand a picture of one of his patients. Then he envisions the patient as totally well, surrounded with love. He suggests that the patient do a similar meditation several times a day. Bob never admits to healing anybody. He says he tries to help people have the will and strength to heal themselves. Although he devotes a lot of time to his patients, he never accepts any payment for his services. I think it's great to have Bob around the house because he's much quicker and more effective than aspirin. He's also gentler on the stomach. The only pain I didn't want Bob to heal was when we pricked our fingers and mixed our blood in order to become legitimate blood relatives.

Mom and Bob are of the belief that people create their own illnesses. They say that a person often subconsciously, and even sometimes consciously, wants to be sick. Their friend Dr. Carl Simonton, a young oncologist, is painstakingly trying to research this theory.

One night when he was staying with us, Carl gave a talk to a whole bunch of people in our living room. The subject was cancer. He said he believed that in some cases people give themselves cancer as a means of socially accepted suicide. He spoke of the regime he designed to help cancer patients become aware of their self-imposed illness. With each patient he would delve into their individual reasons for creating the disease. Then together they would re-focus the patient's will to live so as to reverse the action of the cancerous cells.

The reaction to Carl's lecture was horrible. Some people poo-pooed, others remained silent, and still others openly criticized him. He withdrew into Jon's room, where I found him crying. I wanted to cheer him up. I wasn't sure what to tell him, but I knew he was sincere and shouldn't have been treated that way. I told him not to pay any attention to that bunch, who probably only come around because of Mom's reputation as a great cook. What did they know about creating illness? They're so wealthy that even if they get cancer they probably think they can bribe a doctor to get rid of it. Cancer's just too far from their present reality. I told Carl not to care about a group of people who'd rather see the psychokinetic destruction of silverware than hear about an alternative approach to disease.

With tears in his eyes, Carl began to laugh. I guess I sounded pretty stupid, being so young and all. But I knew he wasn't laughing at me to ridicule me. Carl, Mom and I stayed up late that night talking and laughing the horrible evening away. Carl jokingly asked me

97

*what I wanted as a gift for cheering him up. "Some-
day when you're rich and famous I want a digital
watch just like yours." He laughed and agreed.*

Dr. Carl Simonton was to come a long way from the tear-
ful young man I consoled in my brother's room. He was soon to
be publicly acclaimed for offering repeated proof that in many
cases cancer stems from psychological problems, and can therefore be reversed. A package was delivered to me much later,
when I was in college. There was no return address, just a note
saying "Thanks" and a digital watch just like Carl's. I felt a
strong connection with Carl and found that his work touched a
chord deep within me. A few years later I was going to play that
chord myself through my own involvement with child cancer
patients and children with catastrophic illnesses.

Carl was one of two people who made a strong and lasting
impact on my belief system. The other person was a man I
thought of as Mr. Biology. He was my ninth-grade science teacher,
who became a very dear friend and important mentor.

*This was my first year with Mr. Biology. I'll never
forget how he frightened me that first week of school.
He certainly lived up to his reputation as a slave driver.
The first day of class I watched him closely as, in a long
white lab coat, he paced among the test tubes and mic-
croscopes. He's a short man with greying hair and
dark brown eyes behind gold wire-framed glasses. Like
my father, he has the making of an executive-type pot
belly. I noticed his determined stride that first day of
class. I vividly remember his opening speech, which I
copied in shorthand into my new ringbinder marked:
Biology. Mr. B. Tamara Cohen. Grade 9. Year: 1973–74.*

*"I will not treat you as children, for you are no longer
children. You might enjoy pretending to be, but this is
not a class of make-believe. This is a class of science.
And in science we study fact, not fiction.*

*"You will be required to learn all the material cov-
ered in this room, as well as to live up to my expectations of you as an individual. This means doing
additional research on your own, participating in class,
and taking the initiative to be an adult.*

*"If you have to go to the bathroom, simply tell me
and then remove yourself from class for the time necessary to attain relief. There's no reason to be embarrassed about the natural process your body undergoes
to relieve itself of waste products. It greatly disturbs me
to see the embarrassment that our society has insti-*

*gated around the natural bodily function of various
excretory and eliminatory processes. Because of this
absurd socialized embarrassment, we repress our need
to go to the bathroom until we can slip away unnoticed.
By prolonging the relief of this natural process, we
create a tension in our body, and too much tension in
the body leads to nervous breakdowns. I shall have no
such nervous breakdowns in any class of mine. We
will talk about bladders, urine, feces, menstruation,
penises, vaginas and various species' sexual activities.
Should you blush at the mention of any of these words
or concepts by the end of the trimester, you will be given
an F for the term. Do I make myself clear?"*

*"Yes" we all mumbled (followed by various nervous
stirrings). I had never heard such a speech in my life.
I needed to carry a dictionary to understand what the
man was saying. He frightened—no, he terrified me.*

*The first couple of weeks I studied as hard as I could
every night so I wouldn't be embarrassed when he'd
call on me in class. Of course, he'd find some way to
humiliate me in any event. But after the second week
something clicked inside of me. I was no longer afraid
of him. I was ready to fight back. I think that happened when I finally realized he thought more highly
of the people who would talk back to him and stick up
for what they thought was correct. He did not respect
the people who would ever-so-meekly give the answer
they thought he wanted to hear.*

*Mr. B reminded me a lot of my father. I was deter-
mined to gain the respect of my teacher. I studied
harder for Mr. B's class than for any other course. He
helped me to love science as I'd never loved it before.
He brought to life all the little things I'd never noticed.
We had long discussions about parapsychology. He was
interested in Uri Geller and skeptical about much
psychic phenomena. But he never said he didn't believe.
He was curious and he had an open mind, although he
tried desperately to pretend otherwise. In our discussions after class he helped give me a new perspective
on life. He made me question things I'd previously
taken for granted.*

*"How can you so easily say that just because you
think of someone and the person calls you a moment
later, it's more than a coincidence?"*

*"Because it happens too often to keep being a coinci-
dence."*

"Why can't there be many coincidences? Is there a limit to how many coincidences one can have?"

"I guess not. But I know I can send a message to someone and, more times than not, the message comes through."

"Okay," Mr. Biology would persist, "let's say you send me a message to call you. About five minutes later I call you. How do you know that (1) I wasn't going to call you anyway at that time, or (2) you didn't merely tune in to something I was going to do anyway, and then fool yourself into believing that you were the force behind the call I would've made anyway?"

"Oh, so at least you believe that I might have been able to tune in to an event that was going to take place in the future!"

"I never said that. I was speaking hypothetically, and you didn't answer either part of my question."

"Well, how can I know these things? All I know is, when I sit down and send someone a message to call me, it works. Who cares why or how it works?"

"That's the wrong attitude to take. There's a scientific explanation for most psychic phenomena. The explanations involve theories of brain waves and patterns, thought frequencies, explanations of the intuitive process, the right and left hemisphere of the brain, and so on. You would do well to read some of these books."

And he'd give me a list of chapters in books on psychic phenomena, biofeedback, and new scientific research methods being done in the field of parapsychology. He even made me watch video cassettes on differing explanations of mind over body (such as Indians walking barefoot over hot coals, sticking spokes through their bodies, or stopping their hearts). He never admitted that he accepted ESP as a scientifically proven phenomenon. However, his knowledge of the material written in the field was enough to make me realize that he was not trying to shake my belief in what I had experienced.

He goaded me during class any time the subject of the supernatural came up. He often infuriated me. We fought bitterly the day he introduced the statement "Man is nothing but a machine."

"But what about a soul? Where do emotions come from? How can you biologically explain love?" I asked passionately.

Almost mechanically he replied "Man's mind created

the idea of a soul. Emotions come from a series of bio-chemical reactions often triggered by social situations. Love is an emotion just like any other."

"Dammit, you're heartless!"

"No, as a matter of fact, I do have a heart, or I would most probably not be standing here this very minute. And if you mean by saying I'm heartless that I don't feel any compassion, then allow me to correct you once again: One does not feel compassion in the heart. The heart is an organ whose primary function is to pump blood through the body. As for compassion, I've been socially taught to have that series of chain reactions in order to feel that emotion when the situation calls for it. You must learn not to use phrases so loosely. You must also learn to keep romantic notions separate from scientific evaluation."

Some people hated Mr. Biology. Some people got sick after his classes. Many students thought him to be cruel and unfair. But there were a few students who felt that, despite his facade, this man was a lot more than just a machine. Mr. B opened my mind to questions, my emotions to fire, and my mouth to debate. He taught me to think twice about my beliefs, and in my double-take to realize my naivete or reaffirm my stubborness.

Mr. Biology helped me create a link between my academic studies and my home life. He also played a role in improving my relationship with my father. In exercising the courage to stand up to my science teacher and gain his respect, I learned a new way to relate to my father. I would telephone my paternal parent when questioning the things I was learning. I began to notice his enjoyment at being able to help me academically. I sensed a fatherly pride that his daughter was beginning to "think." I was coming to understand that, in the years I spent trying to connect with my father's lap, he was yearning for me to connect with his mind. So I found myself crawling off his lap and into his head, where finally we touched.

It was in ninth grade when I wrote an *A+* paper on chivalry in the Middle Ages. It was the first thing I'd ever written that I felt like showing my father. I sat before him as he read the thirty-page paper. I watched carefully for any hint of reaction. I longed for my father's pride and respect. He never seemed to expect anything of me. He had so many expectations for Jon. Didn't he care about my future? Was my own father a chauvinist? Did he think I was a simpleton only cut out for housework?

My thoughts were interrupted as I heard the shuffling of paper. My eyes caught his hands turning the last page into the fold of the rest of the manuscript. He was finished. It was over. There was silence. He held the paper in his lap as he leaned back in his chair. Finally, after an unbearable eternity of three seconds, he looked at me and said "Tam, this is wonderful. Has your mother read this?"

"Uh huh, she did. You really liked it?"

"It's excellent. I'm very impressed. Come here." And he reached out his arm to me. I crawled onto my father's lap and he kissed my forehead. I had never received such a compliment from him. He even called my mother to tell her how impressed he was. I heard him telling her that maybe I was going to be a writer when I grew up. I was stunned. I "knew" I didn't have the talent to be a writer, but that didn't concern me. I couldn't believe he though that I might have a profession. My father finally recognized me as a person. That meant more to me than any of the results I'd every gotten on all the ESP tests I'd taken.

Such was the beginning of my friendship with my father, with Mr. Biology, and with the field of reasoning. Was it a coincidence that my math class that year was "Logic and Geometry"? My mind was learning how to think, and my eyes were learning how to see more than just what was put in front of them. It was time for me to notice and develop my peripheral vision.

14
A DREAM COME TRUE

It was frustrating that I couldn't have any secrets. How could I do anything pubescently rotten with all the psychics parading around our apartment, or with my mother "visiting" me? With the realization that I could intuit the thoughts of others came the threat of the vice versa. Consequently, I attempted to close my mind to all external intrusions. These intruders included those whose unconscious thoughts slipped into my mind, and those who consciously entered my mind to shoplift my own thoughts.

In seventh grade, my friend Kit and I decided to take a shot at petty theft. We went into a five-and-dime store and stole a bag. We were caught. The store detective brought us to the manager. The manager looked through Kit's wallet and saw a picture of her stepfather. The manager recognized him as being one of the store's regular customers. Kit burst into tears. She pleaded that it was her first time shoplifting and that she'd never do it again. I tried to calm Kit. I wasn't crying. I couldn't cry. It was like my never being able to cry at a sad movie. All the tears would build up inside me and sit there, while my friends created rivers in the theatre aisles. (Kit, for instance, cried every time she had a bowel movement.)

I didn't cry in front of the store manager. I tried to soothe Kit. As a result, the store manager decided that I was a petty theft professional and that Kit had been my nouveau accomplice. I denied the charge, telling him that it was a first for both of us. He didn't believe me. He proceeded to call my home. I was terribly nervous and upset. I tried to force tears out of my eyes but they just wouldn't come.

I could hear the phone at home ringing through the receiver next to the manager's ear. I was on the edge of my chair. The manager was tapping his foot. The tension was building. Kit was sobbing. The ringing stopped.

"Hallo!"

"Hello. Is Mrs. Cohen there?" (He figured that since my last name is Cohen, so was my mother's. I didn't set him right.)

"Why no she ain't. She's out shopping."

"Well this is the manager of a store where her daughter has been caught and charged with petty theft."

"Pretty what?"

"Petty theft."

"Ain't that nice. Do you wanna leave ya' name?"

"No thank you."

CLICK.

I thanked God that Hattie had answered the phone. She couldn't have written down the name or message even if he had given it to her. The manager was somewhat confused, as is everyone who talks to Hattie on the telephone. He told us to consider the event a "warning." We promised never to steal again. The situation had enough impact on us to ensure that we would hold true to our promises.

When I returned home that day, Hattie told me someone had called for me. When I asked what the person wanted, Hattie said she thought he was selling pretty charge cards. I gave her a huge hug and kiss and helped her with the meatballs. For the next couple of days, Kit and I jumped every time we heard the phone ring.

A few months after this event, my mother, Bob and I went to England to visit friends of the family. During our stay there, we visited our friend Ena Twigg, who was a professional psychic medium. A year earlier Ena had given Mom information about Nana's life in the afterworld, and she foretold Bob's aptitude for psychic healing. I was petrified that she would find out my secret about the petty theft, and reveal me to my parents. During the entire visit with Ena, I flooded my head with other thoughts in order to block her from finding that one. I don't know if she saw my secret. If she did, she respected it and kept it. I can't even remember the reading she gave me. I was too busy flooding my brain. It was a dangerous thing being around all those psychic mediums. You'd either develop a personality complex or a very strong superego. I became extremely aware of all my conscious thoughts.

It seemed that the more psychic intuition I consciously pushed away, the stronger my subconscious pushed it back at me. What I wasn't intuiting in ordinary awareness, I began to see in the unconsciousness of sleep. I found myself awakening to a reality that I was unable to separate from my dreams, and a free will I was unable to separate from fate.

In seventh grade, I dreamt that Kit and I got out of science class early. We went straight to the cafeteria where we saved an entire table for our friends. Soon everyone came to lunch. The table filled up and we were all having a great time. Suddenly Janet was standing at the end of the table. She had her tray in hand as she stared directly at me. She asked me why I hadn't saved her a seat. I looked around and realized that I'd forgotten to reserve a chair for Jan, one of my best friends. I apologized and suggested she share my seat. She did and all was well, at which point, I awoke.

I went to school with the dream nagging me. I saw Kit and told her about it. She said not to worry and reminded me that we never got out of science class early. In fact, we were usually the last ones to lunch on the days we had science. "Besides," she said to me, "even if we do get out of class early, we'll make sure to save Janet a seat." I was reassured.

When the time came to go to science class, I almost forgot about the dream. We got to class and found out that it was cancelled because our teacher was sick. Kit and I looked at each other. "Well, we'll go to the lunch room and save a special seat of honor for Janet." We darted downstairs to the cafeteria.

Everyone else was still in class. Kit and I typically reserved a whole table and carefully designated a seat for each friend. I pointed to the chair to the left of me and said "This seat's for Jan." Kit, seated across from me, nodded in acknowledgement.

The bell rang. Suddenly a flourish of people crowded the lunch room. There was a lot of noise and commotion. Food was being passed along the assembly line. Silverware was clanking against trays and dishes. The papers from the straws were being shot in all directions. People were yelling out their meal card numbers. Our table was bombarded by friends. I glanced over at Janet's seat. It was still waiting for her.

"So how was science?" Hugh asked, as he sat down on my right.

As I proceeded to tell Hugh that our teacher had been sick we were abruptly interrupted.

"Tammy!"

I looked up to see Janet standing at the end of the table.

"Why didn't you save me a seat?" she complained.

"I did. It's right he. . . ." My words were cut short as I swung to my left and pointed to the chair beside me. But instead of my hand's hitting the empty air, it hit a boy seated a few inches away. I looked at him and asked "Where's Janet's seat?"

"Oh, was that Janet's seat? Sorry, the table was so crowded I pulled out one of the chairs and put it at the other table."

My heartbeat doubled. I stopped breathing. I swung around to catch Kit's eyes. For a moment we shared emotion, our reactions mirrored in each other's eyes. I broke the freeze and told Jan that it was a mistake, and to share my seat with me. She did and everything was fine.

But everything wasn't really fine. Kit and I could hardly talk about it after lunch. I was scared. I felt helpless. I had tried so hard to change the course of events. I did everything I could. But I couldn't do anything. So what good was it to dream something before it happened if I didn't have any say in the course of events? It frightened me. I began to wonder if I had say in anything that ever happened to me—or if anyone did. Were we all just pawns in an already written play? Was there no post script? I decided to push the entire experience out of my mind, but it forcefully pushed itself back in again.

I dreamt I was looking out my window. Cars were whizzing by on the street below. There was a feeling of tension. All of a sudden CRASH! BANG! SKID! Two cars had collided. A man cried out in pain. He was lying in the street. His legs were crushed. I was shocked. I ran to the den where Mom and Bob were talking to guests. I tried to get their attention but they told me not to interrupt them. After much persistence, I dragged them to the window. We stared at the scene outside. One side of one of the cars was crushed. I was stunned. Mom and Bob tried to console me. I was crying.

I woke up. I was in a fog as I got up and dressed myself, but I looked out the window and all was calm. I breathed a sigh of relief; it was just a dream. It was 11 a.m. I had slept for a long time and it was time to say good morning to Mom and Bob. I turned my back to the window. Then CRASH! BANG! SKID! Silence.

I think I'm frozen. I can hear the beat of my heart resounding in my ears, pounding in my head. Should I even bother taking a look out the window? Maybe it's nothing. Maybe I'm imagining things. I've got to move from this spot. I don't want to, but I feel compelled to look out that window. (I tell you, just forget it. No, I can't do that. I've got to see what happened.) I wish I could turn away from the window. Why do I have to run to it? Can't I take this slowly? It's happening too

*quickly. Oh God, there it is! Glass is all over the street.
Those two cars crashed at the intersection. But it
doesn't look so bad. Why not? (I should be thankful it
doesn't look bad. Why am I asking "why not?") Those
two drivers are really screaming at each other. They
should be grateful they're not hurt. That guy's window
is demolished and they both have slightly dented cars,
but other than that nothing looks serious. Wait a second, there's a man still sitting in the passenger seat in
one of the cars. He seems fine. Someone's talking to
him through the open window. Why doesn't he get out?
Something's very eerie about this. I don't believe that
everything's all right. Why am I shaking? I've got to
talk to Mom and Bob.*

*Where are they? They're not in their room. The den!
There goes my heartbeat again. Yes, I can hear Mom's
voice. Oh no, they have guests. What a nightmare!*

*"Hello everybody. Yes I'm fine, thank you. Mom and
Bob, could I please speak to you for a moment? It's important. PLEASE."*

*Phew, they believe me. They're excusing themselves.
Thank God for that. Maybe it isn't like my dream after
all. I mean, in my dream they wouldn't listen to me,
but here they realize that this is urgent.*

*I'm in the hall, telling them about my dream. I see
that they believe me. They know I'm upset; they're paying extra special attention to what I'm saying.*

*I can't believe they didn't hear the crash. It was so
loud. I have to pull them to the window. We all look
outside. They think the situation looks under control.
No it isn't! I know someone's hurt! They keep trying to
reassure me. They can't.*

*"I know an ambulance is coming. It's not what it
seems. I know someone's hurt." Are those the only
words I can say? Why must I keep repeating them over
and over again? Maybe they're right. Maybe everything
is fine. Maybe I'm putting more emphasis on my
dream than it deserves! NO! "I know an ambulance is
coming. It's not what it seems. I know someone's hurt!"
There I go again with those same words. I can't help
feeling this way. I think their guests are a little freaked
out by all this. But not nearly as freaked as I am.*

*I'm glad Bob is going downstairs to see if anyone's
hurt. That'll straighten this thing out. But I know the
outcome. Let's look out the window again. From our
vantage point everything seems minor. Wait—what's*

that? It sounds like an ambulance. "Bob, wait a minute! Come here! There it is!"

The ambulance is pulling up to the car with the man in the passenger seat. It's stopping. Maybe it's just a routine run, for insurance or something. Do they do that sort of thing? The paramedics have a stretcher. It looks like they're opening the door next to the man. It's hard to tell because the driver's side of the car is facing this way. They're moving in front of the car. Now I can see a bit more clearly. They're putting the man on the stretcher. It looks like he can't move. Yes, something's happened to his legs!

We're all at the window now. The ambulance has just left. Now there's a tow truck on the scene. They're moving the car that the injured man was in. Now I see. Now we all see. The other side of the car is totally smashed in. There are no windows. That man must have been crushed in there.

Well, I'm glad it's all over. But why did I have to watch that accident twice? It was bad enough to dream about it. But twice is unbearable.

Once again I was frustrated that I had to stand by helplessly and watch an event take place, having no apparent say in its cause or outcome. My only say was my insistence that there was more to the situation than everyone thought. I felt a strong connection with a Greek myth thousands of years old. Apollo gave Cassandra the gift of premonition. Later, when angered by Cassandra, Apollo could not retract his gift, so he added a twist to it. Whenever Cassandra warned anyone of impending doom, no one would believe her. Perhaps the myth was an archetype of my precognitive experiences. I was developing great compassion for the Cassandra complex.

After several more "real" dreams, I only wanted to live in the present. It seemed that knowledge of the future removed me from the complete experience of the present. When I knew what was going to happen beforehand, I watched it happen in a daze, as though I were dreaming it again. So I consciously begged my unconscious to keep its precognitive information to itself.

As the precognitive dreams subsided, a new twist occurred.

On a vacation with my mother, we shared a hotel room. One night I fell asleep as my mother remained absorbed in a book. I began to dream that I was flying one of those Red Baron-type airplanes. I was dressed in 1920s pilot attire. The plane began to lose control. I was heading for a collision with the ground, several hundred feet below me. My plane crashed! The explosion jarred me awake. My mother noticed me jump, and asked what was wrong. As I described my dream, she looked at me in disbelief.

"What's the matter?"

"That's exactly what I was just reading! You became the main character in the scenario I was reading!"

"Great. Now will you put down the book so I can get some sleep?"

But putting the book down wasn't good enough. It became apparent that I was even picking up my mother's dreams and incorporating them into my own. When I'd awaken from such a dream, I would know it was hers because it made no sense to me. In one such dream I was in my grandmother's attic. I was wearing a dress I didn't recognize and talking with my grandmother about redecorating. When I awoke from the dream, my part of the conversation made no sense to me. I felt that I had said things that were foreign to my tastes and couldn't see what the dream had to do with me. I didn't even recognize the other people in the dream. As I was relaying it to my mother, she told me how it ended. It seemed that we had had the exact same dream, but I'd deposited myself in her place. It was *her* old dress, the people were familiar to *her,* and my conversation reflected *her* likes and dislikes. No wonder I was perplexed by it—it wasn't even *my* dream! I reprimanded my mother and suggested she get ear plugs to contain her leaky dreams.

It happened that there was a dream telepathy experiment underway at Maimonides Dream Lab. The experiment entails a "receiver" and a "sender." The receiver is connected by electrodes to a machine that measures REM (rapid eye movement) as a means of detecting when the subject is in a dream state. The sender, in a separate room, is given a randomly selected closed envelope with a picture in it. The sender opens the envelope and tries telepathically to communicate the contents of the picture into the dream of the receiver. Naturally, my mother and I were recruited.

At fifteen, I was reluctant to participate in the experiment, but my initial hesitation was conquered by monetary temptation, as we would be paid for our participation. However, to be chosen for the experiment required that we get a direct hit on a pre-series trial night. So my mother and I packed our nightgowns and headed to Brooklyn for something far from a good night's sleep.

Due to our personal history with dreams, my mother was to be the sender and I was elected receiver. As my mother was comfortably set up in her room with an envelope, I was placed in a separate, shielded room and told to relax into blissful sleep. The only problem was that my head was so hooked up to gooey electrodes that I couldn't move. What they really meant was that I should sleep like a corpse. After a long time of thinking about people waiting for me to fall asleep, despite the discomfort I passed out.

I was abruptly wakened by a sickly sweet voice oozing from a speaker in my soundproof room: "Time to wake up... You were having a dream..." I was? Could've fooled me. I don't remember a thing.

"Could you tell us about your dream, Tammy?" the alien voice asked.

"No."

"Nothing?" the voice ever so sweetly pursued.

"Uh uh," I insisted, "I just don't remember."

We played out that scenario twice more. I was precariously balanced between my annoyance at the voice that kept waking me, and growing embarrassment at not being able to remember any dreams. On my third awakening, the voice literally startled me out of a dream. As it dragged me out of slumber, I watched the last remnants of the dream slip back into unconsciousness. All I could remember was that it had something to do with my stepfather, Bob. I found myself dealing with an internal pressure. I felt that I had to "come through" in some way for the sleepy person behind the cloying voice. In my mind I could see his bloodshot eyes transfixed on my rapid eye movement and I began to feel guilty for destroying his dream by not disclosing my own. But when it came down to it, Bob was all I could remember. So when the voice asked again "Tammy, what were you dreaming?" I ad libbed.

I said I dreamed I was at a carnival and I described rides and clowns. It was short, just enough to make the voice sound happy and allow me to sleep the rest of the night undisturbed. The next morning I was given four pictures and told to rate them according to my dream: The picture that was most like my dream was to be labelled #1; the least similar, #4. Much to my surprise, there was a picture of a carousel, a lithograph of three minstrels, a drawing of a tiger, and a painting of a woman.

Now I was in a bind. I knew that all I really remembered was Bob. And I knew that Mom and Bob had a personal joke about tigers—but I didn't think Mom would know I knew that. At any rate, the independent judge who would later be rating the pictures with my dream description would never know about Bob or the tiger. It seemed obvious that the carousel went with my carnival, so I rated that picture #1. Then the minstrels were like my clowns, so they came in second. The tiger was closer to the spirit of the vision than the woman, so it got third place, while the woman fell completely out of the picture into fourth place.

After I finished the paper work, the target was disclosed to me: It was the tiger. My mother later told me that when she saw the tiger she thought of Bob. But she didn't think I knew of their intimate joke about it, so she tried sending me the mental picture of the animal. While doing this, however, she was unable to remove Bob from her thoughts, although she did not include him in her written description. So, to the world of science we flunked the test, disqualifying us from participating in the series of experiments. This was actually a relief to both of us, as we agreed that no monetary value could be placed on a good night's sleep. Besides, we both quietly knew we'd shared in a dream come true.

Judy and Bob.

15

Traveling Companions

Js

In early 1973 I was beginning to feel like a whirling Dervish. Family responsibilities, growing involvement with the Institute of Noetic Sciences, attention to our own Foundation for Para-Sensory Investigation and my now-committed teaching career at New York University commanded 200 percent of my time. There was a continual flow of people through our apartment, all sharing the same deep interests. One of my friends, a writer for the *Village Voice,* referred to me in print as "the den mother of parapsychology." I was furious and, when I told her that, she assured me I was taking on too much and had lost my sense of humor. I was becoming increasingly familiar with excitement and decreasingly acquainted with peace. I developed a severe peptic ulcer that did not respond to conventional medication. The gastroenterologist who had administered the GI series warned me that if I continued living at such a rapid pace I would soon need an operation. My friends in the newly emerging field of holistic health exposed me to varied programs to assist healing. Nothing seemed effective and I was often in pain. On a balmy afternoon I suddenly collapsed on the floor in my apartment. The stomach pain was excruciating and, since I could not move, I could not reach the telephone for help. I lay in the fetal position, afraid to breathe. I envisioned internal hemorrhaging and started to speculate on the results. I imagined myself losing consciousness and being found later by my family. I knew they would rush me by ambulance to the hospital where I would undergo an emergency operation. I fantasized awakening in a room filled with flowers and sunlight. Heaps of interesting novels lay on tables to be read. There was a hush in the room, and a sign NO VISITORS. There was no telephone, no meals to prepare, no hordes of people to entertain, no overnight guests who stay for a week, no classes to be taught, no conferences to be organized, no radio and television appearances...in short, heaven.

I lay on the floor smiling throughout this vision. It seemed like salvation. It suddenly dawned on me that I had made my existence myself in a frenzied treadmill of self-imposed activities. I had given myself an ulcer to escape. With all that I had been learning about the relationship between attitude and illness, the wonder was that I had never applied this information to myself. All this raced through my mind in a much shorter time than it takes to relate it. By the time I had made the connection between my mind and my body, the pain was gone. I picked myself up off the floor and telephoned my physician. I announced that I wanted to have another series of tests done as I knew I was healed. He thought I was crazy. I insisted I wanted proof. He suggested he call my husband to ask his permission. I was outraged, but realized my doctor thought I had lost my senses. We finally agreed to repeat the GI series later that week. I was not surprised to hear my doctor's conclusion: No trace of an ulcer, probably due to a misdiagnosis of the former X-rays.

The exhilaration I felt over my "self-healing" lasted only a short while. I released some of my activities and curtailed more of the travel. I became vaguely aware of a growing sense of dissatisfaction with my life. This feeling escalated to reveal an emptiness and lack of fulfillment. It seemed paradoxical to be feeling this way. On the surface my life was everything I could have wanted. My work was challenging and had been rewarding, my entire family shared the same interests. We were all in good health and did not have financial worries. Yet something vital was missing and I could not identify what it was. I began to have dreams that were a continuation of my earliest mystical experience. This time there seemed to be an underlying message in them that I wasn't hearing. In the dream state I would feel an all-embracing, universal love accompanied by a peace which was elusive upon awakening.

We were sitting at dinner on September 3, 1973, discussing a Parapsychology Association conference to be held the next day in Virginia. I really wanted to go, but Bob felt it would not interest him. I was loath to go without him, as at that time I was not used to traveling alone. Bob thought it would be a good idea for me to attend, as all my new friends and folks I wanted to meet would be there. During this conversation, Tammy was listening and absorbing it all. "Bobby, you'd better not let her go alone," she interjected. "Why not?" Bob wanted to know. "Because she might get involved with a tall, handsome man," she responded. Bob didn't take the bait. He smiled at Tammy and shrugged. "If she does, she does." Twenty-four hours later the prophecy was fulfilled, but not at all in the way Tammy had foreseen.

I didn't go to Virginia alone. My good friend Douglas Dean escorted me from my home direct to the conference. On the way there, we had to change planes in Washington, D.C. As we awaited our flight to Charlotte I spotted Russell Targ and Hal Puthoff from California coming across the waiting room. As I ran to greet them, Douglas grabbed my arm. He pointed to a silver-haired stranger marching purposefully in our direction. "Oh, look, Judy," Doug said, "There's that doctor I told you about. You know, the one whose house I stayed at when I was in California." I vaguely remembered Douglas' story about a child psychiatrist who was interested in hyperkinesis and ESP who had offered him a place to stay in a village called Tiburon near San Francisco. Douglas greeted the physician as I embraced my friends Russ and Hal. We began to chatter excitedly in anticipation of their presenting the Uri Geller research. Our flight was called; we proceeded as a group to board the plane. Douglas made the introduction casually. "Judy, this is the man I told you about, Dr. Jerry Jampolsky." We howdoyoudooed and Jerry reminded me that he

Dr. Jerry Jampolsky.

115

had once, not too long before, contacted me about the possibility of his working with Uri Geller when Uri was in California. When we reached our destination I was aware that this new acquaintance was not going to let us go. As we were all checking into the hotel, he invited us to join him for dinner.

Jerry seemed particularly interested in accounts of Tammy's ESP. He had memories of early childhood experiences himself and was curious about research that had been done. I was impressed with his openness and his particular focus on hyperkinetic children. He was thinking of investigating the relationship between ESP ability and hyperkinesis, since those were traits he recognized in himself. It was so gratifying to discover a medical professional who was willing to pioneer this arena! The more we explored our mutual interests, the more enthusiastic we became to learn about each other's work. Jerry was especially eager to meet Tammy and I invited him to New York City at the conclusion of the conference. Tammy liked Jerry's California casualness and agreed to try to perform experiments if I would take her to California when I flew there to attend board meetings of our newly formed Institute of Noetic Sciences.

Jerry and I began to join forces to address various conferences and workshops on the interface between psychiatry and ESP. He introduced me to the California climate of acceptance regarding these ideas. Having a traveling companion who shared my professional podium was enormously stimulating, but something sinister was developing. I found myself unusually combative with facets of Jerry's personality, which left me ashamed and puzzled. The qualities I began to criticize in him were aspects of myself. I could find no rationale for my mounting irritations with a person I so appreciated as a working partner. Jerry's attitude towards me was always supportive and caring. I was alarmed at this apparent split in my own personality.

To complicate the tensions, within a short time I found the pace of my life even more accelerated as I accepted an increasing number of invitations to speak about parapsychological research worldwide.

In California to explore the focus of my doctoral work with the Humanistic Psychology Institute in January of 1975, I telephoned my friends Vera and Harold, who had recently moved to Berkeley and were engaged in writing a book together. They were good playmates and I was taking a day's vacation from work. Vera answered the telephone and, in a voice filled with urgency, insisted I immediately accompany them to the newly formed ashram of Swami Muktananda. When I arrived at their home it was evident that a great change had come over the two of them through their association with this Indian teacher.

It was not the first time I had heard about the strong influence this Easterner had on the lives of friends. About a year before, Bob had to have eye surgery for a detached retina. It necessitated a trip to Boston where he was hospitalized for a week. While attending him there I met an Indian couple from Bombay who were at the Eye Institute for the same purposes. The four of us made an immediate connection despite the language and cultural barrier and we invited them to our apartment in New York City for the husband's recovery. Living together was an opportunity to absorb firsthand the effect of the teachings they followed. They were ardent disciples and supporters of a guru they called "Baba" and we learned the name Muktananda through their constant referrals to him. Both Bob and I were impressed by their devotion to and reverence for their Master, and felt it to be a positive influence in their lives. They returned to India in a few weeks, leaving us with happy memories of the blending of our spheres.

On the way to the ashram in Piedmont with Vera and Harold, I told them the story of how I was introduced in advance to their new teacher. I had the premonition that this person was about to play a major role in my life. I was ripe.

But to me the meeting was uneventful and uninspired. I witnessed a sizable group paying respect to a lively man who spoke through an interpreter. I was glad to have met the important focus of my friends' lives, but was touched not at all myself.

Weeks later, back in New York City, I answered a call from one of Swami Muktananda's devotees. The sect had opened an ashram in New York City and he was going to visit there soon. They had been informed that we had a large apartment available for meetings and wanted to know if we would host an evening dedicated to introducing Muktananda to our own community. We were glad to serve in this capacity, mostly as a tribute to our Indian friends and the effect they had upon our lives. I carefully prepared our place to receive the guests. More than one hundred people were invited and when the time arrived it seemed as if all had accepted. Our home was jammed with those eager to experience the Eastern teacher. The meeting had been called for 7:30 p.m. I had myself prepared a vegetarian selection of snacks and tables were heavy with the repast to be served following Muktananda's speech. I had been told in advance which foods he preferred and the colors of his choice. The house was decorated with an abundance of orange, a raised platform with a special seat resembling a throne was built, and he was eagerly awaited. We had rented folding chairs and our rooms were set up as an auditorium. The assemblage was getting restless. The swami had not yet appeared and it was past 8:30. I called the ashram to inquire when he would be arriving and was told it would be still a little while. Uneasily I faced a murmuring audience to explain. Some of the people had driven more than a few hours for the occasion. Finally, the great man presented himself. He breezed into the room where we were all congregated and seated himself on his throne. He proceeded to ask through the interpreter if there were any questions. People were dismayed, as they felt the need for hearing his message first. In the stunned silence the swami stood up and announced "Well then, if there are no questions, I will leave." I couldn't believe this was happening. I quickly jumped up and stopped him and rapidly told the story of how I had first been introduced to his philosophy. It seemed to break the ice and his interpreter convinced him to make a short presentation. He did so in what seemed a curt manner. A few tentative questions were raised that he answered abruptly. He arose once again, and left. The entourage accompanying Muktananda expressed their disbelief at what had just occurred. They insisted his actions were totally atypical and they had never seen him behave in this manner. I was disillusioned, embarrassed and tired. I served his favorite foods to the equally annoyed invitees. The evening was over, and it was not a success. I did not want to hear about it again.

A small gathering was being arranged at the Tarrytown Conference Center in New York State. It was to be low-keyed and unobtrusive in order to give shelter and confidentiality to the two dozen invited international scientists who would be presenting research papers on Uri Geller. Our Foundation's participation was needed to help fund this endeavor. Bob and I attended the proceedings for three days and were stimulated by the variety of work that had been done in more than six countries by this group of people, many of whom were meeting each other for the first time. Uri Geller's television appearances in England, Japan, Germany, Australia and Holland had a contagious effect on many young children who had watched the program. As Uri instructed his viewers to pay careful attention to his directives and imitate his actions, many children found they were able to get the same results in metal bending. The scientists assembled had studied some of the children and dubbed them "Mini-Gellers." There was an abundance of shared research to enthrall us and much speculation by the presenters on how to proceed in the future. At the end of the formal exchange the participants were seated in a room chatting about their conclusions. One of the physicists made the statement that their ideas were extending beyond the realm of physical reality as we define it today. He continued to explain his understanding of the pre-eminence of mind over brain, describing the brain as the physical computer upon which the mind acts. He continued with an analogy that mind triggered a psychokinetic effect in the brain through thought. People around him nodded their heads in agreement and someone picked up the thread. "We know how brain originates in matter, but where does mind come from?" Someone else responded, "We can hypothesize a vast field of consciousness akin to Jung's theory of a collective unconscious." This seemed to be accepted and then someone persisted, "So individual mind differentiates from the vast sea of the unconscious. Well then, where does this unified, limitless consciousness originate?" A pregnant silence ensued. For a long few moments no one spoke. Then a nuclear physicist quietly offered "Some call it God."

I can't say why this affected me so intensely. Certainly the remark was only of an average profundity. And yet I somehow felt as if I had traveled long enough with science. I would need a new traveling companion, but I didn't know where to begin to look.

*Black Building,
Columbia University
School of Physicians
and Surgeons—where
the Course was born.*

16
GOING HOME

Js

My mood was continuing to darken and I felt as if I was sinking into an abyss. The emotional pain was heightened by the rational knowledge that I had no reason to feel this way. I continued to repeat my blessings as a daily liturgy to lift my spirits. I sought a competent therapist who I believed would help to explain this growing despair. The psychiatrist enjoyed my life's story, and at each session she was more and more eager to hear about the soap opera I was living. I began to wonder which one of us was the more confused. I no longer knew what I wanted or where I was going. I was even considering separating myself from my marriage.

Dr. Douglas Dean.

Feeling as depressed as I did, it was no wonder I wanted to back out of a commitment made two months earlier to be introductory speaker at a conference on Kirlian photography at the New York Academy of Medicine. Now that the date was upon me, I desperately wanted to cancel my appearance. And yet I knew there was no way I could. And so I dragged myself across town to speak on healing and the importance of bringing non-traditional methods into the mainstream of medical treatment.

After the conference I went straight home and got into bed. I felt I was at the lowest point in my life. Alone in my bedroom I began to weep, and without even knowing where the call came from, I let out a desperate, wrenching cry: "Won't someone up there please help me!" The words surprised me, for I had never used them before, or even had thoughts like them before.

Two days later, around nine o'clock in the morning, my telephone rang. A friend from Detroit was in New York, and said it was very important that I see her, and could I possibly meet her for lunch at a mid-town restaurant. When I arrived at the appointed time she was waiting for me, accompanied by a man of about forty-five. She introduced him as her teacher of metaphysics, and told me he had remarkable talent as a numerologist. Knowing nothing about numerology, I only half-listened as she told how his amazing abilities had helped her find a more peaceful outlook on life. As we were leaving, my friend handed me the man's business card and insisted that I have my chart done. The man looked directly at me and said "I really do want to do your chart; it will be my gift."

The conversation puzzled me, but I truly believe there are no accidental meetings in life, and I felt I was to comply with my friend's wishes. Rationalizing, I told myself that numerologists, like tarot-card readers and others who attempt to read the future, can be very gifted sensitives who are simply using the tools of their trade to focus their abilities. Perhaps this metaphysician was "sent" to me to tell me something that would help resolve my stress. In my anguish, anything was worth a try.

And so the next morning I called and made an appointment to see him that afternoon. The numerological chart he had prepared based upon my name and birth date, which I had given him the day before, accurately described some of the most important events that had transpired in my life. He then said I would soon meet a much older woman who would become my teacher for as long as she lived and that within a year I would publish one of the most important spiritual documents known to humanity. When I told him that in no way was I about to write anything, he said "I didn't say you were going to write it; I said you were going to publish it." I told him that was ridiculous, as I wasn't in the publishing business. He smiled warmly "You'll see."

The next morning I was awakened by a phone call from my friend, Douglas Dean, who had been chairman of the conference at which I had spoken a few days before. Douglas said he had two reasons for calling: First, he wanted to know if I were feeling better, and second, he wanted to tell me that a professor of medical psychology at Columbia University's College of Physicians and Surgeons had been introduced to him at the conference, and had invited Douglas to come up to the University for lunch to discuss some topics of mutual interest. "Would you come with me, Judy?"

Even though I wasn't feeling well, Douglas insisted that I accompany him. I said I would go, for I had long been extremely anxious to talk to those within the orthodox medical community about holistic approaches to healing. This seemed the perfect opportunity to present our ideas to a professional with one of the most prestigious medical institutions in the country. After I hung up, I began to think about what material I could take with me that might intrigue the professor enough for him to help us forge some kind of link between the medical professionals and individuals who had healing abilities.

On May 29, 1975, Douglas and I drove to the Medical Center on upper Broadway in Manhattan to meet the professor, Dr. William Thetford. I felt somewhat apprehensive about the meeting, for I had no idea what sort of man to expect. Douglas had only spoken to him for a few minutes at the conference, and had had no time to get any kind of a clue to the man's attitudes or specific interests.

Judy and Dr. Helen Schucman.

Walking from the car through the flow of pedestrian traffic towards the crowded entrance to the Black Building at the Medical Center, I said to Douglas, "Oh look, there he is, waiting outside on the steps." I pointed to a tall, slender man. Douglas was stunned. "Yes, that's Dr. Thetford, but Judy, how do you know? You've never seen him!"

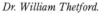

Dr. William Thetford.

I couldn't answer Douglas, for I hadn't thought before I said it. However, after I spoke the words I felt quite certain I already knew this person.

After the usual introductions, Dr. Thetford led us to the faculty cafeteria. In the lounge, he introduced us to one of his colleagues, Dr. Helen Schucman, a slight, short, late-middle-aged woman who couldn't have weighed much more than a hundred pounds. She was Dr. Thetford's co-worker. Both professors told us to call them by their first names, and Bill led us to a relatively quiet table.

Dr. Kenneth Wapnick.

After the usual small talk, I brought up the subject I had wanted to discuss, but neither of them showed any interest in holistic health. Bill and Helen kept talking about research in general, and the more they talked the more I wondered what I was doing there. Then I began to feel there was something on Helen's mind that she was not revealing, though for the life of me I couldn't imagine what it might be. All I knew was that it didn't have anything to do with the research designs she was discussing. And then, as we were eating our desserts, I heard myself saying something I couldn't believe. I turned to Helen, and out of my mouth came "You hear an inner voice, don't you?"

Helen blanched, and there was a strained look on her face as she said, very faintly, "What did you say?"

123

Bill pushed his chair back from the table, saying "Why don't we all go back to our office? I think we'd be a lot more comfortable there."

I didn't know whether to repeat what I had said to Helen, but I didn't have to concern myself, for as Bill led us from the cafeteria he very pointedly became our tour guide. He described, almost non-stop, all the various sections of the hospital as we passed them, until we finally arrived at his office. There we were introduced to their associate, Dr. Kenneth Wapnick. Bill then shut the door, locked it, and asked quietly "You will keep what we say in this room confidential, won't you?" Both Douglas and I gave him our assurances, though I couldn't guess what could possibly be so secret.

Bill and Helen spent the next two hours telling their story of the past ten years. The events they described did not seem bizarre to me, and I did not feel these people were strangers. In a way I could not explain, it appeared that I was being reunited with old friends, and what they were telling me seemed very natural, as though it were a continuation of events with which I had already been associated.

As their story unfolded, I found myself identifying not so much with the details of their life's journey but rather with the sense of predestination I gleaned behind their search. Helen and Bill supplied pieces of the collage that was their joint life both on a professional and personal basis. Married but childless, Helen's work was her focus, and she gave it her all. Professionally they seemed to make an excellent team, but they had marked personality differences. The younger by fourteen years, Bill was scholarly and introspective, with an excellent sense of humor and a pleasantly mild demeanor. Tall and handsome, his gracious way of listening must have earned him the respect and friendship of colleagues. Small, intelligent, snappy, critical and articulate, Helen seemed an excellent foil.

Helen told us that when she was in her late forties in 1959, she was hired by Bill for the position of research psychologist at Columbia University School of Physicians and Surgeons. Bill was then Director of the Psychology Department of Presbyterian Hospital. Immediately upon seeing Bill she had felt, "Oh there he is, he's the man I'm supposed to help." She was used to those inner insights and often accepted them despite the suggestions of her more rational mind. For, in the case of her joining the staff at Columbia, Helen accepted the position although she had more lucrative offers elsewhere.

They told me they had worked together for six years, surviving the vicissitudes of academia, their personal relationship worn but intact. Both of them often wondered how they had maintained their willingness to continue, as it was getting more and more difficult to weather their private storms.

One June day in 1965, after a particularly trying staff meeting, Bill and Helen returned to their office. Bill said he felt acutely frustrated by the stress-reflecting attitudes held by themselves and associates, and even more resentful at the way in which they interacted with each other. At this point in their story, Helen chimed in to describe the confrontation. "Bill wanted to say something which he evidently found hard to talk about. He drew a deep breath, grew slightly red-faced, and actually delivered a speech. Based on the past, he hardly expected a favorable response from me. But he said he had been thinking things over and had concluded that our approach to relating to others was wrong. He said vehemently 'There *must* be another way, and I am determined to find it.' The new way Bill suggested was cooperation rather than competition. He was going to look for the constructive side in all his relationships and not let negative feelings prevail. Somehow Bill's gravity and sincerity struck a chord deep within me and I knew he was right. Though he obviously expected ridicule, I jumped up and told Bill with conviction that I would join with him in the new approach, whatever it might be."

Helen and Bill told Douglas and me that this joining represented a real commitment that was unprecedented in their relationship. It seemed to be the signal for the beginning of a series of remarkable events that occurred during the summer of 1965. Helen had begun to have both sleeping and waking dreams (or visions) which were three-dimensional and in color. She told us this was not an unfamiliar occurrence, as she had many times in the past caught flashes of inner pictures which she likened to black-and-white stills. These new pictures were heightened by color, and she was included in the action. Helen indicated that she was frightened by the emotional power of these mental movies and the fact that they seemed to have a deep spiritual significance. It was not close enough to the scientific path for a respectable research psychologist. As they related to us the variety of these inner experiences, I felt recognition kindle my enthusiasm. Something was happening inside me as I listened to the fascinating sequences of the dramas. It did not seem in the least strange that these two professionally proper people had embarked on such a mystical trip. I savoured the anecdotes and knew they were an important part of the story. I had a thrill of happy anticipation, as if I already knew the outcome of their tale would affect me for the rest of my life.

After three months of what seemed like 'cosmic' preparation, Helen had told Bill she was about to do something very unusual. She did not know what this would be, but the thought of it discomforted her greatly. One evening while she was sitting in her bedroom, an inner voice with which she had become familiar began to give her definite instructions. Afraid, she telephoned Bill. "It keeps saying 'This is a course in miracles. Please take notes.'" In a kindly and supportive manner Bill suggested that Helen, with her excellent shorthand, might just as well sit still and let the inspiration flow. He promised to meet her in their office before the staff arrived and listen to what she had taken down. Still dubious, Helen assented. She settled herself in an attentive position and listened. That first night Helen was given the introduction to *A Course in Miracles*. As Bill had suggested, she brought it into their office the next morning whereupon Bill agreed to type it as he was the better typist, while Helen read her notes out loud.

Douglas and I listened, fascinated, as they continued their narrative, reliving the days when Helen acted as a scribe to the inner voice with Bill as her collaborator. The material they transcribed, through a process Helen called "inner dictation," eventually comprised three volumes and was revealed to them in the form of a self-study course in spiritual psychotherapy. The purpose of the course was to heal relationships and bring about inner peace.

As they told us of its emphasis on forgiveness as the process to remember one's true identity in God, I felt a force begin to stir in me that I had unknowingly long suppressed. An ancient call so very familiar was resounding in my mind, almost drowning out the details Helen and Bill were sharing. I heard them say the *Course* consisted of a text, a workbook for students and a teacher's manual, and that it had taken them almost ten years to complete the project. I listened to the stories of its origin and its message, which certainly were gripping. Yet I felt an impatience building within me to see the manuscript immediately. Bill revealed that they had shown their secret work to very few, not wanting to share it with their professional community. Suddenly I realized I had come there that day for just this. I would have time, much time, to savour the details. Now I needed to slake my thirst. Bill opened his locked filing cabinet and brought out the seven heavy black thesis binders housing *A Course in Miracles*. I reached for the first volume and scanned the introduction:

> This is a course in miracles. It is a required course. Only the time you take it is voluntary. Free will does not mean that you can establish the curriculum. It means that you can elect what you want to take at a given time. The course does not aim at teaching the meaning of love, for that is beyond what can be taught. It does aim, however, at removing the blocks to the awareness of love's presence, which is your natural inheritance. The

opposite of love is fear, but what is all-encompassing
can have no opposite. This course can therefore be
summed up very simply in this way:
>Nothing real can be threatened.
>Nothing unreal exists.
Herein lies the peace of God.

There are too few moments in life when one is really aware
of the powerful present and its slighter handmaidens, past and
future. This was one of those holographic instants. In nonspace
and nontime, I gave an impassioned sigh of gratitude. I knew
absolutely this was the answer to my call for help. I held *A Course
in Miracles* in my hands and trembled as I recognized that,
miraculously, I had been handed my map home.

When I left Bill and Helen's office it was already late in the
afternoon. They had given me the entire manuscript. Carrying
the load in a shopping bag, I walked lopsidedly to my car. I now felt
I could carry any weight effortlessly, as I myself was being carried by an excitement that gave me wings. I had never known
such a buoyant feeling, as if I were supported by a current of air
which would never falter. I couldn't wait to read this treasure. I
burst into our apartment with such enthusiasm I startled my
family. All of them had to sit and listen to the story exactly as it
had been recounted to me. A bubbling feeling within made me
wonder if I was about to explode. There was no doubt that something truly unparalleled had happened in my life. Even before
dipping into the contents of the *Course* I already knew it was to
be my life's work.

I did not go to sleep that night. I could not possibly devour
a half million words at one sitting, but I made a good attempt. At
one point I recall pausing to give my mind a chance to catch up.
And the old refrain from my childhood vision echoed "Now you
know, now you know, now you know."

What I did know was that it would take years of studying to
master the discipline revealed in *A Course in Miracles*. I vowed
to make the effort.

My thoughts dwelled on the curious combination of events
which had brought me to this day, reunited with my intended
fellow travelers in the hands of my Great Travel Companion.

The feeling was so compelling that I wanted to pray. On the
blackboard of my mind flashed my father's favorite Hebrew
prayer. I uttered it first in the familiar ancient tongue and then
translated it out loud for emphasis:

"Blessed art thou, O Lord our God, King of the universe, who has kept us in life, and hast preserved us
and enabled us to reach this season."

At last I had found my way.

17
ON COURSE

Js

Everything that happened to me before the *Course* is "B.C."
From now on it's strictly "A.C." I remind myself that A.C. also
stands for alternative consciousness, and that's what it's all about.

As I began my new study, it became apparent that I was
dealing with the essence of spiritual truth—the same truth that
has always been. But the *Course* has woven this truth into spiritual and psychological themes in a specific and organized way.
Throughout our lives we are constantly urged "Love thy neigh-
bor." *A Course in Miracles* tells us how. It seemed to me the definitive spiritual "How To" book. Its primary emphasis is on
removing the blocks to our awareness of love's presence. The
process for accomplishing this goal is called forgiveness; it is the
blueprint to heal our personal relationships. In forgiving others,
we forgive ourselves, and so gradually become aware of the One
Self we all share.

Shifting my perceptions away from ego identification was
the immediate problem I had to overcome. The *Course* jogged
my memory of the transcendent experience which I already knew
as my reality. With that focus I totally understood that we have
never really been separated from our Source or from each other.
There was no question I had been given this document to help
me out of the sinking quicksand of misperceived relationships.
I intended to use it for just that.

Racing through the text of *A Course in Miracles,* I started to reel from the impact of the emotions it generated within me. It seemed an impossible task to extricate myself honorably from conflicting personal commitments. That very first night I had read:

> When you feel the holiness of your relationship is threatened by anything, stop instantly and offer the Holy Spirit your willingness, in spite of fear, to let Him exchange this instant for the holy one that you would rather have. . . . Whoever is saner at the time the threat is perceived should remember how deep is his indebtedness to the other and how much gratitude is due him, and be glad that he can pay his debt by bringing happiness to both. Let him remember this, and say:
>> "I desire this holy instant for myself, that I may share it with my brother, whom I love. It is not possible that I can have it without him, or he without me. Yet it is wholly possible for us to share it now. And so I choose this instant as the one to offer to the Holy Spirit. That his blessing may descend on us, and keep us both in peace."

I called Jerry in California to tell him what had transpired. I was jabbering so fast on the telephone it was a wonder he could hear my words. Perhaps he didn't and heard my heart instead. We agreed to review the document together on my next trip west, which was imminent. I knew big changes were ahead and it was not without some fear of the unknown that I anticipated that trip.

The *Course* did not seem to kindle Bob's enthusiasm. He was still following his own process of guided writing and utilizing the effect in trying to help people overcome pain. I wanted to share my treasure with the world. But first I had a debt to pay. I called Kevin, the numerologist who had predicted I was going to meet a much older woman who would become my teacher. I had to tell him the history of events and that I did indeed recognize Helen, twenty-two years my senior, as the teacher for whom I had longed. We made an appointment to meet at his home so I could show him the manuscript. Kevin was unmoved by the material itself but gratified that his "sight" was so clear. He knew his own metaphysic was his particular path and acknowledged that it certainly seemed as if I had found mine. And then something so strange began that trying to recapture the sense impressions of that time is like attempting to catch a sunbeam. Kevin identified himself as my tutor in mysteries I had not yet grasped. He advised me he had been "instructed" to help me experience personally many of the paranormal feats I had studied and witnessed. He cautioned "Until you have recognized in the deepest part of your being that we *all* have limitless psychic capabilities you will continue to treat those who evince these traits as 'special.' They are no more special than you. You need to know this in order to advance." I must have been under the spell of his unusual prophecy, which had already borne fruit, for I agreed to start the training.

In two intense months of visits I was ushered into a speeded up unfoldment of part of my self I had never met. In the very first session Kevin had me practice a breathing exercise that relaxed me into an altered state of consciousness. Though still aware of my surroundings and in full control of myself, I did not resist his powerful suggestions. The first task I was assigned was to write upon a piece of lined paper everything that was internally visible to me in a room in his apartment I had not previously seen. I did not impose barriers to this knowledge, but extended myself beyond my body through my mind into the darkened room. I described in detail a desk, photographs of Kevin as a child, a beautiful framed portrait of his mother, the color of the carpet, the fabric and design of the bedspread, the placement of a mirror and a Louis XIV chair. When I had finished, Kevin had me take my list and enter his den. I don't think I was at all surprised to be standing in a room I had just visited, and accurately described. Kevin asked me to practice the technique at home often and to "travel" to places farther away, in partnership with friends who would give me feedback.

Not long afterward I had to travel to Slippery Rock State College in Pennsylvania to address a group of educators. I was assigned a lovely guest suite in an empty dormitory. After I settled in, it became apparent that I was truly alone in a building that usually housed five hundred students. I lay in bed, hearing every sound acutely, wondering if I was safe. I wished at least one other person were there so I could release my anxiety and go to sleep. I got up and walked down a long hallway to a public telephone to call Bob, back in New York City. There was no answer. Then I dialed Jerry in California. He was not home. I tried Kevin's number and heard only an extended, hollow ringing. I was getting more and more nervous, and slightly desperate. So I counseled myself to take my mind off foolish fears and practice the "distant travel" which Kevin had taught me.

I relaxed with my meditative exercise and visualized myself visiting Kevin in his apartment in Manhattan. I did manage to imagine his living room clearly but it was darkened, as were all the other rooms I explored in this manner. In my mind's eye, I sat on his couch to await his return. Somehow it was more comforting to my psyche to be in his sheltered place than vulnerable in this big empty building. All at once I "saw" Kevin's front door open. A shaft of hall light illuminated the entrance and I saw him standing there in a pink oxford shirt, wearing dark grey slacks with a light-colored sports jacket slung over his arm. As he flicked on the overhead light I jumped up to greet him. In a flash my mind remembered that I wasn't there and I brought my consciousness back to my dormitory room at Slippery Rock State College. It had all seemed so very real. I wanted to know immediately if I had been dreaming. I dashed to the public telephone and called Kevin's number. He picked up the phone with "Hello, Judy. Why did you leave so quickly? Did I frighten you?" It was hard to accept, but it *had* happened—to *me!* I quizzed him as to the clothes he was wearing and I was perfectly correct.

Kevin next taught me how to summon my own inner resources for psychokinesis and healing. By practicing an ancient ritual of "gathering God's force" into my being, I astonished myself by bending and splitting my favorite heavy sterling ring set with a huge amethyst stone. Kevin had never seen it or touched it and when I used the process at home I could scarcely believe the results. I was more than a little frightened, and I suddenly felt compassion for the physicist from the Rockefeller Institute who witnessed Uri Geller's feats and "saw but would not believe."

A few days after this incident Bob suddenly took ill and began to have a convulsion. He was trembling violently on his bed, in a cold perspiration with teeth chattering, and barely conscious. I knew I had to summon help instantly but I had an impelling conviction that it would be too late. I pulled off his shoes and, using my new "technique," placed each of my hands on the soles of his feet while internalizing a prayer. Slowly the shaking subsided and in a few more moments he sat up, feeling fine. He was as surprised as I, and neither of us knew what had come over him. Later he jokingly remarked that the universe was providing ample means for my testing myself and he was glad to be a part of the plan to help me acknowledge the "inner healer." After all, hadn't he been doing just this for years?

The most amusing aspect of my indoctrination into psychic self-worth was the rapport I developed with Tammy's dog, Saki Toomi. A pampered, prideful, cat-like Shih-tzu, Saki seemed to take everyone for granted. He just did not act like a dog. I resented the years of care I had squandered on him and the fact that the outcome was indifference. Kevin had taught me faith in my own telepathic process, especially message sending. It was the middle of the afternoon and I was working in my library. It was hours before Saki's dinner time and his famous meatballs were not yet prepared. I was seized with the urge to play a game.

I stopped what I was doing, concentrated on an image of meat-balls and rice and called in my head with great conviction "Saki, dinnertime!" In a few seconds I heard the pooch dash from our bedroom, where he had been resting on a purple velvet chaise lounge, through the long hallway, into the kitchen and then into the utility room where he was always fed. No dinner. I could hear him shoving his empty bowl around the floor and then he trotted all the way back into the bedroom. I waited about five more min-utes and gave it another zap. He repeated the performance, then slunk back to his nap. Ten minutes more, and I struck again. This was getting to be fun! He made the final dash into his feeding room and then, instead of returning to his slumbers, marched straight to where I was sitting, gave me an annoyed "gruff" and lay down at my feet, watching warily. I tried it once more, to no avail. This canine was not to be fooled—ever again. But from then on, I was more keenly aware of his moods than before, and he responded just a little bit to mine.

As I was concurrently studying *A Course in Miracles* with Helen, Bill and Ken Wapnick as my advisors, I began to measure everything that was happening to me in the terms of the *Course*. One of the early useful tools for me was the *Manual for Teachers*. I needed to put my recent activities into a perspective which fit the philosophy of the *Course*. Helen suggested I read what the manual had to say in the section entitled "Are 'Psychic' Powers Desirable?" I read:

> There are, of course, no "unnatural" powers, and it is obviously merely an appeal to magic to make up a power that does not exist. It is equally obvious, how-ever, that each individual has many abilities of which he is unaware. As his awareness increases, he may well develop abilities that seem quite startling to him. Yet nothing he can do can compare even in the slightest with the glorious surprise of remembering Who he is. Let all his learning and all his efforts be directed toward this one great final surprise, and he will not be content to be delayed by the little ones that may come to him on the way.
>
> Certainly there are many "psychic" powers that are clearly in line with this course. Communication is not limited to the small range of channels the world recog-nizes. If it were, there would be little point in trying to teach salvation. It would be impossible to do so. The limits the world places on communication are the chief barriers to direct experience of the Holy Spirit, Whose Presence is always there and Whose Voice is available

but for the hearing. These limits are placed out of fear, for without them the walls that surround all the separate places of the world would fall at the holy sound of His Voice. Who transcends these limits in any way is merely becoming more natural. He is doing nothing special, and there is no magic in his accomplishments.

My work with Kevin was finished.

The preceding summer I had enrolled in the Humanistic Psychology Institute's doctoral program and was now preparing to choose the subject for my dissertation. The glow surrounding the prospect of my degree was beginning to fade as I recognized just how much time I wanted to devote to studying the *Course.* I had to make a choice. I wanted to follow through with my plans for higher academic standing but I felt the magnetic pull of *A Course in Miracles* waiting to be tackled. Helen was aware of my ambivalence and helped precipitate a resolution. Using the language of the *Course* she prompted "Why don't you turn the whole problem over to the Holy Spirit and see what happens?" I was still relatively uncomfortable with the Christian terminology of the *Course,* although I knew its message was certainly ecumenical. The *Course* defines the Holy Spirit as the "Voice for God" and describes it as a mediator between illusions, which are of *this* world, and the truth, which is of God.

I mused on the situation while visiting with my parents at their home in Brooklyn during the Jewish High Holidays. I attended synagogue with my father and recited from the prayer book. At one point I was reading in the familiar Hebrew and my eyes stopped at an expression I knew so well in that language: *Ruach Hakodesh*—translated, the Holy Spirit. I had neglected to interpret the English phrase into my own tradition and I thrilled to the sudden recognition that I had *always* been listening to God's Voice.

After a family dinner that day, I retired to think out my problem in quiet. In my father's book-lined study I lay back in a recliner with my eyes closed, calling upon *Ruach Hakodesh* to help me. I expected a miracle and I got one. I felt a strong compulsion to rise from the chair and walk toward one of the bookcases. I did not know why I was to do this, I just followed the inner directive. As I walked, I held out my right arm in front of me and, when I reached the bookcase, grasped the first book I touched. I looked at it in surprise as I had never seen it before. It was Gershom G. Scholem's *On the Kabbalah and Its Symbolism.* Why had I been led to this particular book while awaiting resolution of my problem? Opening the book at random, I saw a symbol of a crown with

the legend "Kether Elyon, the supreme crown of God." The
description attributed these signs to the *Zohar,* which represents
Jewish theosophy, or mystical doctrine. A laser beam flashed
through my memory, searching for a familiar connection. Suddenly it rested upon the image of a simple gold crown handed to
me by the spirit of my Grandmother through Ena Twigg four
years before. I did not know what it meant then, but now, as I
scrutinized this volume which I was to read from cover to cover
many times, I saw the connection and heard the message. "Your
way is to be united with God. The crown represents that achievement." There was no more conflict. My problem was solved in
this illumination. I resigned from my doctoral program to study
A Course in Miracles fulltime.

It was during this period, right after Helen and Bill had
given me the manuscript, that I began to see clearly the sequence
of events in my life that were such a gentle preparation for my
life's work.

I did not yet know my role with the *Course.* I was so involved
with the process of studying the document—and fifteen hundred
typed pages, richly profound in every sentence, took a great deal
of concentration. The instant unity of the four of us—Helen, Bill,
Ken and me—was such that we were encouraged to spend a great
deal of time together. We adopted a routine of meeting daily for a
few hours as they were on their way home from the Medical
Center. We used our large living room overlooking the park for
our "club house" as we started to discuss the future of the *Course.*

At one point I asked Helen why she had freely given me
A Course in Miracles when it had been shared with so few. She
replied that she and Bill knew the material was not for them alone,
although they were reluctant to give away their deep, dark,
"guilty" secret. The inner Voice told them someone would come
along to "take it on its way." Bill interjected that two years earlier
he had first seen me as moderator of a conference on Kirlian
Photography at Town Hall. He remarked to himself at the time,
"I'm supposed to meet her, but not right now." He didn't see me
again until I was on the program with Douglas Dean and he remembered that flash of intuition. Then, after meeting me, Helen
asked the Source if she should give me their work, and the answer
was strongly affirmative. Helen wanted a more specific answer,
so she asked "Why her?" And she spoke to me the words of the
reply: "Because she is now ready for her spiritual education."
Which of course I was.

I realized from the beginning how lucky I was to have three
experts available as I crammed my head full of the *Course.* They
were as anxious for me to reach their level of learning as I was,
although it would be many years before I would feel that kind of

familiarity with it. They were all equally helpful, although I formed different relationships with each, according to the way our personalities meshed. Bill became my beloved, earthly elder brother—consoling, explaining without judgment, teaching with patience and humor. Helen appointed herself the adopted mother-to-my-mind, and demanded a daughter's attentiveness that I found hard to meet. She did not coddle me, insisting upon an attitude of nothing withheld intellectually, emotionally or personally. With a force like Helen, I couldn't stand still. Ken became the trusted, brilliant younger brother—Helen's chosen son. As I had been raised in a household that absorbed so many varied relationships, there was no competition when I added a few others. And so my days became even busier, but this time with a focus so obviously missing before. Peace began to peek around the corners of my life.

A few months after I received the *Course,* I began to have an unusual series of dreams that mystified me, yet left me feeling exalted. I would often awaken in the night, aware that in my sleep I had been "hearing" ten tape recorders simultaneously speaking whole passages from the text. I knew that in my sleep state I heard and retained all the messages despite the cacophony. Awakening, I would grasp for the elusive passages, deeply knowing that in my sleep I had understood their meaning. Even though it would have been impossible for me during ordinary consciousness I was convinced by my feeling of elation that in my sleep I was truly being taught, and I came to call the experience "learning through decaphonic sound." I had no regret that this could not be captured at will, and I came to trust the process unquestioningly. "After all," I rationalized to myself, "if I can't suspend judgment perhaps the phenomenon will be blocked."

While I was musing on this, a business associate of Bob's dropped by. This young entrepreneur in the gas and oil industry had been achieving great financial success, and had as his goal retiring from his professional life as soon as possible so he could devote the rest of his days to serving and learning with Swami Muktananda. We were not yet well-acquainted, and I had kept my views of his teacher to myself.

Yet, without preamble, this Baba enthusiast interrupted his business conversation with Bob to address me. "Judy, when I had a private audience with Baba Muktananda the other day, he said a strange thing. I wonder if you know what it means." I waited for him to continue. "He said he had heard about *A Course in Miracles,* and that I should tell you he was glad you had finally found your way." The mystery, unsolved in my mind months before, as to why this popular guru had set the stage for a fiasco in our home was revealed. I gave an astonished gasp of respect as I recognized the insight and knowing of such a seer. I certainly had been searching for a guide to higher knowing, and I was sure Muktananda had knowns that guide was *not* to be him.

The disciple added, noting that I was speechless, "Oh, by the way, Baba says the message in both his teaching and the *Course* is identical. Only truth is true, and the form is irrelevant. However to avoid confusion the seeker should choose only one form and consistently practice it." Once again I marveled at the feeling of release such a disclosure offered, and I said a silent thank you to the Eastern holy man.

The newest members of my "family" also became Jerry's teachers, as we both struggled to apply *A Course in Miracles* to our intense connection. The first glimpse of the *Course* touched the same chord of recognition in Jerry that it did in me. Although he had found academic discipline difficult throughout his years of professional education (due to dyslexia), he had an intense desire to absorb the wisdom of the *Course* and apply it in his personal and professional life. In fact, he became so dedicated to learning its message that we began a daily program of reading the material and discussing difficult portions on the telephone. I started to get a glimmer of the direction in which our relationship was headed. Jerry was a perfect study partner for me because he constantly questioned content and meaning, forcing me to clarify the *Course's* epistemology for myself. I invited Helen, her husband Louis, Bill and Ken to accompany me to California for part of our first summer together, so they could meet the people I had come to call my "California consciousness community." Jerry and I knew that many of them would eagerly welcome the form of truth the *Course* offered. We invited groups of individuals to meet the psychologists from Columbia and to be introduced to *A Course in Miracles.* It was extraordinary how many people showed up. My close friend James Bolen, who published *Psychic* magazine, was one of the first to realize what the *Course* meant to him—a very personal answer to his continuing quest. He formed a rapport with Helen which, through their appreciation of each other, started to set the next step of the plan in action.

So many came forward for copies of the *Course* that there was a need to share it in a more convenient manner than fifteen hundred loose photocopied pages. We had it reduced photographically and split into four more-manageable volumes. We could not keep up with the demand. Through our nonprofit Foundation for ParaSensory Investigation, I distributed copies to those who appeared. We ran out of sets so quickly we were aware that the *Course* was beginning to spread exponentially. Two acquaintances in the publishing industry offered to publish it. It seemed like a good idea, but the *Course* was considered too lengthy to be commercially successful and they recommended cutting it. As it had not been edited for simplification, it seemed it should not be edited for profit-making, and we knew we had not yet come across the appropriate method for printing and distributing it. We entertained the ideas of a slew of people who were useful in showing us what *not* to do as we waited patiently for some kind of guidance.

On Valentine's Day of 1976 Helen, Bill, Ken and I were discussing the apparent need to publish the *Course* quickly. We were in a quandary. We knew what we *didn't* want, but we didn't know what we should do. We decided to consult the inner Voice as a group. Perhaps we would get some answers. We agreed upon a question: "Should *A Course in Miracles* be published now?" and each with closed eyes turned within for inspiration. When we opened our eyes each of us felt that the internal answer was a powerful affirmative. That was easy. Next step. The question was formed: "Who should publish this material?" We canvassed ourselves for the reply. Helen had heard that those who will devote their lives to this alone should do the job. I had heard that it should be a nonprofit organization, so those who could not afford the price could receive scholarship copies as a "gift of love." Bill added that the *Course* should not be changed in any way from the original, and Ken's directive was that somehow or other we must all be involved.

"Well, where are we going to find a group that meets all these criteria?" Suddenly we looked at each other in amazement. *We* were to do the job. It was clear that we would be devoted to the *Course* for the rest of our lives. We knew we did not want it edited in any way. We wanted to make it available to those who could not pay, and Bob and I already had the structure of a nonprofit entity in the Foundation for ParaSensory Investigation. We all affirmed that this was the most sensible plan.

One obstacle yet remained: the money. Our foundation had about eighty dollars in its bank account. How could we possibly raise such a huge sum? We knew publishing three hardcover volumes had to cost more than fifty thousand dollars. Once more we asked a question in a meditative state: "Where is the money to come from?" I was flabbergasted by the answer. Too stupefied to report it, I waited until all assembled had given their input. Helen had felt that "Judy will be told what to do" and neither Bill nor Ken received a clear response. Finally I was able to choke out what I had heard. It was very simple. "Make the commitment *first*." I was willing to use all my assets to make this happen, and I quietly pledged "I will."

The next morning my first call was from Reed Erickson, a man I had briefly met twice before. He telephoned from his home in Mazatlan, Mexico to tell me how important the manuscript of *A Course in Miracles* had become to him. One of his associates, my friend Zelda Suplee, had given him the bulky typescript and he had been studying the lessons for months.

"You must print the *Course* in a hardcover edition as soon as possible," he urged. "It's just too difficult to manage this way." Erick was president of the Erickson Educational Foundation and a close friend of Stanley Krippner. I told him we had already received that advice in the form of inner guidance, and just the night before I had pledged to publish.

"But I don't know where I'm going to get the money, Erick."

"Well, Judy, that's the reason I'm calling. I was directed by my internal voice to sell a piece of property last week and I want to donate the entire proceeds to your foundation to publish the *Course.* The amount should completely cover the first printing of five thousand hardcover copies." It was then I knew the true meaning of "Make the commitment first."

With the commitment to publish the *Course* and the funding to make it possible, events began to occur at a remarkably rapid pace to set this program into action. I had always suspected there were no chance meetings and that life was not a random process, but rather an unfoldment of learning opportunities. Evidence to support his belief system was consistently offered during the united effort to make the *Course* ready for wider dissemination. Individuals came forward who felt they had some part in this particular plan and identified themselves and their function. I did not have to search for a printer. Knowing little about typesetting or graphics, it was gratifying to me that a student of the *Course* offered his professional services in preparing the document for publication. With an intense dedication and deep personal connection, Saul expedited the operation so that five thousand hardcover sets of *A Course in Miracles* were ready for distribution within four months—a feat of acceleration certainly astonishing for this industry. On June 22, 1976, precisely within the chronology Kevin had predicted, students were receiving their three-volume sets. We gave a party to celebrate the occasion, and the synchronicity of that date falling upon Douglas Dean's sixtieth birthday seemed most appropriate. With great joy we all toasted both Douglas' important role as a catalyst in the venture and the birth of the latest form of the *Course.*

*Louis, Helen, Judy,
Bill, Ken in
California.*

18
BITTERSWEET SIXTEEN

I celebrated my sixteenth birthday this year. That is, everyone else celebrated it. I cried. This was the worst of all birthdays. It seems, for some reason, that everyone has always spoken to me about a sixteen year old being an adult, and I don't want to grow up.

Tammy and Cindy.

One reason I was so upset about being sixteen was a game Cindy and I used to play when we were six. We'd make believe that we were sixteen and were tall, mature-looking and beautiful. Now here I am, sixteen years old, looking like twelve and far from beautiful. It's pretty depressing. Mom got really annoyed with me when I covered all the mirrors in my room. I don't think she understands that I love myself on the inside (I'm my own best friend) but it's like I've betrayed my inside by the way I look on the outside. The only part of my body I like is my eyes, because my inside can pour out of them.

I know it's ironic that, although I don't want to grow up, I also don't want to look like a twelve-year-old. There's a group of girls at school who glop on gobs of makeup to look adult. Do you have to wear a mask in order to be sophisticated and grown-up? How do I reconcile the fact that, although I hate being five-foot-nothing, I refuse to wear high heels to make me five-foot-something?

Too bad I didn't get a growth spurt on my sixteenth birthday. I did get a chunky gold pin. It was a figure of a Chinese man, carrying a stick over his shoulders. Dad had been saving this present for me especially for this birthday. He knew that I would "absolutely adore it. It reminds me of you, Tam. It suits you perfectly." I was eager to see what my father thought was "just me." I opened the velvet box and froze a smile on my face as my mind raced. (Do you know who I am Daddy? Does this present really represent me to you?! I know you've given this to me with so much love, and I'll cherish it. I just wish you knew me a little better.) "I'll cherish it always Daddy," I said aloud. Luckily I didn't have to wear it because Mom put Dad's gift in the vault for me. Dad was pleased to know that I was taking such "mature" care of it. This maturity bit is sure confusing.

Even Jon, who I always thought knew me the best, considered this birthday to be a mark of budding adulthood. So instead of a new record or tickets to a movie, my brother decided to educate me with a good dictionary and thesaurus. My own brother . . . a traitor! No wonder I'm so reluctant to grow up! Where's the fun of it?

The most frightening thing about being sixteen was a promise made to me by Mom. When we were having one of our numerous discussions about sex, Mom told me she would take me to have a diaphragm fitted when I was sixteen. So many of my friends have already lost their virginity. Mom thought it best I be prepared (Never be underdressed for an occasion."). I swear, my mother is the complete opposite of any parent I know! For instance, all my friends have to fake being sick if they don't want to go to school. Either that or they cut school and forge notes from their parents. MY mother often tries to convince me to stay home with her. She knows my grades are high so she rationalizes that a day or two here and there couldn't hurt. In fact, she insists that I can learn a lot by staying home among the kooks once in a while. Usually I explain to her that I have to go to school—or, more often, that I want to go. What we have here is a case of complete role reversal. I tell you, it's crazy! But the craziest was when I found myself begging out of the contraception offer. "I don't want to be sixteen! I'm still short and stumpy. I don't think I'm a gold-chunky-Chinese-shlepper pin person and I don't want to use a thesaurus. I'm not ready for a diaphragm. I'm still a kid!" Mom agreed to postpone the gift of the contraceptive device for another year or so. I gave a sigh of relief on my sixteenth birthday. It was over.

It figures that I got a stomach attack shortly after my birthday. I've been having these damned attacks for the past few years. They're horrible. What happens is that my entire digestive system gets blocked up until it backfires. My digestive tract undergoes convulsions and I usually vomit sporadically for ten to twenty-four hours. I've had upper and lower gastrointestinal series. I've had barium enemas and X-rays. Nothing ever shows up and no doctor has ever been able to relieve my pain during the attacks. The psychics around the house say I'm repressing my "psychic," Dad says I'm repressing my "sexual," and Mom says "a little of each." I don't know what's going on—I don't even want to know what's going on. And yet, I know what's going on. It's just that there's so much energy inside me, I'm afraid that if I really let go it'll be like opening Pandora's box.

Sometimes I think I'd rather open Pandora's box than open our front door! I didn't think it possible, but with Mom and Bob's involvement with A Course in Miracles, *there's been a greater influx of people ringing our doorbell and telephone. The* Course *has become extremely popular by word of mouth. It seems that one mouth will talk to another mouth about the* Course *and then the other mouth will inevitably call us. Whenever I answer the phone now, I'm usually stuck answering an hour long question about the* Course. *If the question isn't about that, then it's probably an hour in-depth story about someone's mystical experience. I can feel their tears dripping into my ear while my foot anxiously taps in the anticipation that the story will climax and end. Many callers focus only on praising Mom—and forget it if the person senses I'm Judy Skutch's daughter! "Yes, my mother is wonderful. . . . Yes, she is beautiful. . . . Yes, I know I'm lucky to have her as my mother . . . Yes, I do know how many people she's helped . . ." Give me a break. Then there are still the calls asking for a psychic healer, but first they have to go into a long description of their illness in order to justify their need for a healer. I never give them Bob's*

143

name. I just take down their names, stories and phone numbers. But usually I just let the phone ring itself out instead of letting the callers wring me out.

With A Course in Miracles, *the atmosphere in this apartment has passed through psychic dementia and entered a mystical dimension. With the growing popularity of the* Course, *the books are already in their second publishing. Mom and Bob have changed the name and nature of the foundation from "The Foundation for ParaSensory Investigation" to "The Foundation for Inner Peace." I think it sounds sort of hokey, but they're pleased with it. The Foundation for Inner Peace is mainly concerned with the publication and distribution of the* Course. *Despite the name change, the Foundation's hierarchy remains the same: Mom is still the president, and Bob the vice president.*

I find the Course *very interesting but I have to admit that I'm getting tired of the whole thing. Mom's always talking about changing perceptions, being guiltless and seeing everything through love. (Bob doesn't say much, but he's constantly loving.) Dad tells me how hard he has to work to pay for my education. When I feel guilty about it, Mom bombards me with her spiel: "You allow yourself to feel guilty." I have to admit it makes some sense. I mean, Margie pays double for something, thinking that the price ensures better quality, but she won't buy my tightbudgeted father's guilt about money. What's hard to imagine is that Mom was ever married to Dad. Talk about miracles!*

A real miracle is that Mom has been reading and practicing the Course *for a year now, and I hate to admit it but she's actually changed a lot. She's become much more peaceful and she leaves all her decision-making to "Holy Spirit." It's pretty funny to hear Mom, Miss Jew of Brooklyn, talking in terms of Christ's message and the Holy Spirit. She doesn't much care for the Christian terminology herself, but she agrees with the* Course's *statement that words are just symbols used to describe a nonverbal state of being. She says that the more you get caught up with names and words, the farther away you stray from the desired experience of peace and love. Of course we should use words to communicate ideas, but actions must be used to communicate feelings.*

With all the peace and love going on around here, this place has turned into a holy sanctuary. Every room you walk into (with the exception of the kitchen, thank God!), you find people meditating. What are they meditating on? Usually world peace, eternal peace, or simply one of the lessons in the Course's *workbook. Then there's bound to be a new person among the crew who is crying somewhere in the apartment due to ending a lifetime search finally satisfied by: a miracle, Mom, and/or* A Course in Miracles. *As my friend Lori has put it, "Love, Peace, Woodstock, Donuts."*

With all this focus on releasing expectations, loving the world listening to Holy Spirit and meditating every hour, it's quite difficult to be a normal bitchy teenager around here. Believe me, I've tried. There have been times when I've come home from school just itching for a good fight. Of course, Mom is my best target, because I know how to bug her and she forgives me all the time. Anyway, at the beginning of her work with the Course, *I knew how to get her to fight with me. I'd follow her around the house and I'd gripe and grumble. Then, just when she would start to get furious with me, I'd say "Ah-ah-ah, remember the* Course! *This is all an illusion. You're not practicing love!" Boy, would that infuriate her! I usually got a door slammed in my face. After a while she'd cool off and I'd apologize because I had gotten rid of the gremlin in me. Those were the good old days. Now she's been working with the material for a year, and when I come home looking for a fight, I don't get one. I still follow Mom around the apartment and I still bellyache my brains out. But her reaction is not the same as it used to be. Instead, she stops whatever she's doing and smiles at me.*

"What's wrong, darling?"

"WHATAYA MEAN 'WHAT'S WRONG?'! I've been telling you what's wrong!

"You're always busy! You're always on the phone! You never have time for your family anymore! Blah, blah, blah."

Her smile doesn't falter as she asks "What's really wrong?"

"Will you cut out that Course in Miracles *loving-attitude crap? You're just adding to the issue!"*

Then my mother will attempt to hug me. I feel her love beginning to melt me and I don't want to be melted. I push her away. She grabs me tightly. I can't help it— I melt. Sometimes I burst into tears and reveal what's really been bothering me. Other times I try to hide a smile as I mumble "Bitch!" at her. She always laughs.

I swear it's no fun being around people who melt you when you want to have a good fight. I'm not saying that Mom no longer has problems and bad moods; she definitely has her goblins and gremlins, and when she does, she takes them out on me. But I have to get back at her. When she gives me grief, I repeat her "love performance." So how do you get into a good fight? It's a very difficult task. Jon takes the brunt of the fight in me when he comes home from college. He's a great fighter. He can hold grudges for days. I can't.

I think that one of my worst flaws is that I can't hold a grudge overnight. I desperately try to convince myself that I won't give in and give up my anger the next day. But when I wake up the next morning, it's a whole new day. The fight from the night before all of a sudden seems so foolish and unnecessary. I hate not being able to hold a grudge, because when I wake up, I feel like a forgiving hypocrite. It isn't that I renege on my stand in the fight, it's just that I release my emphasis on the importance of my stance. I'd gladly give up pride for the sake of peace and friendship. I'd probably forgive a friend for killing me if I woke up the next morning in afterlife.

Although A Course in Miracles *has inhibited the good scraps around here, it's also helped me gain more independence. Mom has always given me my freedom, but she often puts up a fuss about going out late at night on my own. I can't say that I blame her for fears about a girl alone at night in Manhattan, but sometimes she grossly exaggerates the danger. She doesn't even feel comfortable about my going down to the basement at night. When I'm going out late, I make sure to tell my mother while she is in front of other people. When she expresses her fears, I reply directly from* ACIM: *"In my defenselessness, my safety lies." Then I tell her that I'll surround myself with white light. A while back, Mom was told that you can protect yourself against harm simply by envisioning yourself surrounded by a white light energy field. Since she was told that, she puts white light around everything— including parking spaces, her car and her children. (Actually, we've all taken to putting white light around ourselves and it really* is *convenient when you want to save a parking space or protect your car from getting a ticket when you're in an illegal space.)*

Mom is in a bind when, at 10 p.m. in front of her guests, I say to her "Mom, I'm going out now. Don't worry, I'll use white light!" She can't tell me not to go out into the cruel city late at night because she has been preaching peace, love, trust, defenselessness, white light and donuts. So she smiles a frozen smile and tells me to have a good time and to take care. As I kiss her good-bye, she whispers in my ear "STINKER!" She is not a hypocrite. She goes out of her way to practice what she preaches. I respect her tremendously. In fact, although I hate to admit it out loud, I really do agree with all the Course's *precepts. Mom brought me up to believe those things way before she ever heard of the* Course. *It's just that, being an average teenager, I really need something to rebell against, so the* Course *has become a good scapegoat.*

Although at home I pretend rebellion against the Course, *I really try to put its principles into effect with my friends. But one day I found out that one of my friends was scared to tell me she lost her virginity to some guy I didn't like. That made me aware of how condescending I can be. I don't like that part of me at all. I'd honestly rather love and support my friends than judge them.*

I've noticed that I have a horrible ability to cut people down. It makes me come off as witty and intelligent at the expense of someone else. Once I publicly chopped a boy to tears and was shaken by the fact that my peers were impressed with me for it. I felt sort of sick to my stomach. It was as though I had begun to practice what I hated Dad's doing to me. After I apologized to the humiliated guy, I returned home in a state of confusion and disgust. How can such ugliness come out of me? What's this stupid game of criticism and cynicism I've taken part in? Is it a game primarily setting me as an opponent to the players with penises? I feel as though I've been brainwashed into believing that a relationship between a girl and guy is like a scene from Love Story *or a Humphrey Bogart/Lauren Bacall film—a constant battle of wits between the sexes. Is this just a trend among Manhattan private-school kids, or are all people my age like this? I've got to un-condition this cutting reflex of mine. It's an unnecessary barrier to hide behind. I love my father, but this is one character trait I don't want to inherit.*

Dad has absolutely no idea what goes on at Mom's,

*Dad vacuums the
tennis court.*

and I don't offer information. My two families are
worlds apart. Dad's house is a museum in which one
must ask permission to sit on certain chairs and walk
on certain floors in certain rooms. At Dad's, the dinner-
table conversations consist of discussing plans for the
future, what bills have to be paid, what centimeter of
area has fingerprints on it (or the painters forgot to
touch up), and continual bickerings between Dad and
Marge. After dinner, Dad and I clean the glass dining-
room table with Windex until it is void of spots and
fingerprints. At Mom's dinner table, we discuss the top
ten miracles of the day, the latest update from Holy
Spirit, and who is going to give in and answer the telephone's incessant ring. It's easy to talk to Mom and
Bob about my life at Dad's because they once had that
kind of life. I find it very difficult to discuss with Dad
my life at Mom's. How can I seriously tell him what
goes on there? He'd think I was crazy in a negative
way. I love him despite our differences, but I guess I
haven't yet given him the chance to love me the same.

Dad makes jokes about Mom's travels. He says he
can't understand how Bob puts up with it. I try to explain that Bob is a "homebobby" who doesn't like or
want to travel. Sometimes I even try to explain that Bob
doesn't feel the need or the desire to control Mom. My
explanations are either ridiculed or declared unsatis-
factory. The most acknowledgment and acceptance the
situation ever got from Dad was when he said, "Well
that's great if they really believe it! I'm sure glad I'm
not still married to your mother, because I know I
wouldn't put up with her traveling!" (It's nice to finally
be glad that things are the way they are.)

Mom took me on one of her trips to San Francisco
this year, where I got to spend time with her friend
Jerry Jampolsky. Jerry is a wonderful man who showed
me all of San Francisco. He's warm, cuddly and
reminds me of a worn-in teddy bear. When he smiles,
he scrunches up and reassembles the flab around his
"shlumfy" eyelids. His grin spreads from ear to ear as
his parted lips display a gap between his two front
teeth. Believe it or not, he's a very attractive man. It
isn't difficult for me to like Jerry, except when he asks
me about my ESP experiences.

Jerry is a child psychiatrist who is just opening up
to the field of parapsychology, and he's like a kid with

a new game. He wants to know everything about it and, can he play too? His enthusiasm for the field is infectious, but I have become immune. I hate talking about ESP because I become so self-conscious. I can't stand it being blown out of proportion. Jerry's soft face takes on a sternness and his usually playful tone is replaced by his professional child-psychiatrist manner as he asks "Tell me, Tammy, why do you think it's easier for you to send a telepathic message to your mother than to me?" The question usually comes from left field, and my eyes dart to Mom in a silent expression of "Oh, not again!" But Mom's smiling eyes respond "Patience, sweetheart, he just wants to learn.'" And I know she's right. So I collect my thoughts and my breath, and I answer Jerry: "I don't know that it is easier, but if so, it's probably because I usually send Mom mental messages when it's imperative. When I don't have to send one, I guess it's harder."

Jerry's reaction is mixed. He seems glad to get an answer out of me, yet I feel that he wants me to try to send him a message. I know I'm oversensitive, but it makes me feel like I'm being tested. I hate that. I gave up playing Scrabble for that very reason. I'd win so much that Grandma wanted to play me against all her friends. When I was expected to win all the time, I felt so much pressure that the game became work. In the same way, I wanted to stop answering Jerry's persistent questions. Yet I knew Jerry was not only questioning me for himself, but also as a means of conversing with me, so one night I finally gave in.

After a day of showing me the sights of San Francisco, we settled down to dinner. Throughout the meal Jerry tested me in little ways, such as asking me what color he was thinking of. He could tell that my impatience was beginning to spill over into my dessert, so he offered a little icing on the cake: He'd give me twenty dollars if I could guess the mileage on his odometer.

Usually, I can't do anything like that for money. I only win at poker when I don't bet money, and I can only guess the winner of a horse race if there's no cash riding on it. But this time was different. I was fed up with all the questions and I could think of no better way to both please and silence Jerry. So I made my mind go blank and waited until the numbers popped

Jerry and Tammy.

into my head. I opened my eyes to see Jerry anxiously awaiting my response. The suspense was building. First I milked the silence, then I rambled off a six-digit figure. I waited for Jerry's reaction. It couldn't have been better. He didn't say a word for a few seconds. Then, grinning ear to ear, he handed me a twenty-dollar bill. I ran to the car to check the odometer. I was correct. I wasn't sure whether I should take the money, but Mom told me I should and Jerry insisted on it. For the remainder of that night we put extrasensory perception to sleep. The next day he asked me how I did it. So it goes.

It didn't help that when I was in California I participated in some experiements at Stanford Research Institute (SRI). I worked with the ESP Teaching Machine. Russell Targ and Hal Puthoff connected the machine to a little computer of some kind. It documented all of my hits, misses and trials. In the beginning I didn't score very high, but I got better as I warmed up. They were pleased with the results because they said that they showed the definite presence of a learning curve. I had a great time. They invited me back whenever I want to do more tests. These didn't feel like tests to me—I was just playing with the box without caring about results. When the machine reads "USEFUL IN LAS VEGAS!", how can I not think it's all a game? It was only after Jerry got interested in me with the ESP Teaching Machine that it became yet another dreaded box. No matter how hard I tried, there was no way to keep a lid on it.

Russell Targ

19

ENDING PHASES, STAGES AND ERRORS

Having completed all required courses by my junior year of high school, I decided to apply to college a year early. This gave me one major advantage over the applying seniors: I had no fear of rejection. If I didn't get accepted in my junior year, there was always a second chance in the year to come. I decided to let fate be the judge.

Only it wasn't quite as easy as all that. It just happened that my high school did its utmost to discourage students from withdrawing their senior tuition from the private institution. My professors were asked not to give me recommendations—or at least not ones saying I was already fully prepared for college. Mr. Biology, my sculpting teacher, and a few others ignored the request. With their encouragement, I sent my application for early admission to the college of my choice, Tufts University in Massachusetts.

After my abrupt decision to take a shot at early admission, I had to take my Scholastic Achievement Tests. In two sittings I finished the quota of three tests necessary for college application. My friend Kit, who had wisely convinced me to take my SATs a year early, still needed to take another test. I decided to wait for Kit at the testing site. Instead of merely hanging around, I talked myself into taking a fourth test. Turning to the back of the booklet where all the exams were listed, I closed my eyes and pointed to one, which turned out to be math, my worst subject. But my preference didn't matter, since I wasn't taking the test seriously; I was simply passing time. Opening the booklet so I would appear to be reading it, I merely made designs on the answer sheet, randomly filling in one of every five holes on each line. When the testing time was over, I handed in the answers. My original intention was to cancel the exam, but curiosity prevailed. And, when the results were announced, I attained a higher score on that scholastic achievement test than on any of my others. I chalked it up as a unique and successful test of my individual achievements!

It was required that I write a descriptive sketch about myself for the college application. Mrs. Leviticus, the girls' college advisor and dean, advised me not to mention anything about my "parapsychological experiments or experiences." She said it would diminish my already slim chance of being accepted. I was upset and annoyed with her. My psychic experiments in California and in Brooklyn had been the bulk of my extra-curricular activities. I knew that Tufts was looking for applicants with a unique hobby or a specifically focused personal field of interest. I had been on the varsity volleyball and basketball teams, I watched many movies, and I devoted most of my time to painting and sculpting. I could have listed only these these things, but it would be like leaving out a chunk of myself. I decided if a school didn't want me because of my background and interests, then I didn't want the school. Mr. Biology convinced me to ignore Mrs. Leviticus. He told me that *he* thought I would get into Tufts despite its extremely low percentage of acceptances from our school. Not only did I write about my participation in parapsychological experiments, but I also enclosed a recommendation from Russell Targ, the scientist with whom I worked at Stanford Research Institute.

In February I was accepted for the fall of 1976 at Tufts. On his Bunsen burner, Mr. Biology boiled some tea for a celebratory drink. Kit cut one of her classes and took me out to lunch. My parents were proud. Mrs. Leviticus congratulated me and verbally patted herself on the back for having told me to place emphasis on my "unique parapsychological interests."

Suddenly it was my last year of high school. It all happened so quickly! I called Tufts and learned that one of the reasons for my acceptance was my "special" interests. Their experimental college had been offering a course called "Altered States of Consciousness." Having been to California a few times during my high school years, I had plenty of experiments to talk about in my applications. What I didn't say in those applications is that I was sick and tired of being a human guinea pig. I was growing restless with producing results for some scientist to prove to some other scientists that something does or doesn't exist. I was aware of solid arguments for compiling data in order to legitimize parapsychology, but I was simply no longer interested in providing the proof.

My experiments at SRI had begun with the ESP Teaching Machine and continued with experiments in remote viewing. There are two participants directly involved with the remote-viewing experiment. One person is the subject or viewer, the other person is the traveler. To oversimplify it, remote viewing entails a subject sitting in a room, trying to see telepathically where the traveler is going. The traveler has been given a randomly selected destination in a sealed envelope. At a designated time, the traveler opens the envelope and heads for the specified location.

Often the subject gets clear images of where the traveler goes, but misinterprets the images through rationalization. An example of this is a case in which a subject distinctly saw two people, each holding an object. The objects were described as oversized spoons that dwarfed the heads of the people holding the utensils. The subject drew a picture of the envisioned setting. In the sketch, the people were equally divided by a long rectangular object. The subject interpreted the scene as having been a dinner-table setting. To any independent viewer of the subject's drawing, it seems clear that the picture is of a tennis game (the oversized spoons being the tennis rackets and the long rectangular object being the net). Indeed, the traveler's specified destination had been the tennis courts. In a case such as this, even had the subject rated herself poorly, the independent judges considered the experiment a "hit" or a success.

I participated as "the subject" in several of such remote-viewing experiments. The experiments generally seem to have a high success rate, even among skeptics. According to the psychic researching scientists, remote viewing is one of the best experiments to provide immediate positive feedback to the participants.

In one of my remote-viewing experiments, I described the traveler as wearing a brown suit. I also gave an account of images of fences and farm animals. I detailed a clown with a cone-shaped hat. I drew a picture of an object I saw that looked like "an extremely fluffy cloud." I also saw a man dressed in blue. When the experiment ended I was given a list of places to select and rate: One of them was a carnival, one was a farm, one was a Baskin Robbins ice cream store. The carnival and the farm made sense to my descriptions, so I rated the ice cream store last.

The traveler for my experiment was a man named Arthur Hastings. After the experiment was over, Arthur told me where he had been. He said that he had gone to Baskin Robbins. At the store, he noticed the wallpaper above the counter. The picture on the paper were of various farm scenes with cows, fields and farmhouses. Then he looked at the assortment of ice cream. He noted a special glass cabinet in which there were upside-down ice cream cones. The ice cream was on the bottom and the cone was on the top. The ice cream was decorated to look like a clown's face and the cone was the clown's hat. Arthur ordered an ice-cream sundae and sat down at a table. He concentrated on the huge glob of whipped cream covering his sundae. When he said "whipped cream," I thought of my "fluffy cloud." At the ice-cream store, he bumped into a friend whom he hadn't seen for years. The friend was dressed in blue. Arthur was wearing a brown suit. I don't know how the rating went, but we considered the experiment a success.

In another remote-viewing experiment, a little twist occurred. I went through my description of where I thought the traveler was. My two main descriptions were of a large Y-shaped path or an air strip, and looking through a huge window at a large sculpture of some kind. Russell Targ was the experimenter. When the experiment was over, the traveler (Hal Puthoff) took me to the site. It was a playground. Although there were a few Y-shaped paths, the site didn't really resemble any of my images. We left the playground and drove to the Stanford University campus.

We toured the campus for a very short time, most of which we spent at the University bookstore. At the bookstore, I found myself looking out a large window. The view was of a big modern sculpture situated on a large path. The path was long and had other paths running into it, thus creating a Y-shape. I recognized the images immediately—sort of like a *déjà vu*. I remarked to my mother that this scene was much closer to my images than was the traveler's original destination. The traveler, as well, came to look out the window with me.

We left the campus and headed back to SRI, where we met Russell Targ. We told him where we had been. I didn't say that the bookstore reminded me of my images. When he heard where we had been, he said that he had been listening to my tape and the descriptions in it reminded him of the Stanford bookstore and the sculpture in front of it. This was one of the experiments that prompted research into precognitive remote viewing, which involves the subject's seeing what the traveler is going to see in the future. The subject records the images and descriptions before the traveler even gets the manila envelope. A large or a short lapse can occur between the subject's viewing time and the time when the traveler finds out and goes to his destination.

These were not the only experiments for which I was a subject in California.

*Jerry has become very interested in the ESP Teaching
Machine. I think maybe he wants to use it with his
child patients, but I'm really not sure. Whatever he
wants to use it for, I'm not letting him use it with me
anymore. I can't believe what I went through for Jerry.*

*For some reason Jerry wanted to test my brain waves
while I was doing the ESP Teaching Machine. He
took me to a clinic somewhere north of San Francisco
where there was an EEG (electro-encephalogram)
machine. I wasn't keen on the idea of being a human
guinea pig for Jerry, but I'd really grown to love him
despite his ridiculous questions and wacky experiments,
so I gave in.*

*In the room where I was to be tested, they set the
ESP Teaching Machine in front of me. Jerry was present, along with a large, strange doctor. I was uncomfortable. Had that been my sole source of discomfort,*
Dayenu.* *The doctor began attaching electrodes all
over my head. Wire connected the electrodes (as well as
my head) to the EEG machine. I couldn't imagine how
I was expected to play with the machine comfortably
without freely moving my head. The doctor switched
on the EEG, only to discover it wasn't working. He
fiddled around, but to no avail. Then he attempted to
remove the electrodes from my head, but no go. The
tube of contact grease he was supposed to have used as
a conductor for the electrodes turned out to have been
some kind of contact cement. Finally he had to tear the
electrodes from my scalp. I'm exaggerating only slightly.
It hurt a lot. I was left with chunks of gluey gunk in
my hair. Had the experience ended there,* Dayenu.

*The doctor then decided to replace the electrodes
with needles. I actually sat there while he pricked a
bunch of needles into my head. I didn't say a word. I
was furious. Jerry looked pained and apologetic. I was
disgusted.*

*Had the doctor stuck electrodes on my scalp with
cement, ripped them off, and replaced them with
needles,* Dayenu. *But he then switched on the EEG
machine only to find that the machine hadn't been
hooked up properly from the beginning. I was past disgust, past furious, and bordering on helplessly frustrated. Had the electrodes been stuck on with cement,*

---

*Dayenu (Hebrew). Translation: It would have been sufficient.

*ripped off, replaced by needles, only to find that it was
not me but the machine that was improperly hooked
up,* Dayenu. *There was one last step to complete. I was
to go through the entire experiment as though under
normal conditions. Silently, begrudgingly, I finished
the experiment. I'm not sure what the results were, but
if they weren't what he wanted Jerry knew better than
to complain. He had a somewhat different version of
what happened to me that day. But I wonder who is
more apt to doctor the story—the person who felt the
pain, or the guilt-ridden person who was indirectly
responsible for inflicting it? In either case, I think what
remains important afterwards is the impact it leaves
on the subject.*

*After my experiment with Jerry, the EEG, the ESP
Teaching Machine, the electrodes, the glue, the needles
and the incompetent doctor, I was beyond* Dayenu. *I
was simply, plainly and thoroughly fed up. My experiments at SRI were interesting, but even they've
reached their saturation point in me. I'm ready to
resign from my role of human guinea pig. I no longer
want to prove anything to anybody. I don't even feel the
need to prove anything to myself. When I was younger,
I used to enjoy the fuss made over my results. I don't
care for that kind of approval or fuss anymore. I've
decided that if I have any special talent, I want to use it
for something more constructive than the creation of
textbook data on parapsychological experiments. I want
to take a longterm vacation from laboratories, scientists, experimenters, doctors, and curious people.*

*I have also grown to dislike being the retriever at
home. Whenever someone is missing something, I'm
summoned to find it. It can really get to be annoying,
especially when I'm preoccupied with something else;
I have to stop whatever I'm doing or thinking and re-
focus on finding the lost object. Finally this year I put
my foot down. Mom had lost her wallet. She came into
my room and asked me to find it. I was in the midst of
writing a term paper and I didn't feel like interrupting
my chain of thoughts. I told her to find the wallet
herself.*

"But I can't."

"Of course you can. It's simple."

"Well, how do you do it?"

*"It helps if the first thing you do is look everywhere
for it. That way you exhaust yourself and your mind of*

all the possibilities. Then, you sit down, close your eyes, and draw your mind to a blank—or as close to a blank as you can. Then you picture the object, and simply get up and walk to wherever it is. You don't think, you just walk to one place, stick your hand in and pull it out. That's all there is to it."

"Okay, I'll try it. But if I don't find it, will you look?"

"No way! I resign. If you have any doubt about finding it, then you'll blow the whole process. Besides, you have to try to remove your investment in finding it. Try to be as detached as possible. It's the easiest thing in the world and it's about time everyone stopped being lazy around here. I'm tired of this game."

Mom left my room knowing very well that if she didn't find it, I'd look for it.

"At least she's giving it a try," I thought to myself.

Moments later, Mom proudly marched into my room with her wallet in her hand. "I did what you said and here it is!"

"It's about time."

As I said this, I felt a slight pang of sadness in that I'd given my trick away. It was only the slightest of pangs, because I know these secrets have to be shared. I've always appreciated the trick Janet taught me: She once said that whenever she can't remember something, she thinks of a princess telephone and imagines it ringing. Then, the first thing that pops into her head after the phone ringing is usually the thought she was trying to remember. It's been a very successful technique in helping me spit out a thought that often sticks to the tip of my tongue.

My pang of sadness in revealing my retrieving technique was promptly drowned by a wave of relief. For, when I looked at what I'd taught, I saw it as a going-away present from me to my mother. To subdue her melancholia over my early departure to college, I unbegrudgingly handed over to her my reigning crown as "Resident Psychic."

At last I was graduating.

*Dina's favorite
painting.*

20
A VISION OF BLINDNESS

 I dreamed I was deaf, dumb and blind. As a matter of fact, I was Helen Keller. All day I was being led from place to place, unaware of my surroundings. I was restless, and annoyed that I couldn't see where I was.

My parents sensed my anxiety. At the end of the day they brought me to a candy store. I was set in front of a huge rack of candy bars. Somehow it was made known to me that I could choose any candy bar I wanted.

I could smell the scent of chocolate but I could not differentiate between the kinds of chocolate bars. My only certainty was that I knew I didn't want to be stuck with any candy bar that had coconut in it. At the height of frustration, I weighed all my options. They boiled down to only one possible plan of action: I flashed open my eyes, grabbed the desired chocolate bar, and shut my eyes again.

I awoke from my dream, laughing. I dreamed I was Helen Keller, and I peeked.

Thanks to Jerry, I've found a medium that allows me to use my intuition other than as a human guinea pig. After the futile experience with the needles and contact cement, Jerry seemed determined to redeem himself. But I was incredulous that he had the gall to ask me to participate in yet another experiment!

"Jer, I love you and all, but how can you even think of asking me to do another experiment? You know I refuse to be poked and prodded anymore!''

"I understand how you feel, but I promise this one doesn't involve any machines. It's completely casual. Really, the only thing that'll touch you is a blindfold. C'mon, I'm just curious to see what happens.''

"Jerry, one day your curiosity is going to kill me!'' I thought to myself. But then I remembered the retort I would give to the remark that curiosity killed the cat. "Yes," I'd say, "but satisfaction brought him back.''

I didn't want to do another experiment. I was fed up. Then again, I doubted that Jerry would ask me to do anything I wouldn't enjoy—especially after last time. Reluctantly I had to face the fact that I was a sucker for his pleading puppy-dog look accentuated by those shlumfy eyelids.

"Okay, Jer," I sighed, "exactly what does it entail?''

"It's simple. Blindfolded, you sit in a chair. I put colored pieces of paper in front of you and you put your hand over each one and identify its color. That's all there is to it.''

"That's it?''

"'Cross my heart.''

"Yeah, and hope to die if you stick any more needles in my head!''

"Don't you trust me?''

"After you made my scalp a pin cushion?''

"If I defend myself I am attacked. Without forgiveness we would still be blind.''

"Damn, now you're quoting the *Course!* Can't anyone have a normal conversation anymore? Okay, I'll do it. But please, make it quick.''

"You're beautiful," Jerry said to me through his wide, gap-toothed grin. He often tells me I'm beautiful—especially after I've been shrewish. When I criticize him he thanks me for pointing out a fault that he has to work on. I roll my eyes when he tells me I'm beautiful.

I cooperated with Jerry and his color experiment. Blind-folded, I put my hand over each paper and identified it as either black, white, red or blue. I found that sometimes I felt a subtle variation of heat according to the color. Other times a picture of the color would flash into my mind. My accuracy after dozens of trials was 98 percent. When the blindfold was removed, my eyes throbbed from enduring it's pressure for so long. Despite my momentary blurry vision, I had enjoyed the experiment. It interested me. I wasn't overly concerned with how or why I sensed colors. My excitement was focused on the possibilities this perception offered. I was challenged to find a milieu in which this type of color perception would be useful.

Jerry suggested I work with blind children. He gave me the names of a few such children in the San Francisco area. I was given the freedom to create my own schedule and program for trying to teach blind children how to sense color. For the duration of the summer, Jerry allowed me to live at the Center for Attitudinal Healing. He gave me his keys and radio, pronouncing me the Center's summer caretaker. In the daytime the building was used for biofeedback classes, meditation sessions and weekly meetings, headed by Jerry, for glaucoma patients. (Instantly it felt like home!) Psychiatrist by profession, Jerry was also founder of the Center. As head administrator, he considered my blind color-perception project an adjunct function to the Center for Attitudinal Healing.

Jerry often got irritated by my disorganization and lack of plans. His suggestions were well-intended, but I found myself acting on intuition. After a while, Jerry gave up supervising and settled for my keeping him regularly informed of my progress with the children.

To be honest, I wasn't sure what I was doing. I had no plans, no structure and most of all, no expectations. All I knew was that I was going to play with colors and blind kids. I ended up working consistently with two blind children, whose parents Jerry had briefed. I was responsible for setting up the plan. Although Dina and Franklin knew each other, they were in most ways worlds apart.

Tammy and Dina.

Dina was ten years old, a beautiful, dark-haired Filipino girl. She was blinded shortly after birth due to lack of oxygen in her incubator. When I met Dina, she had no idea why I'd come to see her. Since her mother speaks very little English, I doubt she fully comprehended Jerry's briefing about my vague intentions. She was just glad to have a few free afternoons a week. Dina, similarly, didn't need any explanations. She was thrilled to have a new playmate.

During our first few meetings, I took Dina on little excursions away from her home. We talked about her friends, my friends, our likes and dislikes, getting to know each other. At our first encounter, I told her I had a fun color game to play with her. I had planted the seed in her curious mind. Each time we met, I talked a little more about colors. By the time Dina felt comfortable with me, she was extremely anxious to play the color game.

"Dina, do you know what colors are?"

"Kind of. I know that everything has a color."

"Do you see colors inside your head?"

"I think so, but I'm not sure."

"Well, do you think you can describe a color?"

"No."

"Don't worry, neither can I. It's very difficult," I assured her. "Do you know what color you're wearing?"

"No." I noticed a pout forming on her face.

"Do you want to learn how to see colors?

"Oh yes! A lot!"

"Why?" I was curious.

"I'm not really sure. But I love to paint pictures, and it would be great to know what colors I was using. Do you think I could learn?"

One of her blue eyes stared at me. The other eye, an opaque gray, was wandering, yearning for definitive direction.

"Of course you can!" I heard the words blurt out of my mouth.

"When can I try?"

"Next time we meet. Okay?"

"Great! I'll meet you on the steps!"

I always found Dina waiting on the steps for me. She had become dependent on our friendship. I knew that after school she usually sat home all day. Suffice it to say that three or four of Dina's weekday afternoons were wholeheartedly given to me.

I brought a couple of packages of colored construction paper and picked out the blues, reds, blacks and whites. I decided to use these particular colors for no reason other than that Jerry had used them with me. Papers in hand, I approached Dina's house as she came running down the steps. If someone were watching at a distance, it would have been extremely difficult to detect her blindness.

"Hi!" she said. "Did you bring the colors?"

"I sure did. Where do you want to go?"

"Let's go eat cause I didn't have lunch."

Dina took my arm as we walked into the cafeteria. After we gobbled tuna sandwiches, I pushed aside the dishes and announced that it was time to play colors.

"Yay! What do I do?"

"First you push your stool closer to the countertop." The countertop was made of white formica. I brushed the remaining crumbs off it.

"Okay, I'm ready!"

I guided her hand to a position a couple of inches above the counter. "Now relax for a moment. I want you to notice any feelings you get from the countertop."

"What kind of feelings?"

"It could be anything. You might feel a sort of sensation in your hand. Maybe you'll get a picture of a color in your head, or maybe you'll notice a special taste in your mouth." I tried not to pre-determine what kind of sensations she would feel. "Well," she said with a grin, "I do have a taste in my mouth—tunafish!"

"C'mon Dina, you can do better than that."

"This is too hard," she complained.

"No, it's not hard. Everyone can do this."

I played on the knowledge that almost every ten-year-old likes to be just like everyone else. I certainly remember my own reluctance to be individual.

"Oh, now I feel something," she said almost immediately.

"What do you feel?" I felt sure that she was pretending in order to please me.

"Well, it's kind of warm."

"That's fine," I encouraged.

"What now?" she asked me. I wasn't sure but I knew I had to think of something quickly.

"Okay, I'm going to put a red piece of paper on the table. I want you to put your hand over it and do the same thing you did with the counter." I put her hand a couple of inches above the red paper.

"It feels kind of warm too."

"Good. Now I want you to compare the feeling of the red paper with the feeling of the countertop. Do they feel the same?"

I guided her hand back and forth, first above the red paper, then above the white countertop, until she knew where the red paper was situated. She concentrated for about thirty seconds. Then she said "They don't feel the same. The table's warmer."

"Okay, now I'm putting a blue piece of paper where the red one was before. I want you to do the same thing as last time and tell me if the paper and counter feel the same."

This time it took her about a minute to answer me. Her face looked very serious.

"Yeah, they feel kind of the same."

"Fine." I replaced the blue paper with a white paper. I told her she was now comparing a white paper with the countertop.

"They feel the same too," she answered, a little quicker than the time before.

I put a black paper in place of the white.

"No, they don't feel the same at all. The black paper feels cooler." She answered in a matter of seconds.

"You're doing great," I said. "Now I'm going to put the blue paper down again and I want you to tell me how it feels in comparison with the table."

"It feels the same, but a little cooler than the counter this time."

"Now the white one."

After a few seconds she said "They feel the same."

"Exactly the same?"

"Yes."

"So what color do you think the table top is?" I held back the excitement in my voice.

"I don't know. Maybe red?"

I realized that she had absolutely no idea what she had been doing. I didn't tell her whether her answer was correct. Instead, I repeated the entire procedure with her but I gave her the colors in a different order. This time she narrowed it immediately to the white paper. I asked the $100,000 question again.

"What color do you think the table top is?"

"White!"

"That's right. I can't believe it! That's fantastic!" I couldn't contain myself. I was stunned. I gave Dina a huge hug and kiss. Then I noticed that she looked a little confused.

"But you said everyone can do it. Why are you so surprised?"

For a moment I was taken aback. Then I replied "Everyone *can* do it, but you do it better than anyone I've ever met."

"Oh!" she exclaimed with glee.

My cover-up answer had made perfect sense to her. It also made her very proud of herself.

After an hour and a half, we were beginning to attract the attention of other diners. It was time to leave. I returned Dina home, dropping her off at the bottom of the steps.

"Dina, I have one last color question to ask you. What color is your dress?"

"Red!" she answered immediately. She was grinning.

"How did you know?"

"I asked Mommy before you came!"

At least I knew she was honest.

"Do you have to go?"

"Yep."

"Will we play with colors more?"

"Of course, if you want to."

"Yeah. I'm real good at them, aren't I?"

"You sure are. By the end of this summer maybe you'll be able to tell what color paints or magic markers you're using—if you practice real hard."

"How do I practice?"

"I'm going to give you four pieces of paper: a black one, a blue one, a white one, and a red one. You can touch the papers, smell them, taste them, whatever. I want you to become familiar with each color. Don't worry about their names—just be aware of the different feelings you get from each colored paper. Okay?"

"Yeah. I'll be even greater next time I see you."

"I'm sure you will! I can't wait!"

I gave her a kiss and watched her run up the steps, waving the four papers in her right hand. I was thrilled. I couldn't wait to tell Jerry what had happened. When I told him, he advised me to keep a record of the data and statistics of my work with the children.

Following Jerry's suggestion, I recorded Dina's actions as objectively as possible. It was very difficult for me to keep my emotions out of the report, but I tried to be as scientific as Mr. Biology. From that day on, while with the children I recorded comments, data, statistics and events as they happened.

After my first experience with Dina and color perception, I formulated the hypothesis that she was sensitizing herself to the differing reflections of light and heat from each color. Although black and white are not considered colors, I put them in the same category as the other colors because they too absorb and/or reflect different gradations of light and heat. I knew that, like most blind people, Dina's hands are particularly sensitive to touch. But unfortunately, as solid as my notion seemed to be, further dealings with Dina did not support it.

The next time I met with Dina, I took her to Golden Gate Park in San Francisco. At the park, we sat under a tree. I had brought twenty pieces of construction paper: five pieces each were black, blue, red and white. I shuffled the papers and handed the pile to Dina.

"I want you to separate these colors into four piles. One pile should be only black papers, another only whites, another only blues, and another only reds. Okay?"

"I'll try."

It took her about fifteen minutes to finish the task. By the time she was done, my heart was pounding. She had put sixteen of the twenty in their correct piles. She put a blue in the white pile and vice versa, and she put a black in the red pile and vice versa. I asked her to identify the color of each pile. She was seventy-five percent incorrect. Only her naming of the red pile was correct. She could obviously distinguish among them but she had yet to connect the correct names to the colors. I put her hand over the black paper.

"What color is this?"

"White," she answered almost immediately.

"I think that you know the feeling of each color but the name you give it is wrong. This color is called black."

"Oh." She seemed disappointed.

"Don't worry. You're doing wonderfully. It's just that every time you think a color is white, you must call it black. Okay?"

"Okay."

I mixed eight white and black pieces of paper and told Dina

to separate them. She did so perfectly. Then I asked her which pile was white and which was black.

She pointed to the black pile. "I thought this was white, so I'm supposed to call it black. Right?"

"Right!"

"But I thought this pile was blue," she said while pointing to the white pile.

"Well, now everytime you think a pile is blue, you have to call it white."

I made her sort the reds and blues. She did it perfectly again but she thought that blue was black. At least she was consistent in her mistakes.

"It's hard to remember which name goes for which," she said.

"I'll bet." I laughed. "White is black, black is blue and blue is white. It's kind of like a circle."

"I think I can remember it. Can I try them all again?"

In her next attempt, Dina got 17 out of 20 in their proper piles. She took a while to remember what name was supposed to go with what color pile but finally she got each pile's name correct. I gave her a huge hug and told her that she was the greatest color player in the world. I made it a point always to call working with colors "playing with colors." I hated the idea of "working" with anything. It seemed very important to keep the dealings with color a game rather than a chore.

"Dina, I want you to tell me which color feels the warmest and which feels the coolest."

She felt all the colors. "The black is the warmest. The blue is the coolest."

"Then what?"

"Which color is the second coolest?"

"The white."

She totally blew my theory. I mixed the colors up a few times. Each time I asked her to tell me the degree of hot and cold, without telling her which color was which (although by this time she didn't need to be told). Each time, she switched around the degree of heat of each color. I tried to salvage my theory by taking into account the amount of sunlight on each paper, but we were sitting in the shade.

The next few times I saw Dina, we played with the four original colors but varied the games. I began to focus Dina's attention on the colors of objects other than paper. I would give her four household objects and ask her which one of the four felt like the red paper. Anywhere from one to four of the objects could be the same as the one piece of paper. Later, Dina would have to tell me how many of the objects were the same color as the paper, what each object was, and what the color of the original paper was. I would always ask her to tell me the heat levels of the four colors but she was never consistent. Finally one day I asked her "Dina, how can you tell which color is which?"

"They feel different."

"How do they feel different?"

"Well," she said thoughtfully, "they remind me of different things."

"What do you feel when you put your hand over the color red? You always seem to recognize red almost immediately."

"That's because it's my favorite color. Whenever I feel red it reminds me of being in bed." She smiled.

"That's peculiar," I thought to myself.

That afternoon when I took Dina home, she took me into her room. Her bedspread was red, and her sheets were red-and-white stripes! Finally I understood the connection. She told me that blue reminded her of her favorite stuffed animal, which I saw was a blue furry cat. White was a reminder of her telephone, and black reminded her of her little black puppy. I asked her mother if she had ever told her daughter the colors of these objects. Struggling with the English words, she replied that she humors Dina by telling her when something is red, only because Dina says that red is her favorite color. Other than that, they never discuss the subject. I knew this to be true when I realized that Dina thought grass blue, carrots brown, and trees purple. She knew the sun is yellow and the sky is blue because someone once told her that when she was drawing them.

I let Dina discover the color of grass, trees, and various flowers, vegetables and fruit, by feeling them and comparing them to her colored papers. I introduced green, yellow, orange, brown and purple. As her ability to sense color developed and refined, she began to decipher light blues from dark blues, pinks from reds, and gray from black and white. The assortment of construction paper had grown to twenty different colors. Everywhere we went, Dina would bring her colored papers until she no longer needed them for comparison. She'd run to each object and shout out its color. She was correct approximately 80 percent of the time.

Towards the end of the summer, Dina told me that she'd see a color in her mind when she put her hand over an object. I asked if she could describe any of the colors she saw in her mind's eye.

"It's hard, but I'll try."

"How about yellow?"

"Yellow is very bright."

"How about purple?"

"Purple looks very soft, kind of velvet," she answered after some thought.

"And red?"

"Red looks very warm and very strong. It's hard to explain."

"You're doing just fine. How about blue?" There was a pause. I looked up and I saw a large grin plastered across Dina's face.

"What's so funny?"

"I couldn't figure out how to describe blue but now I've got it. . . Blue looks warm, but not in the same way as red. It looks more comforting than strong. But that's not really it either. Blue is *mellow*."

I couldn't hold back my laughter. Over the course of the summer I had taught Dina the meaning of the word "mellow" in reference to music. Whenever we'd hear a tune on the radio Dina would ask me whether it was mellow or not. Now she had used it in reference to the color blue. I couldn't have described it better myself.

In fact, if I had given it much thought, that is how I would have described the color blue. That is exactly my feeling about blue. As a matter of fact, I probably would have described red, yellow and purple in the way that she did. It struck me for the first time that an extraordinarily powerful telepathy might have been occurring between us. Even though she said she could tell colors at home, I wondered if her accuracy was as consistent as it was when she was with me. At this juncture, my summer with Dina was just about over. There was no time left to exclude the possibility of telepathy. I concluded that even if she was in tune with colors through telepathic communication with me, at least it was an introduction to color for her. If she could telepathically pick up a picture of a color from me and then give the proper name to the color she was picturing, what's the difference if it was telepathy or not? She finally seemed to have distinct pictures of colors in her head and was able to identify them. I think that even if it was telepathy in the beginning, once she was able to identify the colors, she could do so independent of my presence.

Perhaps telepathy was even a factor between Annie Sullivan and Helen Keller when Helen first understood the connection between objects and the symbols—words and sign language—representing those objects. But after Helen Keller made the connection between the two and knew the names of various objects, her knowledge became independent of Annie Sullivan's presence.

Dina and I had gone through many art books together. She would put her hand over a painting and she would tell me whether or not she liked the mixture of colors in it. She would also state the predominant color in the painting. She said that Van Gogh was her favorite artist because she could sense a tremendous amount of energy emitted from his paintings. She could usually distinguish the Van Goghs from other paintings in an art book.

Was it a coincidence that Van Gogh was my favorite artist as well?

One of the last questions I asked her at the end of our summer together was for her to tell me what color shirt I was wearing. She put her hand a few inches from my shirt sleeve. It took her a little while to answer. I was tricking her because I was wearing a striped shirt. Finally she answered "Blue and white lines." Once again, she stunned me. I told her that she had peeked, but she didn't get it.

Tammy and Franklin.

Franklin was totally different from Dina. The day I met Franklin was the day I changed my own perception of disabled people.

I walked up the stairs to Franklin's house and rang the bell. A tall, very good-looking black-skinned boy opened the door. He was about my age—seventeen years old. His smile beckoned to me to come inside. I followed him into the living room.

"You heah to see Franklin?"

"Yeah. Is he around?"

"No honey, he's out riding his bicycle. He should be back any minute." This came from a round-bodied, middle-aged woman. I noticed she had the same friendly smile I'd seen on the boy.

"I'm Franklin's Mama. You must be Tammy. Nice to meet ya."

"Same here. Franklin's doing what?" I was sure I hadn't heard her correctly.

"He's out ridin' his bike. He'll be back in a second, I'm sure."

I was too embarrassed to ask whether he was blind. He was *supposed* to be. Perhaps I had come to the wrong house. But they seemed to have been expecting me, and they knew my name. I decided to sit and wait for Franklin. A little uncomfortable, I studied the family photos on the living room table.

"Why, ain't she cute?" Mrs. Franklin asked Franklin's older brother.

"She sure is."

I smiled and began to blush. They laughed. All of a sudden I felt extremely uncomfortable in my skirt. I was used to wearing coveralls, but I hadn't wanted to make a bad first impression on the family. I should've worn my overalls.

"How many children do you have?" I asked Mrs. Franklin.

"Eleven—but only nine of 'em live heah."

Mrs. Franklin glanced at the window and stood up. "That there's Franklin now."

I looked through the window and saw a boy on a bicycle. I saw the boy jump off the bike, park it by the side of the house, lock it, and then trot up the stairs in front of the house. He opened the door and walked into the hallway.

"Frankle, Tammy's heah to see ya."

A boy shorter than I walked into the living room. His hair was cropped close to his head. He was dressed in blue jeans and a navy blue jacket. His eyes looked intact but unfocused. I was slightly taken aback when Franklin walked up to me and offered me his hand to shake.

Yes, Franklin is blind. When he was born he had an infection that permanently damaged his left eye. The doctors said that his right eye would eventually go blind as well. They weren't sure whether complete loss of vision would occur in a few years, or thirty. Then, when Franklin was eleven years old—two years before I met him—he was blinded while playing basketball. The ball hit him in his good eye and broke a blood vessel. Due to the vulnerability of his eye, the damage was irreparable. In very bright light, Franklin can sometimes detect faint shadows, but not clearly enough to decipher color or shape.

During his first year of complete blindness, Franklin was miserable. He didn't want to go to school, he wouldn't see his friends, and he hated to leave the house at all. Yet, as most kids do, Franklin finally bounced back from misfortune. He developed a tremendous drive to overcome the obstacles his blindness had set for him. He made himself conscious of every inch of his neighborhood. He finally worked up the self-confidence to ride his bicycle locally. His friends, relatives and neighbors looked out for him. His parents allowed him the freedom to explore his own limits. They were caring and supportive, but not over-protective. "Impossible" was not a word given much credence in Franklin's household.

I played with colors with Franklin, but he wasn't too interested. He didn't see how they'd really serve any purpose in his life. He remembered colors from when he could see. He knew the labels of the colors in his mind's eye were accurate. As a matter of fact, it was at first extremely difficult to teach Franklin how to sense color *because* he was already familiar with it. He tended to rely much more on reasoning than on intuition. For example, the first item I ever asked Franklin to color-identify was a napkin from his mother's kitchen.

"Well," said Franklin, "I remember our kitchen's green, and Mama matches everything, so this napkin mus' be green."

I hated to admit that he was correct. Franklin already knew the colors of trees, grass, fruit and vegetables. I had to deal strictly with objects of which he was color *un*conscious. I also had to deal with releasing my own desires and expectations for Franklin to sense color. After my first experience with Dina, I found it difficult not to want Franklin to be able to repeat Dina's performance.

Despite Franklin's disinterest in color perception, he was not indifferent to our friendship. But, unlike Dina, Franklin would not be waiting on the front steps for my arrival. It usually happened that *I* would wait at his house for *him*. Franklin was extremely independent. He had many friends of his own and plans of his own. He had to go out of his way to fit me into his busy schedule. If I had not taken an immediate liking to the boy, I probably would not have continued my work with him.

I often went to the park with Franklin because he liked being outside. We spent most of our time talking and laughing. Only a minimal portion of our visit together was devoted to color perception. Franklin had a knack for telling the differences between black and white. He would get 95 percent correct out of twenty trials of black and whites, but he couldn't have cared less. I gave him a deck of cards and told him to sort the red cards from the black. He put twenty-three blacks and five red cards in the black pile, and twenty-one reds and three blacks in the red card pile. He was a bit more excited about his success at cards because he figured that maybe he could win some money from his friends and family by doing this trick.

Franklin was kind, gentle, considerate and funny, but also very tough. Since he had little interest in color, I saw no purpose in making it our primary focus. My friendship with Franklin taught me more than I could ever have taught him. His attitude about his disability forced me to be as nonchalant about his blindness as he was. In the early stage of our friendship, I was extremely conscious of phrasing my sentences. I tried to avoid the word *see* as much as possible. Once I was so wrapped up in a conversation with him about sharks that I asked if he had yet seen the movie *Jaws*.

"Sure. I make a point to see every new movie that comes out."

I realized the stupidity of my question. Although I was relieved he couldn't see my face reddening with embarrassment, I knew he could sense it.

"Ooops. Sorry, Franklin. I got a little carried away. I hope I didn't hurt your feelings."

"Damn, no! It's about time you forgot I'm blind! I can heah, y'know, and I really do go to movies that have good sound and music."

He was always putting me in my place.

Towards the end of the summer, Franklin had succeeded in making me so comfortable with blindness that I was even able to tease him about it. He would often tap me on the head and say "You sure are short for your age!" Eventually, I started to poke him back and say, "Frankle, you sure are blind for your age!" Much laughter would follow.

He was an imp. Sometimes he'd trip me as we were walking down the street and then say "Hey man, you've got the eyes, why don't ya look where y'going?" I took his teasings for a while, and finally began retaliating with lines such as "You're the one who better start watching your step!" Then I'd trip him back. We both stumbled down many a street in fits of laughter.

Franklin's big passion was music. He played the drums. Towards the end of the summer, I was invited to watch Frankle and his sisters and brothers at their band reheasal. I was surprised how good they sounded, but I was even more surprised by the way everyone treated him.

Franklin's drum set was in a corner of the living room next to the organ. He had to walk around the microphones and squeeze by the piano in order to reach his drums. As he passed the piano, he knocked over a glass of milk which had been precariously resting on the edge of the piano. "Frankle, will you watch it!" his oldest sister yelled. She's about twenty-three and the lead singer, composer and keyboardist of the group. "Sorry," mumbled the boy as he went to get a towel to clean the mess.

I learned so much from the Franklin family. They didn't make me feel uncomfortable for being a stranger. They didn't make me feel different because I'm white. They also didn't ignore the fact that I'm white. Sometimes they teased me about it. In the same vein, they didn't make Franklin feel alienated because of his blindness, and they didn't pay any extra attention to him because of it.

Whereas Dina taught me that perhaps it's possible for the blind to see, Franklin taught me something I value even more. He showed me that people must be given empathy rather than sympathy. I realized, for the first time, that when you offer sympathy to a person, you are only supporting that person's weakness. You are sorry for the individual. What benefit can be derived from feeling sorry for yourself or someone else? In contrast, when you give empathetically, you are identifying with someone's strength. You are being helpful in a positive way that offers results. Franklin's family did not pity him. They emphasized his strong points and encouraged him to live up to his potential.

One of the last times I saw Franklin that summer, we went to a place where there was a trampoline. Franklin crawled up on the trampoline, and I watched him as he walked clear around it to get a sense of where the canvas stopped and where the strings and edges began. Then he walked to the middle of the trampoline. He began to jump. He jumped higher and higher. He lost his balance a few times, laughed and got up again. He was jumping so high that his head was nearing the ceiling. I yelled to him to watch the ceiling. He yelled back that *he* was blind, so *I* should watch it! Then he reassured me he was aware of it a few inches higher than his jumps were reaching.

I watched Frankle bounce higher and higher above the trampoline. Each time he was in the air I could feel his confidence and soaring sense of freedom. In the air, there seemed to be no limits. But each time he came crashing down on the trampoline, my body would become tense. I was fearful of his falling off the edge. Then, after a while, I began to focus on the sound of his laughter and the sight of his smile. I could sense the limitless feeling again. As his jump peaked, so did his sense of confidence and denial of the impossible. I knew he was aware of every molecule of air and space surrounding him. Then, as was to be expected, he came down on the trampoline. Yet this time, I noticed that my body did not tense. The bottom had become as unrestricting as the top. And thus I concluded the summer as I leaped to join the boy whose awareness accepted no bounds.

Tammy off to Tufts.

21
READY, BUT WILLING?

*Humphrey the Car has been loaded. Bob is ready.
Mom is in the car. Saki is coming with his little travel
bag of meatballs, custom-made by Hattie. Hattie, how I
wish I could take her with me. Well, at least I'm
equipped with Odette, my diaphragm. I call it Odette
because it's an oddity that, as a virgin, I have it.
Humphrey's revving to go. Larry, the doorman, slams
the car door shut and waves goodbye. Am I excited?
Happy? Sad? Nervous? No. Simply dramatic. I feel as
though I'm in a movie. I try so hard to give everything
as much meaning as possible: moments, people, things.
But it's so intellectual, and inside I'm laughing at how
emotional I'm acting. I'm playing a game. Roll the dice
and land in high school. Pick a card and advance to
college. Look around you and make everything seem as
real and unforgettable as possible. But nothing seems
real at all. Deep down I feel detachment. Maybe that's
what allows me to have so much fun playing sentimental.*

*"We're off to St. Fut!" sings Bob as he pulls out of
the streets of Manhattan and onto the highway. Bob
has insisted that I'm starting off at St. Fut and when I
graduate I'll be graduating "Tufts." He loves to spell
everything backwards. He doesn't have dyslexia or any-*

thing, it's just that since he was a boy he's loved to spell names backwards just to find out what they sound like. One of his biggest thrills in life is the fact that his own name "Bob," is pronounced and spelled exactly the same in either direction. So, we were off to St. Fut!

After a five-hour drive, we pull up in front of my dormitory. Mom is by my side. God, I'm so nervous. Here I am, starting a whole new phase of life. Yet another error. Why am I here? I'm just a little kid! Mom's holding my hand. I'd better not let her. How can I walk through these college halls with my mother holding my hand? Look, she has tears in her eyes. She thinks she's losing her baby. How can she be so emotional at a time like this? HELP! She is losing her baby! Take me home! Why am I here when all my friends are in high school? I wanna go home now!

"Where's my room, Mom?"

"What does it say on the key?"

"405."

"Then that's your room. Let's go."

We're climbing a few flights of stairs. Mom's cracking jokes. She's really trying to make me laugh and she's doing a good job of it, but the thought of my new living partner gives me the chills. I got a letter from her over the summer. It read: "Hello! I'm Alice from New Jersey. I like horseback riding—do you? I like anthropology—do you? I like archeology—do you? I'll bring an electric hot plate, you bring the stereo. My bedspread is blue. I hope yours matches." Bedspread? Who has bedspreads in college? What am I getting myself into? Help!

Uh oh, here we are. Room 405. Well here goes . . . I put the key in the lock. I turn it. I open the door. What?! She's been here already! Alice has not only gotten here before me, but her bed is made up! I dump my junk on the inferior bed—my new place of rest. The phone reaches her bed but not mine. Figures.

"Let's get the stuff out of the car."

We walk out of the room and close the door. Ooops! I left my key in my room! I locked us out within the first five minutes of college life. "MOM, STOP LAUGHING!"

Just then a girl asks "Are you Tammy?"

"Yeah."

"Hi! I'm Alice," says my new roommate. She is short, but taller than I am. She's on the lighter side of

*plump and heavier side of thin. Her face is round, her
hair is short and brown, and her eyes are hidden by
glasses.*

*"Hi! I just locked the key inside the room. Sort of
embarrasing, huh?"*

*Deadpan, Alice opens the door for us. I notice that
not only does my new roommate have her key on a
chain but also her entire side of the room is completely
organized. I get my key. We leave Alice and her mother
spraying Lysol disinfectant in her bureau drawers.*

*As we re-enter the room with some of my belongings
both Mom and I begin to choke on clouds of Lysol. I run
to the window and open it. I watch Alice's mother dis-
infect her daughter's bed. She offers to do the same
for mine, but I graciously decline. Mom makes small
talk with Mr. and Mrs. Alice as I cough and Bob drags
in my stereo and trunk. Everything is happening so
quickly. Mom and Bob are leaving already.*

*"Please take me home with you. I'm not ready to live
with the Lysol Queen. I'll be gassed to death before I
even get to my first class," I whisper with vehemence.*

*"I'm sure Alice doesn't like Lysol either. You know
how fanatic parents are about their kids' cleanliness."*

"You're not that way, Mom."

"Oh, that's right. But your father is."

*"Yeah, you're probably right. I'll bet she was embar-
rassed that her mother was doing that."*

*"I bet you'll get along with her just fine." Tears are
beginning to glaze Mom's eyes.*

*I give Bob and Mom each a huge hug and a kiss.
Then I give them another hug and kiss. Then some
more. After the goodbyes are over, I watch them get
into Humphrey and pull away from me. Bye Saki. Eat
lots of good meatballs.*

"My little girl!" cry Mom's eyes through the window.

*"I'm just a little kid," I mumbled. "Oh my God,
they're gone."*

*I walk back to my dorm, up the stairs, and into my
new room.*

*Alice's parents are gone as well. I attempt to break
the ice. "The Lysol's gone?" I ask her, in a manner
that takes for granted she's also relieved by its absence.*

*"No, I have two economy-size cans in the closet if
you want some."*

*"Uh, maybe later." Oh God, Mom was wrong—this
girl's serious. She may not indulge in cigarettes, but*

*her clouds of disinfectant are enough to smoke me out
of our room. Well, at least Dad will be thrilled to hear
that I'm living with the Lysol Lady.*

*I begin to sort through my belongings. My things are
sprawled over the entire room. I feel Alice's eyes glar-
ing at me as I stumble and fumble through my flot-
sam and jetsam. After a short while of redistributing
my odds to my ends, Alice impatiently says "It's time
to go to dinner. Make sure you have your key this time."*

*I can't believe this girl. She's acting like my mother,
and even my mother never acted this way. I'll bet this is
some kind of cosmic justice for never having a bossy
maternal figure. Uh oh, I can't find my key again after
all. It's under one of these piles, I'm sure . . . . Alice
rolls her eyes in disgust.*

The second day of school, I made a conscious effort to
organize myself. Any remnant of clutter on the floor, I either
hung on the wall above my bed, or shoved under it. I had scarves,
hats, candy boxes, twigs, many pictures and other miscellaneous
items nailed to my wall. Alice was convinced I was out of my mind.

The nonverbal war began when I noticed that not only was
my roommate inpeccably neat but she also made her bed every
morning before I woke up. She had notes to remind herself about
everything. The pink notes were to remind her of daily appoint-
ments. The blue notes were to remind her which pink note she
should read for which day. It was time for me to rebel.

I made it a point not to make my bed for the first three
weeks of school. I left clothes on the floor. They were eventually
Lysoled to death by Alice. I played three Grateful Dead records
every time she finished listening to Michael Murphey's "Wild
Fire." She talked about being an archeology major while I talked
about meeting new friends. She was realistic, responsible and reserved. I was frenetic, flighty and outgoing. Our water-and-oil
combination didn't mix until the third week of school, when I was
fed up with being polite.

It was mid-afternoon and I didn't expect Alice to return for
another hour or two. I was in one of those crazy moods in which
I talk to entertain myself. The gremlin in me took over as I
dumped our garbage can upside down and began to throw the
rubbish around the room. "YAY! GARBAGE! FREE THE
GARBAGE! GARBAGE INDEPENDENCE DAY!" We didn't
have anything sticky or gooey in the waste basket that day—just
a bunch of papers, most of which were Alice's pink and blue
notes. I paraded around the room, throwing paper and singing a
stream-of-consciousness song about the world's prejudice against

garbage: "It's time to love our rubbish, what's wrong with being slobbish? Why should we resent, garbage in our presence? LA, LA LA, free the garbage, LA, LA, LA, it's free at last, LA, LA, LA!" Suddenly I was aware of being watched. There in the doorway stood Alice. Her stare condemned me to a sanitarium.

My mind had to work quickly. "Al, it's about time you threw some garbage somewhere other than the waste paper basket!"

"Are you *crazy?*"

"Sure am! C'mon Al, throw some paper around!" I handed her a bunch of paper. "Throw it!" I used a tone of voice learned from her. She timidly flicked it in the air, and laughed out of what seemed to be extreme self-consciousness.

"No, Alice, you've really got to THROW it. Like this!"

I grabbed some papers and flung them at her feet. She picked up a few draggles of garbage and threw them at me. We began a garbage fight yelling "YAY GARBAGE!" Finally we collapsed on the floor amidst the liberated debris, and we laughed together for the first time since we met.

It was time for a truce. I agreed that I would make my bed and keep the room a little cleaner, and she agreed not to make her bed on Sundays until after 11:30 a.m. I also insisted that the Lysol be permanently removed from our room. It was a fair compromise.

From that moment on, we became closer. But, although Alice and I shared a friendship in our room, we moved in very different social circles. She hung around with friends I considered "too pristine" as I raced about with a crowd she judged "too wild."

My close confidants consisted of: Albert, an attractive redheaded boy from Chicago, who was hell-bent on transforming the Tufts Film Series by incorporating off-beat films into their repertoire of strictly box-office sensations. When the Film Series didn't concede to Albert's wishes, he began his own alternative series, inspiring us all to join him in the crusade. Then there was Albert's roommate Tom, who was a dark-haired Missouri sophomore—kind, intelligent, always up for a party, refreshingly naive in the ways of women and love, and perpetually boyish and enthusiastic. Third, was Leesa, a black-haired, hot-blooded, quick-witted Italian would-be actress. She was bullheaded, and dramatically presented herself as tough, rebellious, and well able to take care of herself. It wasn't difficult to see that underlying her facade was a vulnerable, insecure little girl in dire need of warmth and affection. Although she guarded her past like Cerberus guarding the gates of hell, a little bird slipped out of Pandora's box to reveal that her mother had died when Leesa was in seventh grade. In an effort to conceal her anger at not having been "mothered," Leesa took on the role of mothering everyone else. These three made up my "family" during my years at Tufts.

After I felt on fairly solid ground with my new friends, I began to open up to them about my family, the work I'd been doing with the blind children, and several of the experiences I'd had. I was secure enough in our friendship to know that my stories wouldn't be doubted. On several occasions I stayed up talking to Albert after Tom passed out from the night's partying. I felt comfortable telling Albert of dreams I had that had come true, and the type of work in which my mother was involved.

Tom and I played more than we talked. We used to go to the beach, or to Boston, or walk around campus, or go out to eat at restaurants. We had many discussions, but the focus was more on laughing than talking. Stories about me would filter into conversations only when he told an anecdote that reminded me of one of my own. Tom noticed that I was good at finding things, so he always called on me when something of his was missing. I usually located what he wanted. It became a joke between us.

It was another friend, Janice, who seemed most interested in getting to know the side of me that I generally underplayed. She wanted to know everything about my involvement with parapsychology. She begged me to talk about it until I was bored to death. One reason she was so intrigued with the field was that she was obsessed with her dreams. Whenver she didn't feel like coping with reality, she had the ability to put herself into a comatose-like sleep and dream whatever she wanted. She could even wake up in the middle of a morning dream, and pick it up that night where she'd left off.

When Leesa was present during Janice's dream renditions and my stories about intuition, Leesa would remain silent. Finally, after a couple of months, she began to approach me cautiously with questions:

"Do you believe there's more to a coincidence than we think?" Leesa sheepishly asked me one day. I sensed that she had the answer for herself, regardless of my opinion on the subject.

"You never know," I said. "But it seems to me, the more you open yourself up to wanting coincidences, the more you allow them into your life. I think they're little bells that chime to indicate you're in tune with people and things around you."

A few days later we were sitting on my bed and I began to talk to Leesa about my friend Janet. I remarked that I had no idea why I was suddenly talking about my childhood friend. I expressed my frustration at not having Janet's phone number. At that moment the telephone rang in my room. Alice picked up the phone.

"Hello. . . Yes, she's right here. . . One second," we heard Alice say, backgrounding our conversation.

"Tammy, there's someone by the name of Jan on the phone

for you." Leesa shrieked as she jumped up from the bed and ran across the hall into her own room.

I told Janet that she'd done it again! She said she'd just called to say hello. When I hung up, I went to look for Leesa. She had locked her door and wouldn't open it. She explained, from behind her door, "I don't want to talk about it!"

That was the first experience I had with Leesa's tremendous fear of the things that happened to me. She often said she wanted to know more about it, but she'd close up whenever we began to discuss it. I wrote in my journal:

> *I feel so silly with Leesa whenever anything happens that shows we are in tune with each other. She seems to freak out even if we say the same things at the same time. I don't understand why she would be scared about something that's so much fun. It's so weird, because I can't imagine that people don't like these sort of little coincidences to happen to them. I can't imagine living without them. Life would be so boring. It never occurred to me that everyone else doesn't feel the same. I've got to keep convincing Leesa that there's nothing to be afraid of—that it's more exciting than scary.*

Whereas I felt that I had something to teach Leesa, she was teaching me about something I never really wanted to look at.

> *So many new feelings have come over me this year at Tufts. The boys call themselves "men," the girls call themselves "women," and I laugh and cringe at the new descriptions.*
>
> *Leesa tells me that I need to have a better image of my body. I insist I'm still waiting for my growth spurt. She implores me to wear dresses more often, but then she chides me when I wear skirts with knee socks, boots, a slip and long underwear. I think it's still a step in some direction.*
>
> *I've been trying so hard to accept my sexuality, but it's such a bummer. I sat in on a conversation with Leesa and some of the girls—"women"—on my floor. They were reminiscing about the high-school experience of whispering about a flame while walking by a class-room for a quick glimpse of him. I felt left out of the conversation, as my high school was too small for such antics. It seemed to me that I'd missed something in life. When the talk graduated to sexual fantasies, it occurred to me that I never had one. I'd always been too busy doing things that I considered more exciting than*

*fantasizing. It never even occurred to me that I was
unusual for not engaging in sexual fantasies. When I
revealed this to my friends, they didn't believe me.*

*Eventually convinced of my ignorance, they persuaded
me to give it a go. Thus, over the next couple of weeks
I decided to come up with a good sexual fantasy. It was
fitting that one came to mind during poetry class.*

*On a spring afternoon, while the teacher's pet was
reading her seventh boring poem in a row, I noticed
one of the guys twiddling a gold chain around his neck.
Unnoticed, from afar, I watched him. I noted that the
chain looked attractive on him, although I didn't
usually like it when males wore jewelry—especially
gold chains. But this particular chain, on this particular boy, attracted me.*

*"This is my big chance for a fantasy!" I thought to
myself. I looked at my classmate and decided that he
was very handsome. There was a real boyish look about
him. Guardedly, I glanced at his brown eyes and his
tousled hair. There was a quality of manliness about
him. He always seemed to be fidgeting, and I remembered once seeing him climbing a tree. I thought that
he was a little crazy, and I liked that. Enough of this, I
was going to have a fantasy.*

*For the next two hours of class, I imagined seducing
this guy just to get the chain from his neck. It seemed
like a real* Samson *and* Delilah *maneuver. So I imagined that once he gave me the necklace I returned it,
insisting that it looked too good on him for me to keep.
(Okay, so it wasn't the most enthralling of fantasies for
most people, but it was my first and I was inexperienced. It wasn't very sexual, but the idea was there,
even though the vivid images weren't.) I watched him
as he occasionally took the chain off his neck and
twirled it around his fingers. I immersed myself in my
fantasy and was surprised to find the class over before
I wanted it to be.*

*As the students congregated around the teacher at
the end of class, I pulled Leesa downstairs and outside.*

*"Leesa, do me a favor and wait with me until one of
the guys from class comes out."*

"Which one?"

*"I don't know his name. He was sitting near you. He
was the one wearing a chain around his neck."*

"Oh, that's Alec. What's going on?"

I proceeded to tell her about my fantasy, and how I

just wanted to complete it by waiting outside for a quick glimpse. We both knew I was being ridiculous, but Leesa humored me.

"I'm so excited that now I have a way to pass the class time quickly."

"Are you ever going to do anything to realize this fantasy?"

"What do you mean, 'realize it?' I realize it."

"No, I mean to make it real."

"Oh. How should I know? It does seem like a great challenge, though—don't you think? I can't wait until next class to think about it some more."

"Look, there he is!"

Alec walked out of the building, accompanied by two girls. I walked near him and uttered the first words I'd ever said to him: "So long. Have a good spring break!"

"You too!" he said.

I smiled and pivoted to walk back to the dorm with Leesa. As I was turning, I felt something hit my hand and wrap itself around my wrist. It was Alec's gold chain. I could hardly think straight. I figured he was just being playful, so I tossed it back. But he threw it back to me and said "Keep it!" as he turned and trotted away.

I was shocked. Leesa screamed. I turned toward her and held up the chain. I was about to say something when she yelled "I don't want to talk about it! Everything always happens to you! I just don't want to talk about it!" When we returned to the dorm, she retreated to her room.

The more I thought about it, the angrier I was. How could this happen? I was so excited about having a fantasy, but before I even got to relish it the end result was accomplished. Is this what they meant by premature climax? I had anticipated its duration for at least a few more poetry classes, but now the thrill was gone. What a bummer! Well, at least I'd bring it to completion by returning the chain with the statement that it looked too good on Alec for me to keep.

I attempted to give the necklace back to Alec after spring break, but he wouldn't accept its return. Later when we became better acquainted, I asked Alec why he'd given me the chain.

"Beats me," he chirped, "I just felt like it." So much for that. Alec was not a man of many words.

I was quite disturbed that as soon as I created a fantasy, my fantasy became realized. I felt uncomfortable with the notion that my thoughts were actualized without the interception of my conscious will. Or was some other will at work?

My freshman class in Greek classics presented me intellectually with the age-long controversy of fate versus free will. What are we people supposed to do—sit back and let everything happen, or go out and make everything happen? Is there a will similar to the will of the gods in Greek mythology? Whose will is meant by "Where there's a will, there's a way?" In an effort to feel control over life, do I fantasize about what I unconsciously know is predestined? Or, if I have the power to create the present, should I exert my will or submit to the flow of events?

I became acutely aware that I seemed able to will that I not consciously receive precognitive dreams. I also knew that over the course of my childhood I had willfully pushed away several of my "psychic" abilities. Had I merely alleviated the pressure of being consciously confronted by my lack of control over events?

The more I focused on this issue, the greater became my desire to release many of my self-imposed blocks to awareness. It soon became evident that my fear of powerlessness was counterbalanced by a fear of too much power. I realized that I'd been nurturing a tremendous apprehension about giving way to the full extent of my intuitive abilities for fear of misusing them. A series of thematic, recurring dreams revealed to me the pattern of my growth process.

First, I dreamed that I stole a pair of sun glasses from a store. When I woke up I was furious with myself, because I knew I had the money to pay for them. Even if I hadn't, my action seemed inexcusable. In my next dream, I saw a sweater that I liked, and I stole it but left money to cover half its price. Again I woke up furious with myself. Next, I dreamed that I bought a candy bar and for my change the cashier accidentally gave me a ten-dollar bill in place of a one. I didn't tell her. Again I woke up annoyed by my actions. The dreams continued in this vein and then shifted slightly.

I saw a man drop twenty dollars. I decided that if he realized it, I wouldn't take it. I gave him a couple of seconds, and when he didn't turn back I pocketed the money. Suddenly he reappeared, inquiring if I had seen his twenty. I handed it to him. But I woke up wondering why I hadn't told him in the first place that he dropped his money. Later my dreams became situations in which I would take something but put it back before anyone noticed. But in every case I could easily afford the object of my desire, so the entire situation seemed my own set-up. In my conscious state, I felt that I was continually testing myself to a point when I'd be sure that I wouldn't misuse any of my abilities for monetary gain, or for distorted ego purposes.

As I grew to trust myself, I felt ready to open some of the blocks I'd created as a child. I thought I'd start by willing myself to have "real" dreams again. So one night, before I fell asleep, I told myself that I was going to have a "real." The next morning just before I woke up I dreamed that I was given a traffic ticket. When I awakened, I vowed to drive exceptionally carefully throughout the day. I even went out of my way to use the car as seldom as possible.

On my last errand of the day, as I was slowly driving down a side street near home, I noticed two hitchhikers. I remembered my ' driver's education rule that, when passing pedestrians, you should always look in your rear-view mirror to make sure you didn't hit them, or vice versa! I looked in my rear-view mirror, everyone seemed intact, and I pulled into my driveway.

Just as I got out of the car, glad that my dream didn't come true after all, a police officer drove into my driveway and called "Hey, miss! Come back here!"

What could I possibly have done wrong? Nothing. The cop probably just wants to ask me a question. Despite my rationalization, I could feel my body trembling as I approached the police officer.

"May I see your driver's license and registration?"

"Sure, but what did I do wrong?"

"You didn't stop at that stop sign on the corner."

Damn! In going overboard to check the safety of the hitchhikers, I didn't notice the stop sign. Despite my pleadings, the policeman handed me a ticket and told me I should drive *more* carefully.

Having to pay for the ticket made the price of a precognitive dream too high. I settled for dreams about friends from whom, upon awakening, I knew I'd receive a letter or a phone call. I had come to the realization that there was some element of free will in my conscious awareness.

It finally occurred to me that free will and fate were as intertwined as light particles and light waves. In physics, light can be looked at in either of two ways: as a particle or a wave. When light is studied as a particle, it displays distinctive characteristics and movements. When light is examined as a wave, it displays a different set of characteristics and movements. And although the properties of waves and particles both pertain to light, they can only be studied one at a time.

Just in this way are fate and free will interdependent. When life is looked at from the point of view that everything is pre-destined, so it becomes. When life is seen as a series of events which the individual personally creates, so it becomes. But somehow both are mutually intertwined, working together to make life *happen.* The choice is in the will of the participant, who can either sit back and let everything occur, or go forth and make it all happen. The doers and the watchers—we are all both.

I found myself entering a stage of many expected accomplishments: I needed to get good grades in college, create and establish solid friendships, continue my work with disabled children, and develop a strong sense of self. With this in mind, I chose the role of "do-er" rather than my previous role as "see-er."

Tammy as "see'er."

22

NEVER MIND THE BODY

Js

Tammy was home from college for the winter vacation, and we spent the morning catching up with each other and planning the holiday. Later in the day I left the apartment to do some errands in downtown Manhattan. In the midst of rush hour, I caught a taxi for home. Stopped at a traffic light about half way there, I heard myself order the driver to turn the cab around immediately and proceed to an address right off Fifth Avenue. It surprised us both, as I had no previous inclination to do that. I wondered why I felt such a powerful impulse to go to a jewelry store where some earrings were being repaired for my mother. She *had* asked me to collect the earrings if I should happen to pass the place, but there was no urgency and I certainly was not nearby. I was angry that my compulsive act as traffic was building up made it take twice as long to get home. At least the earrings were ready. My mother would be delighted that I remembered them.

Tammy met me at the front door. "Did you get Grandma's earrings?"

"Don't tell me that was *you!*"

"Well, you could say it was both Grandma and me. She called a while ago and wondered where you were. She said she would love to wear her earrings to the opera tomorrow night, and when I told her you were already downtown she asked me to send you a message."

"Well, it looks like nothing's changed. Welcome home!"

I had been concerned about the repeated bouts of intestinal illness that plagued Tammy for many years. The condition could not be diagnosed, but its effects were appalling. No one likes to see another person suffer, but when it is your child there is an added dimension of frustrated helplessness. Now Tammy told me about an episode that had significant bearing on her problem. She described a full-blown mystical experience that impressed me much more than it did her.

She had been relaxing in her dorm room when she felt transported into an intense rainbow of light. She was aware that the light was limitless, extended forever into space, and that it was a brilliant white. At the same time she was able to "see" the full spectrum of colors in it. There was a knowing that this somehow was a perception of God and that she was both a part of this extension and also her small Tammy self. She felt capable of asking this greater part questions that had been troubling her. "Is reincarnation true? Have I really a memory of past lives shared with my Mother?" The answer was direct. "In a way, the only way you can now perceive, you have lived many lives and your Mother was a part of many of them. But in the overview, all lives are but One life, and in this sense you are now living all lives that ever were, are now and will be."

"What are these painful attacks that I have been having?"

"They are resistance to your higher knowing."

"Will they ever go away?"

"As of now, they have already disappeared."

I believed that this had happened and Tammy assured me that she had not had a recurrence since this insight. The interesting part of the event was the contrast in styles: I was deeply affected by the story and still am. Tammy was moved at the time and then seemed to let the incident casually slip away.

We had a lot of catching up to do. Although we spoke on the telephone often enough, there are some things that just must be shared in person. Intricate stories about new friends, plans for the future, inner experiences—all in a more adult camaraderie as my daughter slipped into womanhood despite herself. I scarcely noticed that I had always thought of both Jonathan and Tamara as mature minds in small bodies. Now the bodies were at their full growth and yet their psyches kept expanding. I felt constantly privileged for the precious moments of intimacy I was allowed. The small crises and perpetual dramas in the lives of two energetic siblings added to the zest of parenting. As Jonathan once remarked after we had accused him of being a non-stop chatterbox, "But I'm never boring, am I?" We had laughingly agreed.

I was trying to do too much, too fast, as usual. People were coming for dinner. I jerked open the heavy wooden clothes hamper as I was scurrying around the bathroom barefoot. Its safety chain gave way and twenty pounds of agony crashed onto my big toe. The shock was compounded by the feeling of stupidity I experienced at the senseless accident. I sat on the floor nursing the blow, muttering obscenities to myself. A few moments later Tammy limped through my bedroom and hopped into the bathroom to confront me. "Mom, I had a sudden jabbing pain in my big toe just now for no reason whatsoever." I pointed to my toe and we burst out laughing. "This is carrying sympathy too damned far." We both agreed I should be more careful in the future for, as she put it, "You'd better take care of yourself, for *me!*"

Later that night I was reading about true empathy in the *Course.* As so often happened, whenever I needed clarification of a problem, some sort of illumination would be provided by the precise section I was studying. This time I found "To empathize does not mean to join in suffering, for that is what you must *refuse* to understand." The *Course* goes on to explain the mistake we make when we choose to join in pain, emphasizing that healing pain is not accomplished by delusional attempts to lighten it by sharing. It suggests once again that we give the situation over to the Holy Spirit, which knows how to use our propensity to empathize. We are promised that if we will merely sit quietly by and let the Holy Spirit relate through us, we will empathize with strength, thus increasing strength and decreasing weakness.

No more would I be tempted to help another person alleviate either physical or emotional pain by feeling sorry for the person— or guilt that I was not suffering as much! Nor would I encourage anyone else to feel that kind of sympathy for me. I promised myself to try to remember the true meaning of empathy and not to forget my strong Friend and prayer. Not too long after this, I gave myself another test.

My scream couldn't be stifled. Bill Thetford came running into the kitchen. I had been cooking dinner for a group of guests who came that afternoon to discuss the *Course.* Everyone was having such a good time, the decision was made to stay on through the evening. Someone had to feed the mob, and I elected myself. Now I had poured sizzling oil over my left hand and wrist. The pain was intense and large blisters were beginning to form. With Bill helping I rushed to plunge my hand into ice water. One of the physicians in the group examined the burns and urged that I hurry to a nearby hospital emergency room for an antibiotic injection.

Bill looked at me calmly. "Do you want to try to heal this?" he asked. Holding back tears, I nodded my assent. While the doctor called the hospital to announce my arrival, Bill asked me to hold out the wounded hand. He reminded me to select one of my favorite daily lessons from the *Course* as a focus. With closed eyes we both concentrated on releasing fear. "I choose the joy of God instead of pain" I repeated over and over to myself like a mantra. My mind started to escape the magnetic grip of the injury. I was conscious of wondering why I had done this to myself. I suddenly realized how angry I was at excluding myself from the interesting conversation by offering to prepare dinner. I could have suggested we all go to a nearby restaurant. I did not have to mother the world! Bill was studying me intently. There were no signs of pain. The redness and blistering had subsided and I felt at peace. My doctor friend burst in on us to tell me it was all arranged at the hospital emergency room. I showed him the almost non-existent burn. He shook his head in disbelief. The incident had ended.

Once again I had chosen suffering. This time it was because of an abscess under a tooth that had recently been filled. Perhaps some decay remained for, within a day, over a weekend, the swelling began. My dentist was unavailable and I was trying to find a substitute when our doorbell rang. I was very glad to greet a surprise visitor. It was my latest friendly physician, who had continued his study of medicine with some unorthodox lessons in Tibetan healing and metaphysics. With him was his elderly teacher, a man in his late eighties who had the look and vigor of fifty. We were chatting when the Oriental mentor pointed to my jaw and inquired about the swelling. "That must be painful. Go, my son, and get the green light."

While I wondered what was happening, my doctor friend rushed out to his car. Returning, he plugged in a large green bulb with a portable reflector and arranged a chair for me so that the light would shine on the infected area. As a good hostess, I didn't want to hurt their feelings by indicating I thought this would be useless—I just needed to have the tooth redrilled as soon as possible. So I went along with their recipe for recovery. Both teacher and student closed their eyes in deep meditation and began a low rhythmic chant which I assumed was a prayer. I conceded their good will and let my mind relax, wondering how I would end this gracefully. Their hands were on my shoulders and I began to succumb to the contagion of peace. In a little while I wasn't thinking any more about the extreme discomfort in my mouth. Instead, I noticed an almost imperceptible taste of mint that was quite pleasant. All at once the session was over. The green light was flicked off and they asked how I felt. I felt my jaw line. There was no swelling left. I touched my tongue gingerly to the gum that had ached. No sensation at all. It felt anesthetized. I stammered my thanks to the beaming duo and we all began to laugh in pure joy.

After my guests left, in a mood of elation I jotted down some of my thoughts about the experience. They sounded too familiar to be original, and when I reread what I had written I found I had quoted the *Course.* "Healing is a collaborative venture," "To heal is to make happy," "My body is a wholly neutral thing," "I can be hurt by nothing but my thoughts." This was obviously getting to me. It was already in my blood. Chuckling, I remembered all the times we had teased Helen when she voiced nebulous physical complaints. Instead of reminding her to repeat a powerful lesson from the *Course* which states, "I am not a body, I am free. I am still as God created me," we taunted her with our own verision: "She *is* a body, she is sickly. Get her to a doctor quickly!" I reviewed my major recent encounters with illnesses in various forms. I had come to agree that healing occurs the instant the sufferer no longer sees any value in pain. My ulcer disappeared when I relinquished my need for it, as did the burn on my hand. "Sickness is a defense against the truth" took on a new meaning as I explored the opportunities I had followed to think ill of someone else, thus separating myself from the other person *and* my Source. I turned to the teacher's manual of the *Course* for more clarification.

It is obvious that decisions are of the mind, not of the body. If sickness is but a faulty problem-solving approach, it is a decision. And if it is a decision, it is the mind and not the body that makes it. . . .

The acceptance of sickness as a decision of the mind, for a purpose for which it would use the body, is the basis of healing. And this is so for healing in all forms. A patient decides that this is so, and he recovers. If he decides against recovery, he will not be healed. Who is the physician? Only the mind of the patient himself. . . .

I may not have perfected the technique of that shift of perception, I thought, but I certainly do agree with the premise. I proved it to myself with loving helpers. And my daughter suggested a motto I could emblazon in my memory: "Never mind the *body,* mind the *mind.*"

*Black Sunday, a
workshop on* A
Course in Miracles
in California

23

Black Sunday, and
Other Dark Thoughts

J s

"Adrenal overload" the doctor dubbed it, when I complained of exhaustion and a sense of burn-out. He recommended that I take a break from almost continuous travel and lecturing. I felt I could afford a weekend off, and I would combine it with a visit to Tammy at Tufts. She was living, with other students, in a large rented home in suburban Massachusetts. The environment was student contemporary and there was a new cat I had to meet—my grandkitty Natasha! Tammy met me at the airport, noticing immediately how beat and dejected I looked. She hurried us to her home and ushered me into an immaculate, sunny room made festive to greet me. The housemates were charming and solicitous. I was kept in bed until I no longer felt like sleeping and then presented with ethnic penicillin—homemade chicken soup. Tammy is an adventuresome cook and never uses a recipe. That soup had things in it I'd never tasted in combination. It must have done the trick for, with a couple of days of tender loving care by that mob (including the cat), I felt renovated, rejuvenated, and ready to roll. Tammy took me to the airport. As I tried to thank her for my resuscitation she stopped me cold with, "Look Mom, I'm glad you're feeling so much better. I'm glad I could help. But remember, this time we chose to come with *you* the mother and *me* the daughter. This is the only role reversal you get!" I stood forewarned.

We had played with the idea of reincarnation before. When Tammy was tiny she once told me that she was afraid to have me leave her. When I replied that mothers sometimes go out but they *do* come back, she sadly shook her head.

"Not one time, Mommy. One time you didn't come back ever."

"What do you mean? I always do come home."

"No, Mommy, one time when I was seven and we were living in that big white place with all the colored stones in pictures on the ground, that time you said you'd come back and you didn't."

I clutched her to me, a four-year-old, knowing what she was saying nearly broke my heart. Why did this single, unsubstantiated remark touch me with such pathos I wanted to weep? What did I "remember"?

From some distant place I imagined I saw a Persian palace, white walls and walled courtyard, colorful tiles in mosaic patterns on the floors both inside and out. I saw a huge golden dome and soldiers coming to take me away as I shrieked for my child, arms stretched out as I begged not to be separated. That was all. The emotion was too strong to be played with and so it was banished. I delved much later into reincarnation literature, particularly the studies conducted by my friend Dr. Ian Stevenson in *Twenty Cases Suggestive of Reincarnation.* My personal court was still out on the verdict, and it did not figure prominently in my belief system.

A Course in Miracles provided me with as much suggestion as I felt I needed on the subject.

> In the ultimate sense, reincarnation is impossible.
> There is no past or future, and the idea of birth into a
> body has no meaning either once or many times. Rein-
> carnation cannot, then, be true in any real sense. Our
> only question should be, "Is the concept helpful? And
> that depends, of course, on what it is used for."

It continues with an explanation that suited me well at the time. The *Course* states that, to some, there may be comfort in the concept, and if it heartens them its value is self-evident. It urges that we consult our internal Teacher for guidance in looking at this within the framework of our present beliefs. Eventually, all that need be recognized is that birth is not the beginning and death is not the end.

With Tamara and Jonathan no longer living full time at home, and Bob's daughter Laura and son Andrew also in college, the apartment began to feel too large. We were still using it for meetings, but with me traveling so much it left most of the maintenance up to Bob. One night in the fall of 1977 he announced that his guided writing indicated we were to sell the apartment and be prepared to move. "Where to?" was my immediate reaction. Bob shrugged. He didn't know, but trusted time would tell. Almost all the office work necessary for the dissemination of the *Course* was now being handled by Bob, who had resigned his position at the brokerage house and conducted both the Foundation's business and his own from our home. It was comforting to know that the Foundation's daily doings were in such capable hands, and that I was free to visit study groups and speak at conferences all over the world regarding the *Course*. The decision to move really had to be Bob's. He was the home front.

Our apartment was placed on the market. It sold immediately. We had six months in which to relocate. I was in a state of shock. I had not realized how attached I had grown to that particular place and lifestyle. Where to go? The anxiety of not knowing where we were to settle was worse than the thought of leaving a place that had housed a family of four-plus-two for ten years. And the accumulation of possessions and records! (For it was also a move of two offices.) I needed all the help I could get and, although the idea of my moving at all threatened Helen as much as it did me, she and Bill were supportive as usual. I looked for new places in New York City. I looked in the suburbs in Connecticut. I didn't even know what kind of a place I should be looking for. Helen suggested I should calm down and ask. I felt I was to keep looking and I would know it when I found it.

Meanwhile, when I was in town we were continuing our meetings.

The *Course* was spreading rapidly and some radio talk shows and television interview programs requested some one to speak about the material. Helen and Bill refused to play the guru roles as they both felt the material should stand on its own. But people did want to know more. It was decided I should represent the *Course,* as I so obviously was still only its student. It was touching to watch Helen wrestle with her ego when she felt there were "funny goings-on." She could not imagine why people were being drawn in droves to a metaphysical teaching as difficult as the *Course*. At one point she remarked that she felt barely eight or nine people would ever truly understand what it meant. I mentioned this to Tammy and said I hoped some day to be one of them. Tammy had absorbed some of this by osmosis. She seemed to have no desire to read the *Course* at all. When she first heard about it from me, she wanted to know what it said. I gulped and asked her how long a summary she desired. "No more than three minutes." I talked as fast as I could and described the major premises. She nodded and said thoughtfully, "Oh, yes. I know that." This time she reflected upon Helen's comment and my determination to truly know the *Course*. "Mom, is it true that the *Course* says only one person is needed to save the world?" I expanded on this idea, telling her the concept is that one wholly perfect teacher of God, whose learning is complete, can so touch other minds because of that person's recognition of his or her spiritual being and limitlessness that all other minds would instantly hold that thought. For, being one, we are so joined. Tammy digested that for a moment.

"Mom, is that likely to happen soon?"

"I'm sorry to say, honey, that in what we know as time, it probably won't be."

"Well, that's a relief, cause I'm having so much fun here!"

I was certain that the world was not likely to be saved by me in a hurry, as I was still trying to heal my relationships, especially with Jerry. Our friendship had deteriorated into a push-and-tug match to ascertain who was in control. Neither was winning. We knew we had to speed up the process, and kept promising to relinquish the entire affair to the Holy Spirit. But we slipped a lot. Helen focused her time with me on increasing my willingness to let go. One afternoon, as I was confiding my unhappiness, Helen queried, "Do you have any idea of what your relationship with Jerry is for?"

"Yes I do, Helen. It is so I can understand the insanity of the ego and through my pain be better able to help others."

"Ridiculous! The Holy Spirit's lesson is that pain and suffering in any form are unnecessary."

I felt humiliated. Of course, I had studied that. I just forgot it often. Somewhere in the back of my mind I knew Jerry and I were engaged in a dance of "specialness." I also sensed that this dear brother of mine really existed in my life so that I could come to understand the power of forgiveness. But I had nothing to forgive him *for!* And that is exactly the *Course's* teaching.

Specialness begins with a misperception of ourselves as discrete from God. It is an insane dream. In that error of thinking, guilt is born—guilt that we *dared* separate ourselves from our Source. The special relationship is born out of the need to project that guilt onto someone else and so misdirect our thoughts away from God. I was keenly aware that falling in love, for me, was an attraction to someone who seemed to have something I lacked. That person was my "saviour" and would make me complete. My feelings of love were not really love at all. I wanted something from that beloved other, and when the other did not continue to supply that scarcity in me, I was no longer in love. That much I had figured out for myself. What mystified me was why that "special love" should turn to "special hate." The *Course* explained it perfectly to my satisfaction. We are not incomplete at all. How could a creation of God lack anything? To mistake another as needed to fulfill that which is already complete is indeed a major error. But to recognize the other as a mirror for yourself; to see in another being God's shining light; to expose our "special hate" relationships as opportunities for forgiveness—then the "enemy" can be seen as a blessed friend. In Jerry I had the possibility of seeing that "all the lamps of God were lit by the same spark."

Bill Thetford was especially helpful to Jerry by reminding him of the meaning of forgiveness. Bill termed it *celestial amnesia:* remembering only love from the past and selectively discarding all the negative emotions. I reminded myself of Dr. William James' remark, *"Act as if* and you will *become."*

We tried so hard. Jerry tried harder than I. In fact, his powerful example of the desire to change constantly inspired me. He had made so many changes in his life already. He had been inner-directed to give up alcohol and he did it cold turkey. He felt the need to eliminate coffee from his diet. I thought that would be more difficult, as I had watched him consume up to twenty-two cups a day! One evening he visualized a steaming cup of coffee in his mind and told himself that he was not to drink it any more. He stopped immediately. Jerry had shifted from an eclectic psychiatric practice to one based openly upon spiritual principles. This was not the same hyperkinetic man I had met in an airport a few years before. When we lectured together on our use of the *Course,* I saw people respond to him in a new way. He was lightening up, and it was more than physical.

On a lovely spring weekend Bill, Jerry, and I were attending a workshop on forgiveness in the Santa Cruz mountains of California. We were the moderators, and I was feeling totally unforgiving. I "acted as if" as long as I could. My ego was giving me a monumental battle. Jerry had done nothing to deserve my rage. I couldn't pin it on anything at all, so I chose to dislike the way he was smiling. Finally I broke away from the group, hiding my emotion, and ran into the woods. I felt as if I were wrestling with a dark side of me I had never truly known. It was horrifying. I wished my friend harm! Bill Thetford followed me into the woods. Dispassionately but in full empathy he put his arms around me and held me as I shook. Between spasms I bared my soul. He smiled and quietly offered, "You should rejoice." I turned, furious at him. "Rejoice! How can I be happy when I'm so miserable and don't even understand why?" "Rejoice because you wouldn't be experiencing such darkness if you weren't so close to the light."

Bill then suggested that my persistent and mounting rage at Jerry was in truth a projection of my own fear of the separation from God. It had nothing to do with Jerry at all. I was making him the butt to escape my own deep sense of guilt over a separation that had never occurred!

I really didn't hear him. But I collected myself and huffily went off to moderate the next panel on forgiveness. When I approached the group there was a refreshment pause and people were milling around. I saw Jerry with a bandage over his eye. He had walked, unseeing, into an open metal cabinet door. He looked at me and said sadly, "Now, are you happy? Or would you like me to kill myself?" I was stunned at the nightmare we shared. I could hardly wait for the session to end. It had been a very black Sunday.

Later that night I was to give a talk about the *Course* to a group of students in Palo Alto. More than a hundred had gathered for the occasion and I felt like a hypocrite. Still heavy at heart, I looked down at Bill and Jerry sitting in the audience as my support team and wondered how dishonest I could be. I heard the hostess introducing me in glowing terms. I didn't believe any of them. Now it was time for me to speak. I couldn't, I thought, I just *couldn't.* In desperation I closed my eyes for a moment to shut out this horrific situation and suddenly remembered to call for help. It took only an instant to say to my internal Teacher, "You take this mess, I can't hack it!" When I opened my eyes, I gasped out loud.

The room was filled with the most extraordinary light. For a puzzling moment I thought the light shining on me was for televising the talk. I heard someone from the back ask the custodian, "Will you please turn that light lower?" There was no external source to the laser-like ray. And then it was gone and I was left blinking my surprise. But oh, that feeling! Released, refreshed, rejoicing. Thanking the world and everyone in the room with a fierce gratitude I had never known. I looked down at Jerry and knew he knew. He was beaming pure love at me. I gave my speech. They liked it. Jerry came up to me as everyone was crowding around sharing stories and waited until I was alone. He whispered softly, "Thank God, it's over." We held hands with tears of joy brimming to the surface of our enlightened eyes. It was the beginning of the end of specialness.

Bill suggested that we open our text to page 448. Together we read out loud:

This holy relationship, lovely in its innocence, mighty in strength, and blazing with a light far brighter than the sun that lights the sky you see, is chosen of your Father as a means for His own plan. Be thankful that it serves yours not at all. Nothing entrusted to it can be misused, and nothing given it but will be used. This holy relationship has the power to heal all pain, regardless of its form. Neither of you alone can serve at all. Only in your joint will does healing lie. For here your healing is, and here will you accept Atonement. And in your healing is the Sonship healed *because* your wills are joined.

24

Public Eye, Private Me

Being away from home all year has shown me that life outside our apartment pales by comparison. Coming home is like returning to a furnace of energy. The phone calls and mail orders for A Course in Miracles *are now coming in by the hundreds. Bob and I have been typing address labels for the mailing of the books, and Grams and I have stuffed and sealed so many envelopes that our fingers are riddled with paper cuts and our tongues are affixed to the roofs of our mouths. I can't help but laugh when I hear people refer to the Foundation for Inner Peace as an organization that distributes the* Course. *I think* disorganization *is a more apt description.*

With the second publishing of the Course *has come the first article publicizing it. The CIM saga was the feature story in the first edition of a magazine called* New Realities. *The magazine used to go by the name of* Psychic, *but they decided to create a new design. Just as my mother's interests evolved from a psychic to a spiritual focus, so did* Psychic *magazine turn to* New Realities.

With the transformation of the magazine, it seemed fitting that its initial issue be about A Course in Miracles *and include a full article on my mother's transformation from housewife to psychic explorer to spiritual pursuer.*

When the first issue of New Realities *was released, there were hundreds of copies in our apartment. The magazine's office is in San Francisco, but it seemed as though we were responsible for its distribution on the East Coast. I sneaked a copy out of a carton. As I flipped through its pages, I was confronted by a full-page picture of Mom. I thought she looked great. After I read the article, I changed my mind.*

Halfway through Mom's interview, I stopped short, taken aback by the sight of my own name. I read that Mom said I was the reason for her delving into parapsychology. I don't know why I have to be her scapegoat. I always get blamed for everything! But even that didn't bother me as much as seeing myself described as "an extremely gifted sensitive, and an intuitive child." Bleck! I couldn't believe my own mother had sabotaged me! I immediately reproached her for bringing me into the article. I told her Dad would sue! In her defense, she said that she merely told the truth. What could I do? It was over and done with.

Finishing the article, I felt the kind of nausea caused by an overdose of spiritual sweetness. Mom is made out to be a mystic whose head is in the clouds. Not once does the article show her human side. They don't say a word about how she still gets angry, still makes mistakes, and still cringes over her father's judgments. And there's certainly no mention of her ulcers, colitis and backaches! They don't even depict her witty, biting humor. In the article she is portrayed as a saccharin-sweet spiritual saint, and the photograph of her loving eyes reinforces the image. That's only one aspect to the real Judith Skutch, and if you ask me it's the boring side. But the magazine seems to be selling well, and the orders for the Course *have multiplied. So what do I know about what people want to read?*

What I do know is that I'd never show the article to Dad. Boy, would he have a field day with it! Actually, that may not be true. It seems he's softening. We finally discussed my resentment about his preferring Jon to me. And, you know, I think he's felt just as hurt by the distance I've created from him as vice versa. So we've begun to patch up old wounds. I think we're getting along better now because he's relating to me more as a person than as a child. Was it Mark Twain who said "I went away to college and when I came home, I was surprised to find how much my father had learned." Ditto.

*Soon enough, my home away from school will be
Dad's. Mom and Bob have put the apartment up for sale
and expect to evict me in a few months. I'm supposed
to start packing up all my years of belongings and
memories. I guess I took it the hardest. Why do we
have to leave? They said their inner guidance told them
in meditation that it's time to move on. What kind of
mixed-up guidance is that? Don't they realize their
inner voices were just kidding them? But the joke's on
me. It's the end of an era that's turning into an error.*

*I hate the thought that new people will be inhabiting
our apartment, and the traces of us here will be papered
over, painted over, carpeted over, washed up, broken
down and disinfected away.*

*One West Eighty-First Street. No more view of the
planetarium. No more looking at the snowfall over
Central Park. No more bedside view of the Thanksgiving
Day Parade. No more big parties and no more open
boarding house. Mom is tired of cooking. Bob wants a
small home. I must admit I think it's daring that they're
picking up everything they've established and dumping
it somewhere else. They trust their guidance so implicitly
now that they'd follow it anywhere.*

*I just can't believe this won't be home anymore. I feel
as though a huge chunk of my life is drifting into my
past and there's nothing I can do about it. There's
something about this apartment that is so full of my
spirit. I'm afraid I'll have to leave some of it behind.
This is just an apartment, but it's me. Why doesn't
anyone understand that? When I come home to this
apartment, it holds all the subtle and blatant memories
of my childhood. I can't hold all those remembrances
in my brain, or my head will be so heavy with clutter,
it'll hang low. In order to hold my head high, I can
take only what I'll be needing later.*

*I think I'll write a note to the new tenants and stick
it in a hidden crevice in my closet:*

*"I've lived here for ten years. I love this apartment.
It will always be my home. Even when you think you've
redone this place, it will always be the same in my
dreams. As much as you think you can cover up the
remnants of the previous inhabitants, we will always
be here in every nook and cranny. I'm hiding this note
just to prove it. I hope you're as happy here as we have
been. I wonder if that's possible. Good Luck."*

From now on, I have to carry my home inside me.

*View of Central
Park West.*

*Photo by
Jonathan Cohen*

25

DOUBLE BLIND

When I got home from college, I paid a visit to Mr. Biology. I waited for the students to pour out before I entered the classroom. Mr. B was still talking to the lingering students. I was thrilled to see him look ferociously at a student who asked him to repeat an explanation already made in class.

"Why should I repeat to you what your science textbook should have taught you already? Haven't you been doing your homework? It's all in there!" He roared "Who's next?" The rest of the students abandoned their questions and quickly dispersed. Mr. Biology turned to me and, trying to hide a smile, growled "What do you want?" I laughed and embraced the big bad bear, reassured that some things would never change.

We sat down at the lab table as we made up for lost time. I focused the conversation on my work with the blind children.

"You should do a controlled laboratory experiment with color sensing," Mr. B told me.

"As a matter of fact, I am. I've convinced a Tufts professor to allow me to do an independent study on color perception. I'm actually getting science credits for it!"

"So you've suckered yet another science compatriot to credit you for your shenanigans!"

I laughed. Did I detect a note of jealousy in Mr. B's voice?

"It would be interesting to determine the factors involved in your blind children's color perception.''

"What do you mean?''

"Maybe they were picking up the mental images of the colors from you by way of telepathy.''

I was wrong. Mr. B had changed. He'd come a long way in receptivity since I first met him. But perhaps I hadn't.

"Who cares about how they do it, as long as they do it?''

"I do.''

"Oh, good. Well maybe you'll do an experiment with them,'' I goaded.

"My hands are tied as it is. Did I tell you that I'm the teacher for the extra-curricular cooking class?''

I couldn't refrain from laughter. "You've gotta be kidding!''

"No, I'm a superb chef. As a matter of fact I was just about to make some tea and soup. Would you like to join me!''

"An offer I can't refuse!''

I gleefully watched my favorite teacher as he boiled water on the Bunsen burner, and then poured the hot water into four cups, two with tea bags in them, and two containing Lipton's noodle soup. We drank and we ate and I realized that I'd never felt more comfortable with him than at that moment. When we parted company, I promised to keep him up-to-date on my continuing work with the blind children.

Shortly after my arrival in San Francisco for the summer, I called Dina. I was eager to resume working with colors, and perhaps that was my biggest mistake. Whereas the previous summer I'd had no expectations of what would happen, this summer I assumed Dina and I would pick up where we'd left off. Holding an expectation, I set myself up for disappointment.

Dina and I had a wonderful reunion. She was glad to see me, but I could tell that she wasn't thrilled about concentrating on colors. When I'd put a colored object under her hand, instead of paying any attention to it, she would wildly guess its color.

"Dina, what color's this scarf?''

"Blue!'' she would answer immediately.

"C'mon Dina, concentrate.''

"Orange!'' she would instantly answer again.

"Yellow, no maybe green,'' she'd continue.

After the first few times I saw her, it became evident that she was feigning interest in color just to ensure my companionship. I knew she had the ability to perceive color, as she'd demonstrated the previous summer, but I could neither force nor persuade her to take interest again. Since I couldn't release my desire to resume where we'd left off, I had to create new incentives.

I organized a group of Dina and two friends with whom she had played "colors.'' Darlene was a large girl with buck teeth who resembled a miniature Hattie. Darlene was going blind and was anxious to perceive colors after the loss of her eyesight. Darlene relayed each color as having a varied sense of texture. She described yellow as "liquidy," blue as "mushier than liquidy," red as "sort of solid," black as "shallow," and "white feels thick." A second friend, Juan was a fat little boy who said that whenever he put his hand over a color he'd get a distinctive taste in his mouth. When his hand touched yellow, he tasted lemon, red was cherry, black was licorice, blue was mint, purple was grape. To each his own.

After blindfolding myself and Darlene, I randomly selected a colored piece of paper and placed it in the center of the circle made up by the four of us. By blindfolding myself, I was attempting to eliminate the possibility of telepathy in accordance with Mr. Biology's suggestion. Whoever properly identified the color on the first try got a point. We kept score and the one with the most points at the end of the day got a prize ranging from bubble gum to a paper hat. The others got booby prizes. Although we rarely all agreed on the paper's color, when the choice was unanimous, the paper never failed to be the color of our choice.

Despite the fact that Dina and I were often joined by her friends, there were many times we spent alone. It was quite apparent to me that Dina could sense colors accurately when in competition with her peers, but when it was back to the two of us she lost interest once again. She'd go back to guessing rather than concentrating, and she'd grow impatient. I began to feel that I was forcing her to do something she didn't want to do. It was at this point I introduced Dina to remote viewing.

"Dina, how'd you like to be able to know what people are doing even when you're not with them?"

"That'd be great. Could I really? How?"

I was happy to see interest. I proceeded to explain remote viewing. I told her that one person would go somewhere and she would follow that person in her mind. She'd tell me everything that person was seeing, either by imagining herself seeing those same things, or by seeing directly through the eyes of the other person.

I asked my summer associate Tanya to help us. When Tanya was the traveler, I would sit with Dina and record everything she described Tanya as seeing.

The first few run-throughs were uneventful, but soon Dina started getting the feel for it. During one instance, Tanya went for a walk with a piece of paper on which to transcribe her sightseeing. Dina was sitting with me. After Tanya left my field of vision I gave Dina the go-ahead to tell me what she was seeing. At first she rambled off a bunch of objects like the ground, her hands, and so on. But then all of sudden Dina stopped. She paused a moment and then said, in a very soft voice with tears in her eyes, "So that's what a tree really looks like." I was taken aback. "What do you mean?" I asked her. She composed herself.

"I see a huge tree with lots of leaves, I guess. It's like nothing I've ever imagined." Then with excitement in her voice she remarked "Now I see a house with a furry dog, and a woman holding it! And now I see the inside of a room and a long line of pictures! There's one of a man!"

A couple of minutes later, our traveler returned. For the first time since I had known Dina, she was silent. Tanya read off the list of images she had seen. One of them was a large tree with thick green leaves, another was a house with a woman and a dog, and then she went into a building that had a hallway lined with paintings and old photographs. When I read Dina's descriptions, Tanya was surprised. She said there had been a photograph of one particular man, but she didn't record it. We were all excited, especially Dina. She wanted to play the game some more. But it was time to go. Subsequently her remote viewing was not always that accurate, but it opened up for her a whole new world of vision.

On one occasion, I met Dina at her house to find her anxiously pacing the bottom of the steps. Upon hearing the car pull up, she shouted she had something to tell me.

"What is it?"

"I did something great!"

"Well, what was it this time?"

"The other day I came home from school and Mommy wasn't there. She's always home when I get home so I was a little nervous. When I started to get a lot nervous, I decided to find out where she was by looking like you taught me. I relaxed and saw her getting her hair done. I didn't really see clear pictures, but I knew that that's what she was doing. So I wasn't nervous anymore. And when she came home, the first thing I said to her was, 'Mommy, I know where you were! You were getting your hair cleaned!' She asked me how I knew, and I said that I saw her the way you taught me! She couldn't believe it!"

"That's fantastic!" I said aloud, but inside my head flowed images of her mother burning me at the stake. Because of her disinterest and poor English, I had never discussed with Mrs. Dina the work I was doing with her daughter. I always figured she considered me a free babysitter who had become her daughter's friend.

"Dina, was your mother upset?"

"At first, but then I explained it to her. I don't think she really understood me but it doesn't matter. She said it's okay if I like to do it. I don't know, maybe she thought I was pretending. But it really happened!''

"I'm so proud of you!'' I was ecstatic that Dina had found a way to incorporate remote viewing into her daily life. It occurred to me that, even if Mrs. Dina *hadn't* been at the hairdresser's, the important fact was that Dina used the method to relieve fear.

As the summer progressed, Dina told me of incidents in which she would know who was on the telephone before she'd pick it up. She told me that she and Darlene would play remote viewing together on the telephone, by guessing what the other one was doing or wearing. What excited me most was that Dina had opened up a whole new world of images parading before her mind's eye. I realized that by releasing my desire to turn Dina into a color-intuiting sensitive I had allowed her to make way for a new mode of learning. I expected that she'd soon tire of this game as well, but I was confident that she would always have it at her command.

When I had called Dina at the beginning of the summer, she was overjoyed, and asked me if I would come immediately to see her. In contrast, when I called Franklin to resume our relationship, he was typically Franklin.

"Hello, is Franklin there?''

"Yeah, this is Franklin. Who's this?''

"Frankle! This is Tammy!''

"Who?''

"Tammy!''

"Tammy who?''

"How many Tammys do you know?''

"I don't know.''

I was getting a little insulted that he didn't remember me immediately.

"TAMMY, Franklin. Don't you remember? We worked with colors last summer.''

"Oh yeah, Tammy. What's happenin'?''

I still wasn't convinced he remembered me.

"Have you forgotten me already?''

"Hell no, I was just confused for a moment. It's hard talkin' on the phone, y'know. Where are ya? Aren't ya in New York?''

I finally accepted he knew who I was, and my wounded ego healed quickly.

"No, I'm in San Francisco for the summer. I want to see you. When can I?''

"Well, I'm real busy tomorrow. How 'bout the day afta?''

Same old Franklin.

"Fine, I'll call you to find out what time you want me to come over.''

"Jus' come over any time in the mornin'."

I went to Franklin's house at ten thirty, only to wait two hours for his arrival. As usual, his family took me in immediately, stuffed me with food, and invited me to spend the entire day with them—with or without Franklin. I noticed a new baby gurgling in a highchair. I asked who I was to congratulate.

"Congratulate all of us, honey!" Mrs. Franklin picked up the infant and bounced it in her arms. I was told that the baby belonged to Daryl, the seventeen-year-old son of Mrs. Franklin. The baby was illegitimate and the mother wanted to give it up for adoption. Mrs. Franklin wouldn't hear of such a thing, so she adopted the child herself. The Franklin family was filled to the brim with bubbly children running in and out of the small house. I helped Mr. and Mrs. Franklin diaper their daughter's baby, their son's baby and their own little girl. Then Franklin came trotting in after a typical morning of bicycle riding.

The boy was wearing tight brown pants with a beige polyester shirt and a brown plaid jacket. I noticed he had grown taller since the last time I had seen him.

"Hey, Franklin. I don't know if I'm even gonna talk to you. I think you've grown taller than me."

"You better talk to me or I'll step on you!"

Still the same old Franklin, just a little older. I was glad to see that even with the onset of puberty he hadn't lost his sense of humor and self-confidence. I had to restrain my laughter when Franklin turned his back towards me and I noticed a hair pick sticking up from the back of his head.

"Franklin, you left your comb in your hair," I teased him.

"Don't you know it's cool to do that?" he retorted.

"Oh, excuse me, I'm just a little whitey y'know."

"Yeah, I'll have to teach you the cool way of life."

"You do that."

Franklin's family laughed and said that there was hope for me yet. It didn't take much time for us to catch up on the year that had stuck itself in between our last meeting. When I asked him if he still wanted to do the "color stuff," he grinned: "Hell, yeah. My brother wants you around cause he thinks you're cute." I wasn't sure how to respond to that, especially since he was talking about the brother who just had the illegitimate child.

When Franklin and I resumed working with colors, we were both a little bored. We had so much fun joking around and doing things together, that it became an effort to do the colors. He was too old to convince that it was a fun game. At this point I got an inspiration.

"Well, Franklin, if you don't feel like doing the colors anymore, how would you like to try something else?"

"Like what do you have in mind?"

I could tell by the snicker in his voice that his mind had changed from child to adolescent. I noticed that he was beginning to develop peach fuzz above his upper lip.

"Franklin, what kind of thought are you letting come into that head of yours?"

"Heh-heh-heh!"

"Cut that out!"

"I'm sorry, I just thought you might like to educate a poor blind boy."

"Better luck next time."

"I hope so."

"Now let's get back to what *I* was talking about. I know you're not interested in colors, but what about if I were to get pictures of instruments. Do you think you might be able to sense what instruments?"

"I don't know, but I'll try anything once."

I knew Franklin's main passion was music, particularly his drums. His family band had been playing night clubs and rehearsing in garages. I looked through magazines and cut out every picture of any instrument that I could find. I ended up with a picture of a flute, a piano, a guitar and a trumpet.

When I presented Franklin with the pictures, he thought I was crazy. "You mean you were serious about this?" he asked.

"Sure! It took me all night to find these pictures. Just tell me which picture is a set of drums?"

I watched Franklin mockingly put his hand over each picture as though he were trying to sense its color. After a few seconds, he turned serious and I noticed him in fixed concentration.

"Y'know, I really do feel something from these pictures."

I awaited a punch line. Instead he sat quietly, flipping through the five pictures.

"Oh c'mon, Franklin, quit clowning around."

"I ain't kiddin'. I really do feel something and I think that these are the drums."

He handed me the picture of the drum set. I looked at it and was stunned.

"Hey, how'd you do that? I didn't really expect you to do that. What were you feeling? Was it the shadowy shape of drums against the clear background?"

"No, man. I didn't really feel nothin' in my hands. I just got the feeling of drums from the picture."

"*What* feeling of drums?"

"I guess it's the same kind of vibration as when I'm playing them. It's hard to explain. It's just a feeling."

"Maybe you were just lucky. We'll try it again."

I took back the pictures, shuffled them, and returned them to Franklin. In three minutes he handed me the picture of the drum set.

"I think this is it," he said to me. "I'm right, ain't I?"

"Yeah, you're right—but it's so hard to believe."

"Hey, what's with you? You're the one who put me up to this and now you ain't even believin' me!"

"Of course I believe you. I'm just surprised. Let's see if you can do it with the other instruments."

I told him to identify each picture. His focus was more intense than ever before. I could tell he was excited to work with this new challenge. Time and again he accurately identified the picture. At first he had difficulty distinguishing the flute from the trumpet. But after awhile, he identified even those with ease. He insisted that each picture set off a specific vibration in his mind that reminded him of the instrument. I expanded his set of pictures, but he was always most accurate with those of guitars, drums, electric organs and pianos. He acknowledged that these were the familiar instruments of his band.

I wasn't sure how to explain it. I remembered Mr. Biology's suspicion that the blind children were telepathically receiving input from me. I decided to test this by closing my eyes, mixing up the pictures, and handing them to Franklin. I told him to make piles for each instrument and to identify each pile by rote. During this entire process my eyes remained closed. The results did not alter. He consistently got over 85 percent of the instrument identifications correct.

Although I believed he was intuiting different vibrations from each picture, I knew this explanation would not satisfy scientists. It was difficult enough for me to explain tactile color perception. I still found myself hiding behind the rationale of "sensitized tactile abilities attuned to varying heat gradations," blah, blah, blah. I decided on the socially acceptable explanation that Franklin's high sensitivity to colors' heat emissions enabled him to distinguish shapes of objects. I was not yet ready to face the skeptics of the world and stand up for what I knew to be truth. I was still hiding behind a socialized wall where I thought if I conformed I would be respected.

I spent much time wondering how I could test Franklin's intuition versus his sensitization. I had to involve something that would interest Franklin and help me distinguish whether he was sensing shapes or intuitive sound vibrations. Finally, a resolution occurred to me. I was flipping through magazine after magazine looking for the perfect picture-subject. There were many models, and I noticed that their attire usually hid the shapes of their bodies. the baggy look was "in," portraying women wearing football jerseys and men wearing sweat shirts and pants. I even found a picture of men wearing kilts. It occurred to me that if Franklin knew the subject of a picture by sensing its shape, he could distinguish a person but not the gender. From the androgynous baggy quality of the model's clothing, how was he to know male from female? If he could identify gender, it would mean he was using more than tactile sensitization.

It was obvious to me that Frankle was no longer a little boy. I knew he was going to get a kick out of this new experiment of identifying the sexes.

"Franklin, I have a bunch of pictures here of men and women. Do you think you could separate the males from the females?

"Are you jivin' me? Why don't you jus' ask me if I know my head from my ass?"

I laughed, "No, I'm not asking you if you can tell the difference between a girl and a guy under normal touchy-feely circumstances. I'm asking you to feel the pictures and tell me which are of men and which are of women. It's not so easy because they're dressed in baggy clothing."

"Hell, that don't make no difference. If you want me to, I'll separate the girls from the women and the boys from the men!"

"That won't be necessary, unless you really want to. Do you want to do this? If you don't, we don't have to."

"Sure I'll do it. I told ya', I'll do anythin' at least once, and sometimes a lot more than that."

When I gave him the pictures, he studied them carefully with his hands. He laughed self-consciously a few times as he sorted the piles.

"Franklin, I could've sworn that under all that black skin of yours I just saw some red. Are you undressing those girls with your eyes?"

"Hell, yeah," said Franklin as he blushed.

Out of fifteen pictures seven were of men and eight were of women. Franklin got thirteen out of fifteen correct. We repeated it several times and he consistently scored above ten correct. Franklin could not go by shape perception alone. He explained very coolly "The ones that stuck to my fingers and felt the warmest were the women, of course." I laughed and he told me more seriously that he had no idea how he did it—he just felt "woman" when he touched the picture of a female and "man" when it was male.

Franklin revealed that he didn't see images of men in his mind, but that he made sure to invent, if not to see, a mental picture of each woman. I made it a point to constantly change Franklin's pictures of men and women. I knew if I introduced new bodies each time, his interest would linger. Indeed, Franklin's enthusiasm for the peep show lasted the duration of the summer.

Near the end of the summer, I got a call from a woman who said that she was very interested in the work I was doing with color perception. She said she wanted to meet me, so we set up an appointment.

I met Mindy in Jerry's office. She was a round woman, without being too heavy or stocky. Her eyes were blue, her hair light brown, and her face cheerful. It was impossible for me not to be taken by her bubbly nature. We talked for a while, and I told her about the work I had been doing with the blind children. She mentioned that she was particularly interested in becoming involved in this type of work because she felt, as she put it, "attuned to color."

Mindy was like a God-sent gift to me. I had been a bit concerned about what would happen with the blind children after I left to go back to school. I hated to just come for the summer and then leave. I didn't want the kids to feel that I was abandoning them. Then, out of nowhere popped Mindy. Things just have a way of working themselves out.

I brought Mindy with me to meet Dina and her friends. They took to her immediately. When I asked Dina if it was all right for Mindy to continue working/playing with her, Dina's reaction was "YAY!"

I took Mindy to meet Franklin, and I came straight out and told him why he was meeting her. He took me aside and whispered in my ear "Is she a fox?"

"Huh?"

"Y'know, is she a foxy chic? Is she nice to look at?"

"What's it matter to you? You're blind!"

"I may be blind but people see *me*. And I'm only seen with the classiest—but I did make an exception in your case," he said.

"Yes, she's foxy," I smirked.

"Well then I'll be happy to work with her." Typical Franklin. I felt relieved that I was leaving them well-cared-for.

26

In Sickness and in Health

In addition to my association with the blind kids, Jerry offered me the opportunity to play with catastrophically ill children. Within the Center for Attitudinal Healing, Jerry initiated a program for children with cancer, leukemia, and other potentially life-threatening illnesses. The function of the program was to congregate the catastrophically ill children in an effort to show them they are not alone in their predicaments. The children get together and openly discuss issues they wouldn't normally discuss with their parents. For instance, they express their feelings about death—a subject that is often taboo among their families. Often there is a silent conspiracy between parent and dying child that death is not a topic of conversation. The children notice that every time they bring up the subject, they're silenced and their parents become cold and secretive. From such behavior, children can get the impression that death is something horrifying. The secretiveness feeds their imaginations with outlandishly frightening images of death. When they are allowed to openly talk and hear about death, many of the children's hidden fears are revealed and relieved. One of the boys who was dying of leukemia developed this opinion: "I don't really think these bodies are real. We just use them for a while and then throw them away in order to go to heaven where we're one with all souls. Then sometimes we can come back to earth and act as a guardian angel." When this child died, some of the children teasingly fought over who would get the boy as their personal guardian angel. By bringing the subject of death into the open, the children feel less alone in their fears, and they even begin to allow themselves to laugh about it.

Before the children join the group, they feel outcast from their peers and siblings. Some of them say they feel like freaks for being the only student in class bald from radiation treatments. They think that they are each unique in their unfortunate circumstances. When they join together with other children undergoing similar treatments they feel less alone and less strange.

One of the foremost principles of the Center for Attitudinal Healing is that in helping others, you help yourself. The group of catastrophically ill children put this theory into effect. By helping each other through supportive discussions of their fears, each child builds a foundation of confidence.

Jerry directed me towards the children who seemed to have the most problems relating within the groups. I was supposed to do nothing more than love the children and be a listener if they wanted to talk. I'd take the child to lunch, to a movie, to an amusement park, or wherever we both wanted to go. The more time I spent with the children, the more I realized that what I could offer them was "childishness." It seemed to me that because of all the trauma they experienced through chemotherapy, spinal taps, and living in the hospitals, the children had become very old before their time. They'd become wise and experienced but (in my opinion) more serious than children ought to be. So gradually my role turned into reminding the kids that they were still kids. I accomplished this by doing juvenile things such as initiating food fights, tickling sessions, and telling silly jokes.

Through laughter, strong bonds developed and I was able to be regarded as a peer rather than a controlling adult. Perhaps it helped that I look so young for my age. The more time I spent with the children, the more I learned about appreciating life for the moment. I knew these children did not enjoy being ill, but at the same time it seemed they were not upset about all the attention being directed towards them.

One day I took two of the children to Muir Woods for a little day hike. Tracy, my favorite of the children, had a bad cold. I asked her if she wanted to get rid of it, and she said yes. Tracy, age eight, and Richie, age six, and I sat in a circle.

"Close your eyes and take three deep breaths," I said to Richie and Tracy.

"Can we hold hands?" asked Tracy.

"No way! I'm not gonna hold hands with any girls," protested Richie.

"Oh c'mon Richie, it won't hurt you. Don't you want to help get rid of Tracy's cold?"

"I guess so. Okay, I'll hold hands, but not for very long."

"Good. So take the three breaths, and relax. Now, I want you to keep your eyes closed and picture a black bird inside of Tracy's head. Can you both picture that?"

"Yeah."

"Yes, I see it," said Tracy.

"What exactly does it look like?" I asked her.

"It's big and black with a long nose," she giggled.

"I can see it too!" chimed Richie. "It has wings bigger than an eagle! And it's flapping them wildly!"

"That's right, and do you know why it's flapping it's wings so wildly?" I asked them. Richie jumped right in.

"Because it wants to fly away, higher and higher until it disappears into space forever. And then it'll have to find food in space and get more fuel for flying power. Maybe it'll open it's mouth and swallow a big comet and then it won't have to flap its wings cause it'll go zooming around with the comet inside it, and then it'll fall to earth and. . ."

I could not believe how much this kid could talk. Tracy was laughing. Ever since we left his house he hadn't kept quiet for a moment, even while eating his lunch.

"Richie, hold it for a second! You'll tell us the rest of the bird's life later. There's something I have to tell you about the bird that you overlooked. The big black bird is really Tracy's cold. And it wants to fly, just as you said. It wants to leave Tracy but she won't let it go. Tracy, why don't you let the bird fly away from you?"

"Okay. I'll open my mouth and let it fly out," she said.

I opened one of my eyes to see Tracy opening her mouth, her eyes still closed. I turned towards Richie in time to see him catch my open eye and quickly close his. I smiled.

"I knew that the black bird was Tracy's cold all the time," said Richie. "I was just going to say that it was going to fall to earth and explode into millions of pieces and become invisible."

"Well that's one way of getting rid of it, but maybe we should be a little less destructive. How do you think we could get rid of it nicely?" I asked.

"I know," said Tracy, "we could imagine it turning into a big beautiful good white bird."

"Is that okay with you, Richie?" I asked.

"Sure! It can fly around doing good things for people, like telling other birds not to doodoo on my daddy's car!"

Tracy and I laughed and agreed with Richie.

"I guess we can open our eyes now. How do you feel Trace?"

"Okay, I guess. My headache is gone."

"The black bird took it away!" exclaimed Richie.

"Of course it did. Maybe the black bird can take away your illness, Richie," I said.

"No." he answered immediately. I was not used to him answering me without a lengthy explanation, but this time he offered me none.

"Why not?"

"Because then nobody would pay any attention to me," he said.

I was stunned. I knew that he had come from a large family of many siblings in which he was neither the oldest nor the youngest. I knew that it was difficult for him to get a word in edgewise when he was at home. I assumed that was why he talked so much when he was with us. But he had reminded me of a man who was ridiculed in our living room when he introduced his speculation that in some cases cancer is self-induced. I couldn't get Carl Simonton and his theories out of my head.

In dwelling on how or why these children derived their diseases, I found myself longing to reverse the process, and realized I was overstepping my bounds. The premise of the Center for Attitudinal Healing was not to focus on the healing of the body, but rather on the healing of the mind. I didn't think I had the power to prevent a child from dying, but I knew I had the ability to make the path more peaceful. Perhaps I was able to deal with death because I had been raised to believe in afterlife and spirits. With my great-grandmother dropping pictures every year on the anniversaries of her birth and death, it was very difficult to regard death as the end.

I guess it really doesn't matter how the kids got cancer. The fact that they have it now is all that matters. I can't heal their bodies. All I can do is swamp the little guys with love. That's where the real healing takes place. I've been introducing them to different religious views of death and I try to help them be happy with life as they have it right now. I don't know if I'm helping them or not, but they sure are helping and teaching me. For some reason, although sometimes I feel sadness, I don't get depressed when I'm with them. If they can deal with their situations, then so can I.

People ask me what I've been doing with my summer. When I respond that I'm working with catastrophically ill children, their reaction is so peculiar. They look at me as some sort of a saint and say "Oh, that must be so difficult! I know I could never do anything like that. It takes a lot of courage." Courage? What in the world are they talking about? I have so much fun working with

*the children. To see them laugh at illness and dying—
what could be more exciting? I don't understand why
people are so afraid of death. The death of a child is
thought to be the most unjust because it's seen as unfair
and untimely. But the unfairness is mostly to the parents. Many of the children feel that they're put on
earth to teach lessons and help people evolve. I know
that I might sound callous but I'm really not unfeeling.
I feel so much empathy for these children; I know they
go through a tremendous amount of physical suffering
and I wish they didn't have to. I'd do anything to relieve
their pain. But why mourn over what I can't do? My
only function is to provide joy and laughter and, in
doing so, aid the healing of their mental anguish.
When they see me in a bad mood, they do the same for
me. How can that kind of relationship be depressing?*

*Working with these kids really shows me that even
I could go at any time. Just because I'm young doesn't
give me a free pass to long life. I still haven't decided
what I'd want done with my body at death. I was thinking of donating it to a necrophiliac so I could give someone a little joy even after I'm dead! When I found out
that's illegal, I figured I'd donate it to science so something useful will come of it. What's the difference what
happens to my body after I've left it? The last thing I
want to do is take up space in a coffin in the ground,
and have people pulling the flowers out of the ground
in order to place them on my grave. I'd rather let the
flowers live. And I'd rather the marble from my head-
stone be a great statue or someone's sink. It strikes me
as so funny that people worry about what's going to
happen to their bodies after they die, so they spend
money reserving plots. I think, especially if they believe
in going to heaven, that they're better off increasing
their chances by donating their funeral-plot money
to charity.*

*I told Jerry if I pre-decease him, for my funeral I
want each of my friends and relatives to be given a
helium balloon with my name on it. After the service
of song and merriment, everyone should release the
balloons into the sky. As my personalized balloons float
upward, they're all to yell: "Hurray! Tammy has risen!"
Jerry liked this idea so much that he tried it out at a
gathering of the children after the death of one of the
group's members. Jerry said it went over with much
laughter. That's the only contribution I feel worthy of
offering: laughter in the face of death.*

*Albert and Leesa
produce fear.*

27

BUSTED BUBBLE,
TOIL AND TROUBLE

Over the summer I had fallen in love with a graduating senior from Tufts, and we indulged in a brief affair before he left for the Midwest. Although it burst my bubble to realize that my first sexual experience was not all it had been cracked up to be, I rejoiced that I had finally taken a step toward feeling comfortable with my body.

Just prior to my loss of virginity, I had one of my stomach attacks. Every few minutes I found myself in the bathroom retching, until I regurgitated only green bile. My innards were so sensitive I could barely breathe without feeling wounded. It was not until the fourteenth hour, as the attacks slowly subsided, that I began to seethe with fury.

"I'm getting sick and tired of these wretched stomach attacks!" I thought to myself. "I've endured them for the past five years. How can I have put up with them so long? They've got to be psychological, since no one can figure out why I have them. I HATE THEM! NO MORE! I refuse to give in to these things from now on. I swear I am not going to do this to myself ever again!

Something registered deep within me, and I felt certain that the days of torturing myself were finally behind me. It wasn't until my nineteenth birthday that I put myself to the test. I was back in college and everyone was waiting for me to join the birthday party in my honor. Mom had come to school to share in the celebration. She was the first to notice my pallor. My stomach began to hurt as though it were the onset of one of my attacks. I reminded myself that I'd sworn not to indulge in these masochistic tortures. As I stroked my belly, my mind repeated my refusal to give in to the attack. Suddenly, for the first time in my life, the attack subsided before it ever gained momentum. They would not return again. It was the first and best birthday present I had ever given myself.

My nineteenth birthday also marked the first time in my life that I felt jealous of my mother. I was so proud that she could enter a room full of my contemporaries and make herself fit in. No one seemed uncomfortable or inhibited by her presence. She joined my birthday party, plopping herself down on a bed amidst people drinking beer and smoking pot. She appeared totally at ease. I noticed that many of my friends, who'd always felt intimidated by adults, were totally relaxed with Mom. Even Albert seemed more comfortable speaking with Mom than he ever was with me. Later that evening, and for weeks to come, I kept getting comments about how great she was. I didn't understand how she could make my friends feel more comfortable than I could. For some strange reason, because I felt a little competition with my mother, I felt a little bit older.

In emulating my mother, I began to find areas in which I realized I had to be my own self. During my involvement with a boyfriend, I found myself preaching to him and a mutual female friend, that I didn't mind their caring for each other. I misinterpreted Mom's practice of the *Course's* precept that "we are all one, we are all love" to mean that exclusivity in relationships is bad. But would it hurt me if my boyfriend and girlfriend made love? The more love, I figured, the better. Love everyone equally.

When they called me on my proclamation by taking it to the limit, I was surprised to find myself furious with both of them. Unwilling to express my anger overtly, I found myself trapped within the bounds of my own belief system. I had to hide behind a frozen smile, declaring that it was just fine by me. But when they repeated the performance, I blew up.

Shortly after this experience I dreamed I was walking in the forest. I turned off a beaten trail onto a more obscure path, and then I noticed rocks turning themselves into steps. The steps led to a small shrine for one enormous tree, overlooking rocky cliffs that cascaded into the ocean.

"You're an interesting tree," I thought as I looked at the branches, intertwining with each other and reaching in all directions. I had never seen anything like it.

"Tell me I'm a beautiful tree," I heard someone say to me.

"Who said that?" At first I thought that there was someone standing behind the tree, teasing me.

"I did. Tell me that I'm the finest tree in all the forest."

It took me a few seconds, but I realized that I was talking to myself, inside my head. I was sure that I was becoming schizophrenic, especially since I didn't recognize my own voice, but then it wasn't exactly like the voice in which I usually talk to myself. "But you're not the finest tree in the forest, all the trees are fine," I continued my own conversation.

"If you don't tell me that I'm the finest tree in the forest, then I won't talk to you anymore."

I couldn't help laughing aloud.

"Aren't you being a bit ridiculous?" I continued the conversation in my mind.

"Absolutely not! Now say it aloud, or I won't teach you that which I have to offer." My curiosity was aroused. What could a tree offer me besides wood, shade or a stump to sit on?

"This is crazy, but OK, if you insist. God forbid I should insult the voice of a tree I'm hearing in my own mind." (OK, I thought.) "You are the finest tree in all the forest. So what?"

"So now you can sit down on me and we can talk."

"How could you have stopped me from sitting down on you had I not said what you wanted?" I asked, resuming the conversation in my head.

"I wouldn't have, but you would not have made any special connection with me, and that would be a loss."

"What do you mean?"

"Well, you have been wanting to love everyone the same. You've been trying not to say you love one person more than another."

"Yeah, that's right,it's my goal. So what?"

"So you can't love everyone the same if you want to learn the lessons of this life."

"Why not?"

"Because you need to make commitments to people through relationships in order for anything to prosper from them. Through your struggling in relationships you learn and grow, but if you remove yourself from acknowledging that you love someone more than others, then you aren't facing your responsibilities. You're shying away from real learning. It's the lazy person's way out to throw everything into one category, without dissecting each component to get a total understanding rather than a general impression. By making a commitment to me, by telling me you think I'm the finest tree in the forest—in effect, singling me out—you've made me special. Thus you will learn from me. By passing me by and lumping me with all trees, you'd have continued on your way, oblivious to the learning that was available to you."

The tree continued to tell me things about my life, and life in general. When I awoke, something had clicked inside me. It occurred to me that I'd been floating along, without the grounding of an anchor. I'd been taking too much at face value and too much for granted. Of course it was easier idealistically to string everyone together and love "people" as a package deal. But in reality the package falls open, as the only strings are those that tug the heart, tying attachments to individual people. Each individual person offers the potential of shared learning. I finally realized that although God dwells in everybody (binding people together as "one"), you must focus on "one" person *individually* in order to see God. The bee must go to each individual flower in order to pollinate. There is no way around it. But from then on, I realized I could only handle being queen bee.

As a result of my encounter with the tree, I perceived that I am separated into two selves: On a surface level, there is my ego self, which struggles, complains, laughs, plays, celebrates and mourns. Then, on a deeper level, there is an eternally wise, loving self that remains peaceful and consistent as it smiles at all the antics of my ego self. Whereas my loving self appeared ancient, my ego self was only nineteen years old. It was my loving self that knew that since we're all one, it wouldn't make any difference if my boyfriend and girlfriend made love. But my ego self rebelled, and rightfully so. It has a lot more years to go before it catches up with the ancient wisdom of my deeper self. I realized that I couldn't propel myself into situations, expecting only my loving self to respond. It was futile to expect my ego to be at the end of a path it had just recently begun. I was not exempt from the age-old stages of ego development. At least I knew I had an inner "fwend'" who helped me laugh at all the dramatic antics of my ego self.

Throughout my life, I'd always heard the laughter and guidance of my inner "fwend." But at nineteen, I suddenly yearned for a glimpse of that self. After much heartfelt mental pleading for my innermost being to show itself to me, my "fwend" finally came out to play.

One day, mid-semester, I was doing a relaxation exercise when I fell into a strange slumber. I had the sensation that I'd lifted myself out of my body and was soaring in the air. I perceived myself as being wide awake but my weightlessness made me think I might be dreaming. Abruptly, I felt myself moving swiftly through a tunnel. At the end of the passageway I saw a brilliant light. As I reached the light I became one with it and that moment I was intuiting all the knowledge of the universe. It was a sensation totally different from anything I'd ever felt. I was pregnant with omnipotent love of a nonpossessive nature. It was a state of being in complete acceptance of everyone and everything in the world. I, as Ego Tamara, shrank to a minuscule dot trapped in a speck of time. Although words diminish the experience, the most apt description of it is "pure, unadulterated joy." I heard the laughter of my inner self so loud, it instantaneously occurred to me that I was (and had always been) my own best "fwend." Suddenly, my ego panicked, as it cried out from the depths of my mind, "What about me? Don't forget ME!" With joyous submission, my "fwend" submerged to its home within, giving way for my ego to regain its usual control.

When I opened my eyes, everything in the room was luminescent. All seemed aglow with the auras of my childhood. I felt absolute peace within myself. I sensed that everything was as it was "supposed" to be, and my life was all right.

I ventured out of my room and, in doing so, tripped over my own feet. Yet even as I fell, I felt lighter than air. I connected with Leesa, Albert and Tom. My sole emotion was unbounded love for my three friends, but I noticed that every time I made eye contact with Leesa or Albert they'd immediately turn away, asking me not to "do that." As they laughed nervously, I was amazed by their fear of love. Later, Leesa admitted that she felt self-conscious because she sensed my gaze seeing right through her. Maybe they thought I was crazy. Maybe I was, but I'd never felt so good in my life.

The experience didn't last more than a day, but its impression was everlasting. I felt tremendously secure in and with myself. For the first time since puberty, I was proud to have my body. Everything was in its perfect place. My petite body housed a larger-than-life giggle. How could I condemn the body that giggle chose for its dwelling?

Unfortunately, with the distancing of the experience, this sentiment faded. But what vividly remained was the awareness that I'd gotten a glimpse of something formerly kept buried in my subconscious. Despite the fact that I needed to suppress it again, I knew it was always there for me if ever I wanted to bring it up.

I felt my life taking on the meaning of a quest, in which my intellectual ego self would continually experience and develop until it reunited with my inner loving self. I could never explain that to anyone. It was a uniquely personal knowledge. I knew my friends would not understand, so I tried not to talk about it. I felt certain that instead of exciting most people it would threaten them. Hence I kept my momentary enlightenment in the dark.

In light of this experience, Leesa's reaction to my coincidences no longer bothered me. Whenever she would scream, cover her eyes, and run into her room I'd merely shrug my shoulders, laugh and continue living. I felt secure in her love for me, and I thought that she'd accept everything about me just as I would accept everything about her. When I made a friend, as I had with Leesa, Albert and Tom, I trusted completely—and took for granted that the trust was reciprocated. I was soon to find out that I had been extremely naive.

Finals week was one of terror. Leesa was in bad shape because her friend from home had just died of leukemia. My Uncle Manny had also recently died of cancer. Exams were taxing our energy and our minds' ability to think clearly. There was tension permeating the air.

We were all anxiously waiting to hear from Albert's friend David, who'd visited Tufts at the beginning of school. David was a free-spirited deviant who, instead of following the crowd to college, took off traveling to the East. Whenever we did anything with great flair, David's name would come up in conversation. It was during finals week that David's name was accompanied by a chill up the spine rather than a thrill of excitement. Albert received word that our friend had died of undetermined causes in Thailand. The news was shocking. Leesa was trembling and I think Albert was numb. I reacted sadly on the outside while inwardly wondering what he was doing at that moment. Although I didn't know him intimately, his spirit had been too alive for me ever to consider it dead.

It was a miserable last week of school. Nerves were on end, and we were all bickering with each other. The arguments finally snowballed into one large explosion in which I felt persecuted by Tom, Leesa and Albert. As my insecurity peaked, I expressed my rage by dramatically storming out of the room. I fell into my bed and cried myself to sleep.

Leesa and Albert were upset. They hadn't been to sleep in over twenty-four hours. Tom was trying to be cheerful in his usual manner. They were still feeling shock over David's death. They began to talk about me and our argument, when suddenly a book fell off the shelf in their room. Albert and Leesa became afraid, and as their fear reverberated off each other they jumped to the conclusion that I had caused the book to fall from the shelf—that my wrath was out to destroy them.

The next day I noticed that Leesa was doing all she could to avoid me. She wouldn't come near me and she pretended not to hear me calling her. I was in a fine mood. It was a new day and, as usual, I couldn't hold a grudge. When I noticed that Albert was also looking warily at me, I asked Tom to tell me what was going on. Always suave, Tom suggested that I go ask Leesa and Albert myself. Since Leesa was blatantly avoiding me, I approached Albert.

Reluctantly, Albert told me about the book. He said to me, "Well, what do you think?"

I felt nauseous and was on the verge of tears.

"What am I supposed to think?"

"Were you doing anything last night?"

"What are you talking about? Yeah, I was doing something. I was sleeping soundly in my bed. What do you think I was doing?"

"I don't know, but I can't explain how weird it was. I've never been so frightened in my entire life. We were shaking!"

I remembered the times my brother and I were alone in our apartment, when we used to turn out the light and turn on the radio. We'd either light a candle or turn on a flashlight. We'd stare at each other until we began to change forms right before our eyes. Then we'd scare the living daylights out of each other by suggesting that maybe Nana's deceased voice would come over the radio.

Bitterly I explained to Albert that fear has a tendency to breed, especially if you're tired and not in the best of moods.

"Yeah," he said, "but it sure was strange. Leesa was so freaked out about it that she can't even talk to you."

"Well what the hell did you think I was doing? Zooming about outside on a broomstick? I admit it! I was in my dorm room brewing a potion in my cauldron to scare the wits out of you for being so mean to me!"

"Well, I can't explain what happened, Tammy," Albert said again, ignoring my sarcasm.

I can't believe that after all the fun-loving stories I told you about my home life, you'd twist them into evil distortions of witchery!"

"To tell the truth," Albert said, poker-faced, "I never really believed any of those stories. I just thought you were making conversation until this thing happened. I just can't explain it."

"Making conversation? I can't believe any of this! You want an explanation? I'll give you *my* explanation. I think you're both asses!" I yelled, concluding our conversation.

I felt violated. How could my closest friends possibly think I was doing some sort of black magic? Didn't they know anything about me? I felt like a victim of a witch hunt!

Suddenly I felt bitter towards everyone. All my trust disappeared, and I began to doubt my own belief system. Maybe everything was just coincidence, maybe people were innately negative, maybe life was just an accident, maybe I'd been a naive fool all along. My principles seemed stupid and without foundation. Had I been a Pollyanna? Was my experience of self just another psychic trick? I was so lost in mental anguish, that for the first time in my life, I couldn't hear my "fwend's" laughter.

After what seemed to be an eternity of damnation, I decided to resurrect myself.

> *Sometimes I find myself creating problems to bring me down from a constant high. When I get involved in these problems, my high becomes low, my smile becomes toothless, and my eyes become solid. It is during these times that I find I've lost myself. Enough! Enough already! Stop all this doubting! So what if no one understands my life? My life is what I make of it. Let them all be miserable and think the worst of everything. If my theories work for me, that's all that matters.*
>
> *I feel that I've never been understood by any of the people here. How can I call these people my friends? What are they so fearful of? Why can't they understand that the "coincidences" that happen to me are fun? Why would they take something so good and twist it into evil?*
>
> *All I know is, I can't keep banging my head against the wall. This has made me headstrong. I wonder if I'll ever open up to them again? I have a feeling this is the first grudge I'm not going to let go of. This is one nightmare I won't forget by tomorrow morning.*

It took some time for me to learn the purpose of undergoing judgment and denouncement by my own peers. In the meantime, I did hold resentment toward my friends for what they had "done to me," but not in a way anyone would notice. After a couple of days, Leesa, Albert and I resumed as though nothing had happened. However I knew I didn't trust them with my self, and I felt bitterness toward them like a seething inner brew.

When school recessed for summer, I sadly realized there was no way I could take home Rubungus, my blue Samurai Fighting Fish. I flashed back to David's buying the fish at the pet store because they were about to throw it away. Without my consent, David convinced the store manager that I would rejuvenate the dying fish, and so I did. Rubungus made it through my freshman year, but after finals, and the news of David's death, the fish began to look pallid.

Upon much deliberation, I decided to emancipate Rubungus by dumping him into the nearby Mystic Lakes. Tom drove my fish and me to "freedom row." After our farewells and best wishes,

I plopped the little guy into the water. Knowing he hadn't been feeling up to par, I hoped that the abundance of water would lift his little blue spirits.

"Swim, Rubungus, swim!" Tom and I cheered and coached from the sidelines. But Rubungus wasn't swimming. Rubungus wasn't even moving. Glub, glub, glub. Rubungus began to float on the top of the water. In fact, Rubungus was dead.

Tom and I gave my pet a few resuscitating pushes and shoves, but they were to no avail. The water had indeed lifted the fish, but not as I'd hoped. I guess we drowned him. Whoever knew it was possible to drown a fish? We left Rubungus floating in Mystic Lakes. It had been a tough year and I knew how he felt.

*Bill, Bob, Judy and
Jerry in California.*

28

JOURNEY WITHOUT DISTANCE

Js

Specialness is not confined to just a few people in our lives. All our relationships are special until we give them to the Higher Guide Who helps transform them through forgiveness into holy relationships. I didn't realize how insidious specialness is until I had my terrible dream.

In it I was sitting on the bank of a wide river. It was an overcast day and my mood was gloomy. I did not know why I felt so deprived. Then my attention was arrested by loud voices and raucous laughter from a barge floating down the river. The barge held a gaily decorated San Francisco cable car and people were partying and singing enthusiastically. I suddenly realized why I felt so miserable. Tammy had died and I was in deep mourning. When this dawned on me I began to wail, rocking and keening, making a racket. All at once I heard someone calling me. The voice sounded familiar. It *was* familiar. It was Tammy shouting to me from the barge. She was wearing a party hat and gaily colored clothes. *Her* mood was festive. "Tammy, Tammy," I screamed. "Come back, I thought you were dead!" "I *am* dead, Mother. Stop carrying on like that!" "No, no, no! I can't stand living without you. Don't do this to me. Come back. *Please.*" As the boat sailed away I heard her clearly in my head. "If you really loved me, you'd let me go. I'm having such a good time."

I awakened with shivers, sure something terrible had happened to Tammy up at school. I was afraid to call her all day, and a pall of sadness permeated my being. Two days went by, three. I was still convinced that if something awful had not already happened, it was about to. Finally Tammy called *me*. "Are you all right, Mom? You sound funny." Relieved, I spilled the whole story. I told her how I grieved when I thought she was dead. I told her how desolate I was and how my life would never be joyous again. I got myself good and worked up. I even started to cry. It all felt so very real. There was silence at the other end of the line for a few seconds. Then I heard my daughter smile and say cheerfully, "Well, I'm glad that business is over. Now you'll never have to do *that* again." I've thought that over many times since and she's so right.

I had reached a new level in my understanding of the role the thought of death plays in this world. I had exposed my fear, realized it was groundless, and let it go. How could I ever be threatened by this bad dream again once I knew it *was* a dream? And I had held onto it, trying to make it real. A passage from the *Course* lightened my mind:

> What you seem to waken to is but another form
> of this same world you see in dreams.
> All your time is spend in dreaming.
> Your sleeping and your waking dreams
> have different forms and that is all.

I also began to realize that there are those we truly love whom we imprison in specialness. I had believed my relationships with my son and daughter were by now those of deep mutual caring, with an honest desire on my part to support their emotional and spiritual growth. I did not feel as if I needed them for anything, or wanted them to be other than they were. I had to face the fact that I was hiding from myself. As long as I wanted anything from them, including the presence of their physical bodies, I was reinforcing specialness. I still had a long way to go.

I began to sniff special relationships in my life with the fervor of a hound trained to track drugs. I wanted no secrets from myself, no dark corners in which to hide. I found a giant fear lurking in a crevice. I did not want to give up our lovely apartment. It had been such a gracious home from which to function. It made me feel as if I were "somebody" in the world. Maybe that was why I had to let it go. I became more and more anxious about where we were to live as the time to move got closer and closer. I asked Bob to consult his guided writing to see if he could find us a new place. What he wrote did not ease my tension. "You will be shown your next move by the end of May." Try as I might, I couldn't get the date speeded up. But Bob did come up with the phrase, "Judy doesn't need to worry. She will like the next place even better than this." Somewhat mollified, I intensified my search.

Helen suggested I try "asking" through the process she and Bob used. I had always been comfortable with the "hearing" part of inner guidance. But I was quite shy of the writing. It seemed much more majestic when it came from the pen of others. I also knew I was not a writer. Nevertheless, it was time to show myself that, with God's help, nothing is impossible.

I was in Washington, D.C. as a guest at the President's Annual Prayer Breakfast. It seemed a propitious moment for my debut. Helen had suggested I pick a time when she could join with me in mind for spiritual support. We decided upon twelve noon. I prepared myself through meditation to quiet my chattering stream of consciousness. At exactly noon, feeling quite calm, I picked up my pen and paper and posed the question, "What should I do about another place to live?" Without an interval the words poured through:

> In stillness and in peace I come to you. Be not afraid.
> For I am here along with all my hosts; your brothers
>   and your friends.
> Listen in quiet recollection to my Voice, for it is so
>   familiar to you now.
> You have but to recall your Father and your home and
>   all life's emptiness will cease.
> You are the chosen child of God who makes the choice
>   for heaven and for love.
> Along the way I stand beside you with a firm and
>   guiding hand so you can hold it as you go.
> And when you falter and you sometimes doubt your goal
> Your holy brother will appear to you in shining glory
>   with a radiant light to clear your sight.
> Be not afraid, for I am one with you and you with Me.
> And all the joy of vision is our truth. Hear me now.
> Your path is certain. Though you know not why, forget
>   to question and embrace the change.
> Your reason will not tell you how to love. My Way is
> sure. It does not matter where the body is. Believe that
>   I will take you where you need to go.
> And in this message is my promise kept. You are at
> home. You are at rest. In happy certainty give praises
> now. And sing to all your brothers of my love.
> Their Father stands beside them as you sing so you
>   may see His face and know that it is true.

At first I couldn't believe I had actually scribed those words. My head was spinning, and I knew I was in an altered state of consciousness. Somehow, though, I felt relieved. I did not need to worry about resettling. I was not in charge. I did not know what anything was for. I felt trust, and peace in that trust. I had let go of my special relationship with our New York City apartment and I was ready to move on.

The finale did not take long to be revealed. I had stopped by to see Jerry while in California on a speaking tour. As we were visiting, Bob called me on the phone. When we had finished our conversation, he asked to chat with Jerry. On the extension phone, I heard him say, "Jer, why don't you help Judy find a place for us to live in *California?*" I couldn't believe the casualness of the comment. I had never anticipated moving cross-country. The Foundation, Helen and Louis, Bill and Ken, Bob's and my combined families—all lived on the East Coast. Jerry's response was, "Do you mean that, Bob? We'll look right away!"

Shortly a charming little house became available for rent. It had not been on the market before; it was brand new and the owners had built it for their own retirement a few years in the future. It was perched on stilts in the water three doors away from Jerry in Tiburon. I called Bob and described it. He felt it sounded perfect. Helen was worried about the distance, but we assured her I could commute as easily from California to New York as vice versa. Bill decided it was time for him to move also. He felt relaxed and comfortable in California and we found a place for him on the same street. Our Foundation assistant, Dotteye, felt she should join us. The move was effortless. Tammy, my mother, and I were the advance crew to make sure everything was in order, while Bob and Dot kept the office functioning in New York City until the last moment.

The day of their departure Jerry and I took two cars to the airport to meet them. There was a ton of luggage and our dog, snooty Saki Toomi. Suddenly I was terrified. "What if they hate it out here?" I wondered. I forgot I was not responsible for their happiness. Guilt got its grip on me. When the planes unloaded I was too busy to think. We piled the suitcases in Jerry's car and I took Dot, Bob, and the dog. Jerry followed. Crossing the Golden Gate Bridge, I had the unbidden idea that I should stop at the designated vista spot for a look back at San Francisco. I argued with myself that it was July. The tourist places were jammed. I'd never get a parking spot. My bigger voice insisted. It would be a wonderful way to welcome them to a beautiful city that was to be their new home.

Against my better judgment I swerved the car into the parking area. Jerry followed, wondering what I was doing. Sure enough, not a place to park. But wait, one car has just pulled out and I can slide in. Bravo! Jerry double-parked. I invited the new Californians to witness the sun setting in the west while the city reflected the bronze beams from white buildings and blazing windows. It was a magic wonderland. I have a quirky habit of looking at license plates. Usually they tell me something. Messages from God. This time my habit proved more arresting than anything else that day. I gazed at the car to my left and felt my vocal chords freeze as I sputtered, "Look! Look at this!" Bob and Dotteye turned their backs to the view, concerned that something had happened. I was acting very strange. Dotteye saw it first. "Oh, my God. I can't believe it. Look at that license plate, Bobby." Bob stared at the six letters. They spelled BOB DOT. Dotteye put her arms around him and gave him a big hug. "Welcome home, darlin'," she said. I was too choked up to utter a sound.

Rational Bob tried to compute the odds of a six-lettered license plate that spelled out their names apearing at just that time in just that space. I spent the rest of the drive to the new house being amazed at how I receive the answers I need even when I don't pray. We arrived at the new house, which Bob had never seen, in a place he had never visited. He had moved three thousand miles away on total trust. I marvelled at the extent of his faith. We walked into the immaculate sparkle of the bay home. A panoramic view revealed the city and the bridge. The picture windows framed Angel Island. Bill lived nearby on Paradise Drive. Laconic Bob smiled his warm, dimpled grin and announced, "Oh yes, this is where I belong."

It was all so right. It was all so familiar. There was a quote from the *Course* that wanted to come to mind. It was stuck on the tip of my memory. It broke loose like a banner before my eyes as I saw, "The journey to God is a journey without distance to a goal that has never changed." How apropos that sounded at that moment. It inaugurated a new phase.

Tammy's artwork.

29

PENNIES FOR MY THOUGHTS

 I was asked to be a paid lecturer at several conferences over the summer of 1978. One, in California, was entitled "Children of the New Age"; I was to speak about myself as a child of the New Age and about my work with blind children. Another lecture in Santa Cruz, California was also to be about my work with blind children. Jerry had recommended me, and he assured me I'd have something of interest to talk about. I felt very uninformed and inexperienced. I had no idea what I would say or why anyone would listen to me. As the time to deliver the lectures neared, I found myself working up a frenzy. Before leaving for California, I sought out my favorite biology teacher in hopes of collecting some words of wisdom.

 "I made you a cake in my baking class," Mr. B told me.

 "You did? What happened to it? I never got it!"

 "I ate it. How was I supposed to mail you a cake?"

 I noticed that his little pot belly had gotten bigger over the years. My father's had grown at the same rate as Mr. Biology's. I noticed something else about my favorite professor. He seemed to have modified the bully facade that he used as a barrier. I found myself able to tell him things that I would normally have sheltered behind my own tough facade. I suddenly welcomed my vulnerability.

 "You know, I'm nervous about giving these talks this summer," I confessed to him.

"What's there to be nervous about? You're just going to be talking about your experiences."

"I know, but what if there are hard-nosed doctors there, or total skeptics who don't believe things like blind children sensing colors and images through their hands? What can I tell them?"

"There's nothing not to believe when you tell them the fact that each color emits an individual gradation of heat, and that these children have sensitized themselves to this property. It's a scientifically acceptable explanation."

"Yeah, but Mr. B, I told you that theory didn't really hold up with the kids. How can you still insist that this is the scientific explanation for their color *and image* perception? You just can't accept that there may be—and probably is—more to it than that, can you?"

He took off his glasses and rubbed them clean on his lab coat. He replaced them over his eyes. There was a pause. There was silence. Then he looked down at me through his glasses as he said, "Still jumping to conclusions without listening to what I've said, are you?"

"Whattayamean?" I asked, feeling belittler than I am already.

"You asked me what you can tell the hard-nosed doctors and skeptics. Your main concern seems to be with convincing the disbelievers, so I offered you an approach to convince them of the validity of your accomplishments with the blind children. You didn't ask me what *I* think is going on with the children and their ability to sense color and images."

"Yeah, I guess you're right."

"Of course," he smiled.

"But how can I lie? If I believe there's more to it than just different heat levels of colors, how can I omit that?"

"You *are* in conflict. It seems to me that you have to make a choice between saying what you feel and standing behind it or hiding behind socially accepted values."

"Which way do you think is better??"

"Neither way is any better or worse. The better way is the one you're most comfortable with. I don't think it's wrong to relay information in its most comprehensible form."

"Huh?"

"Well, let's say this time you give them the explanation of heat gradations for tactile color perception. Perhaps next time they'll further expand their minds to accept the possibility of color perception directly through the mind. It's a type of preparation, leading gradually from A to B, instead of jumping straight to B. Although, knowing you, I have no doubt you'll be dealing with C soon enough."

"But Mr. B, do *you* believe the blind kids are using more

than their sensitized hands to perceive colors and images?"

"I don't *believe* anything—I simply know what is and isn't." His "bully" facade was rapidly returning.

"Well, what do you really think?" I persisted.

Mr. Biology looked at me with a Cheshire grin on his face as he said "I think I should be getting back to work."

End of conversation. End of yet another meeting with Mr. B.

My first talk was to be given at a two-day conference sponsored by the Family Guidance Center and California State University of Continuing Education. The conference, as it was advertised, was to "Explore the Transpersonal and Holistic Orientations in Psychotherapy and Education with Children." Whatever that meant, I was right in the middle of it.

The highlight of the two-day conference for me was that I was given my own hotel room with two double beds. Since I hate to waste anything, I placed a wake-up call for two a.m. When the operator rang my room, I woke up and switched beds. I thought myself very shrewd.

On the day of my talk, I hoped that no one would show up. When it began to get late, I was insulted that no one had showed up yet. I decided that, as long as my talk was being taped, I would deliver a wonderful speech to myself. Just as I began to clear my throat, people started piling into the lecture hall. I don't even remember what I talked about. I put myself on automatic pilot and babbled for a few hours. I know that I delivered an introductory course in color perception. They were a remarkably open and fast-learning group. I came to realize that the people who attend consciousness conferences are not those who would challenge my every word. These were people who already "believed," and they wanted to hear what was new and who was who. In this realization, all my fears dissolved. I had no problem standing up for what I believed. Among these crowds, I could stand taller than I'd ever been.

In the middle of August I was to give my talk at U.C. Santa Cruz. Jerry would be moderating the conference, and delivering a lecture of his own. He was bringing an entourage of catastrophically ill children to appear alongside him. Jerry suggested I share his method of Show and Tell by bringing Franklin. I immediately took to the idea. It would be fun to have Franklin with me and I was thrilled that he would use up some of my talking time. Franklin readily agreed.

Just before Franklin and I delivered our joint lecture, Jerry lead the conference in a moment of meditation. I was seated beside Franklin holding his hand. Jerry requested that everyone close their eyes. I noticed my partner's eyes were open.

"Franklin, didn't you hear what Jerry said? Just because you're blind doesn't mean that you can cheat and keep your eyes open."

"Well, if yours were shut then you wouldn't know that mine were open!"

"I'll close mine when you close yours!" A few seconds passed, and I whispered to him "Are you nervous?"

"Hell, no!" he answered. "I don't have to look at any of these turkeys. For all I know, there may be no one but us in here when we flap our gums."

"Maybe I should keep my eyes closed when I talk to everyone. I'd seriously consider it if we weren't going to be videotaped. Uh oh, here we go."

I stepped up to the podium and began to speak of my work with the blind kids and a little of my background leading up to it. Of course I hadn't prepared any kind of speech. I spoke a little of Franklin and our work together. I told how the first time I met him he was riding his bicycle around his neighborhood. But then I began emphatically to stress the point that he was no different from the children who were ill—or from anyone else in the auditorium. Franklin merely had a situation with which he had to cope, so he coped. He did so well because he didn't make such a big thing about being blind; in fact he made fun of it and often even ignored it. I told of my blunders with him when I met him and was shy of using the words *see, blind,* or *eyes.* I explained that now I tease him for being blind and he teases me for being short.

When I introduced Franklin at the podium, he put his arm around me and he said "Thanks, Shorty." He was a natural comedian. He repeated in his own way much of what I said, the whole time holding my hand. When it came time for questions from the audience, Franklin had a funny comment for each. One person asked him how he rode his bicycle around his neighborhood. "Very carefully," he answered. He had the audience in the palm of his hand.

The talk ended and Franklin and I left the auditorium. At this point he was on a roll and couldn't be stopped. A lady came up to us and began to over-praise his ability to do things despite being blind. It was as though she had missed the message of our talk. When she was finally through, Franklin very graciously thanked her, and as she was walking away he quickly asked me "Is her hair tied back?" "Yeah," I answered, "it's in one of those clips."

"Hey miss," he called to her, "your clip is falling out!"

She thanked him and continued walking. It didn't even occur to her that he never could have known that, and that it wasn't falling out at all. I watched her readjust it and move on. The two of us laughed wildly. I knew I'd better get Franklin out of there before he got us into trouble. But a man approached us and asked us if we had seen a red fountain pen in the auditorium.

"Yeah, I saw it," said Franklin. "It was in the aisle."

The man thanked him and entered the auditorium. I dragged the little devil away.

That afternoon I took Franklin and some of the catastrophically ill children to the Santa Cruz amusement park. Of course, Franklin was the only one on the roller coaster who wouldn't hold onto the safety bars. The rest of us screamed and held on for our lives.

When I returned Franklin home, I gave him a big hug and kiss goodbye.

"Why Franklin, I do believe your Black is turning pink," I laughed.

"That's just my sunburn," he said. "Thanks for taking me with you. I really had a great time."

So did I. Our work together had concluded but our friendship continued.

30

Tricks or Treats

*Although my summer activities showed me I don't
need to hide my experiences, I've come to realize that
there's a time and place for everything. And back at
college, I know to keep my mouth shut about anything
out of the ordinary. I used to feel such a compulsion to
tell everyone everything, but no more. I've learned
that lesson.*

*I've declared myself a religion major, focusing on
Eastern religion, mysticism, and the pursuit of the
self. In my class on mysticism in literature, we've been
reading articles and books written by people who fre-
quented our New York apartment. I never used to give
much thought to the professions or the literary accomplishments of our houseguests. To me, they were merely
friends with varying personalities. But in this class,
we've been studying many of their philosophies of
religion, mysticism, and altered states of consciousness.
I get tickled inside every time a student asks a question
like "What do you think Stanley Krippner means
when he says. . . ?" I giggle to myself that if my classmate really wants to know what he means, I'll just call
Stanley and ask him! But I never say that aloud. I keep
a very low profile.*

At college I'd become introverted and guarded about anything having to do with psychic. Here, I was taken aback when my grade-school friend Janet called me during the semester to tell me about a paper she was writing on parapsychology.

"Tam, you're not gonna believe what happened the other day!"

"What happened?"

"Well, I had to do a report for one of my classes about something unusual, so I decided to write about parapsychology. I was looking through a book on the subject when I saw your name! I was so startled I screamed right there in the library and had to apologize to everyone!"

"What books are you talking about? I've never read any of them."

Janet disclosed the titles. I remember that a man had once written a chapter about me, but he changed my name upon request. It was a book on psychic children, and in no way did I want my name in it. More than that, Mom knew that Dad would probably sue if he ever saw the book. Stanley had also sent me a book of his in which my name was used in reference to an experiment I did with him at the Dream Lab in Brooklyn. Jon's work with Kirlian photography was also described in that book and Mom was mentioned for something having to do with the Foundation. All I needed was for someone at college to see my name in a book, and who knew what strange reactions would emerge.

"Jan, if you come here, never mention this."

"Why not? I was so excited! I think it's great!"

"They're just books. I've never even looked at them."

"Well, I think it's great to be so far away from you and to find you sitting in my school library! You, and Mom and Jon!"

I had almost forgotten that there were people, friends of mine, who knew, accepted, and even loved that whole side of me. I hung up with Janet, feeling less lonely than I'd felt in a while.

As much as I tried to conceal my little "coincidences" from my college friends, sometimes things slipped out unexpectedly.

A friend, Bill, and I were showing each other card tricks. As we went along we began to get sillier and sillier and make up tricks that became extremely elab-

orate. I decided to show him the trick of all tricks. I told him to pick a card, any card.

"Okay, now what?"

"Don't show me the card. Just put it back in this messy pile of cards on the ground. Now gather up the cards and shuffle them however you want. Then hand them to me."

"How are you going to pull this one off?"

"Just wait and see," I said, taking the cards and shuffling them myself. I planned to put him through the longest card trick in history, and at the end of the trick admit to him that I had absolutely no idea what his card was. I cut the deck of cards and sorted them into five piles. I told him to pick a pile and then I put that pile on top of the four other piles. I shuffled them again and divided the cards into ten piles. I did every maneuver I could until he began to lose patience.

"C'mon, you don't know what my card is?"

"Be patient, we're coming to it!" After more shuffles, cuts and what-nots, I went through every card until finally I chose at random the eight of hearts.

"Here is your card!"

Bill put his hand to his head, collapsed backwards in hysterical laughter, and screamed "I don't believe it!"

I began to laugh at his reaction to my having put him through a ten-minute card trick with no intention of knowing what his card was. We both laughed for a while, until I began to realize we weren't laughing about the same thing. He kept repeating "How did you do that? How did you know?"

"Know what?" I finally asked, while wiping the tears from my eyes.

"I could've sworn that you didn't know what my card was!"

"I didn't! I was just teasing you."

"What are you talking about? You guessed the right card!"

"You're kidding!"

"No, I swear it! I couldn't believe it!"

We looked at each other and I think that I became more surprised than he was. He asked me to repeat the trick but I refused. A while later, Albert came home from classes and Bill told him about my attempts at being a magician.

"Tammy, will you show me the trick you did for Bill?" Albert asked.

"Oh, c'mon," I said, "It was just a silly joke."

"But show me what you did."

I dropped the cards on the floor, all face down, and told Albert to pick a card, put it back, and shuffle the deck. As I repeated an abridged version of my original trick, I described the process to Albert. ". . .So, after going randomly through all the cards, I pull one out like so, and say "TA DA! Here is your card!" In jest, I threw the card at Albert.

"I can't believe it!" yelled Albert.

"What can't you believe?"

"That's my card!" he said.

I didn't even look to see whether his disbelief was genuine. It seemed evident that the joke was on me. I knew he was mocking me, and I was furious.

"Oh shut up," I said cynically.

"I mean it! That was my card!"

I could take this sort of abuse no longer. All my repressed anger from last year surfaced. I looked at him with hatred as I yelled "You bastard!" After which, I ran to my room. In a couple of minutes, I heard pounding on my door. "Open up!"

It took half an hour for Albert to convince me he was telling the truth and, how dare I think he was lying to me! I didn't know what to believe. Had I become so self-protective that I couldn't even recognize when someone was truthful about this sort of thing? Was I so paranoid that I had come to expect my best friends at school to mock me? YES. Not only did Albert insist that it was indeed his card, but also that he had changed since the previous year. He didn't mistrust me anymore and he was really growing interested in these "paranormal things." I cringed. Would they always be referred to as out of the normal? In any event, I realized that I was so tightly holding my friends in the past, that I wouldn't release them to share in my present.

It was Leesa who became the most instrumental in helping me release my grudge. Although I wouldn't have believed it a year earlier, Leesa had actually become very interested in things like meditation and telepathy. At her request, I began to teach her relaxation techniques and remote viewing. On one occasion, Leesa suggested that we try remote viewing to see where Tom was. Neither of us had any idea of his whereabouts. I guided Leesa through the process. She said she saw Tom in her mind, walking into his Freshman dorm *room. When Tom came home, he remarked that he'd paid a visit to his first-year living quarters. Leesa's reaction was not the yelp of terror I'd anticipated. Instead, she pulled me aside and shyly requested me not to tell anyone about it. She didn't want a big deal to be made over it, nor did she want to face any skepticism. I couldn't believe that my partner in crime was none other than my previous judge.*

How could anyone have changed that dramatically in such a short time? I suddenly felt an overwhelming love for Leesa. She had taught me one of the most valuable lessons of my life. She initiated my realization that people come to terms with these sorts of things in their own way and in their own time. I can't pry them open, and must not judge them for the way they choose to define their life. This notion gave me a tremendous sense of relief. I finally felt absolved from the responsibility of distinguishing a "trick" from a "treat."

Dad and Tammy.

31

To Know Is to Love

I learned to accept that some people need to negate the
"mystical," but I remained doubly intolerant of those who considered a mystical experience the be-all and end-all. It seemed to
me that, without the release of one experience, there would be no
room for the entrance of another. In the same vein, on a more
spiritual level, when people focus on an external God, it's very
difficult to readjust the perception inward. It was at a seminar at
Carleton College that I frustratingly learned that most people
don't take responsibility for the God within; they'd rather look
without.

At a five-day conference in Minnesota I led a workshop for
children. I was to introduce them to telepathy, remote viewing,
color sensing and meditation. The children were the offspring of
parents attending the conference focused on *A Course in Miracles*.
Originally, when they asked me to lead the children's workshop,
the conference coordinators didn't realize Tammy Cohen's connection to their prospective conference leader, Judith Skutch. My
mother and I enjoyed the idea of participating in a lecture series
together, yet independent. We brought my grandmother along for
the ride.

> *Mom is the main attraction at this conference. She*
> *had to give* A Course in Miracles *workshops and lec-*
> *tures. I've been attending her lectures in the afternoon*

but I really can't stand it anymore. Everyone has become fanatic over her. I know she's an excellent speaker and a fantastic person, but these people have made her into a goddess. One person actually came up to me the other day asking permission to touch me because I am Mom's child! That seems to be the attitude of most everyone around here. It makes me nauseous.

I'd love to get up in front of all these people and tell them that she gets irritable, and occasionally swears. I think even that would shock the people here who consider her so saintly. They've made A Course in Miracles *their Holy Bible, and my mother the living representation of all the* Course's *precepts.*

Mom and I haven't been getting along too well, due to my intolerance of this behavior clashing with her undying patience. Grams' attitude toward their idolatry is different from mine. She's pleased to see that Mom is so well-loved and can make people sob during talks. Grams is thrilled that everyone thinks her daughter is "inspirational."

I know I shouldn't dump my feelings about these people on Mom, but I haven't been able to curb my repulsion. Poor Mom is over-worked, over-tired, and similarly disgusted by her position on the pedestal.

The tension mounted until, on the third day, my mother asked that I attend an afternoon lecture. Par for the *Course,* my mother stepped on stage and walked to the podium in the auditorium crowded with people already applauding. The microphone was a bit too high for her short self, but instead of adjusting it she did something that made me admire her tremendously. She took the three volumes of *A Course in Miracles,* dropped them on the floor, and then stood on them to reach the microphone. There was complete silence in the auditorium except for a few gasps here and there. The silence was broken by the sound of my mother's voice: "This is to illustrate that the principles of *A Course in Miracles* don't live in these books but in our hearts." She explained that the *Course* was for everyday use, and that the books could get filthy but the principles would never soil. She continued that if people chose to work with the *Course,* they should not misinterpret it by projecting it onto a special person. The creation of a "leader" is not one of the precepts of the *Course,* which honors only the teacher within. She said that there was no difference between herself and the audience except that she was talking about the *Course* and they were hearing about it. "But," she stressed, "it's the inner dialogue on which the emphasis should be placed." My mother spoke of her personal struggles and attempted to underline her humanness for her worshippers by listing her own faults. I don't know if anyone noticed it, but I realized that my mother was giving them a loving reprimand.

Her lecture was well-received and, as usual, people surrounded her afterwards. Despite her message, there were some who approached me to comment on the holiness of my mother and ask if they could touch me! As on the occasion of my lecture with Franklin, few people seemed to digest the message of the talk. They saw what they wanted to see and heard what they wanted to hear.

I was tempted to be furious at their ignorance, but something clicked inside me. I suddenly realized that in some cases my mother served as a catalyst for these people, and in other cases she was filling a very empty place in their lives. Who was I to judge the way in which they brought joy into their lives? My anger shifted to compassion. I knew my mother's work was worthwhile, but I felt a sigh of relief that I didn't need to follow in her footsteps.

I watched my mother as she smiled and talked and made time for each and every person who pursued her. She sneaked a wink at me, and I returned it with a truce-making smile. Later, I watched her again as we gorged ourselves at dinner, sneaking away from the conference and into town for a "real" meal. Even later, I watched her curse the dormitory bed as she collapsed onto it and said "I don't want to see another person for the rest of my life—or at least until tomorrow—whichever comes first. I think I'll dream that I'm put in solitary confinement." And it was after all this that I knew my mother to be the saint everyone thought. But I doubted that anyone knew the whole of it.

I further released my judgment of people on pedestals when realizing my own propensity for pedestal projection. It was Thanksgiving when I arranged my first reunion at my mentor's home.

I'm never nervous when I visit Mr. Biology at school, so why should I be so jittery to meet him at his apartment? Well, here it is, and here goes nothing.
"BBBBRRRRRIIINNNNNG!" sounds the doorbell. I hear voices. Now I hear footsteps. The door knob is turning...
"Hello, I'm Tammy."
"Hi, Ean is expecting you. Ean! Tammy's here!" It was one of the most shrill voices I've ever heard in my life. I have to keep myself from jumping. So this is his wife. She's nothing like I would've expected. She has such short hair and such an angular body. Why doesn't

she talk to me? I feel a cold shoulder. Oh, here comes her other half, thank God.

Mr. Biology was wearing a white apron that reminded me of his lab coat, which relaxed me a little bit. I gave him a peck on the cheek.

"Don't get too close to me—I'm full of turkey grease and stuffing," he warned.

"Ean! Don't neglect the turkey! The oven's heating! Come back here!" yelled the shrill voice that had apparently moved to the kitchen.

"I hope you don't mind talking to me in the kitchen," he said to me apologetically.

"Of course not. Are you making the turkey dinner for tonight?"

"Certainly."

"Where's the Bunsen burner?" I teased.

"I had it built into the oven," he smiled.

He began to season the turkey, dress it and stuff it. As I watched, I recounted the events of my summer lectures.

"So you said everything that you believed?" he asked me as the turkey gobbled his arm up to his elbow.

"Yeah, but it wasn't that I was so courageous. The type of people attending those conferences come with a thirst for new alternatives in perception. They drink up what I say. But I do tell some people the explanation of color and heat that you suggested."

"Like whom?"

"Oh, people like my father's friends, who think I'm a straight, level-headed person, and skeptics like...YOU."

"Me? I hope you'd never tell me anything but what you believe!" He shook the large turkey at me threateningly. I laughed. He reminded me of a combination of Captain Hook and Captain Cook.

After the bird was in the oven we went to the living room, where I filled him in on my work with the blind and the catastrophically ill children. As we talked, I noted that I'd never seen my biology teacher look so soft. It wasn't that his features were any different, or that his pot belly was any larger, he just had an air of quietude about him. He wasn't even in the mood to banter with me. His completely straightforward kindness put me a little ill at ease.

As his wife passed the living room she barked: "Ean, take off your apron, for God's sake. You're in the living room!"

"Yes dear," he answered passively.

I was stunned. Mr. Biology took off his apron, revealing his blue jeans and T-shirt. When I noticed his clothes, my mind flashed back to the time I saw him at high-school graduation. I remembered noticing something that wasn't "right" about him, until I realized that I'd never seen him in anything but his lab coat. His appearance in jacket and tie jolted me into the realization that he was a man with a life outside of school. I could adjust to that, but I had trouble with the fact that he jumped in obedience to the orders of his aggressive wife. It, too, reminded me of an image from the past. When Mr. B gave an order at school, each student's facial reaction reflected the look I was seeing on Mr. B's own face when he acquiesced to his wife's command.

> *Mr. Biology a henpecked husband? Can't be. But ever since I got here she's been ordering him around, and he follows. Unbelievable! It's as though he plays the role of bully at school because he has to be woolly at home.*

We continued our conversation about the possibility that many physical illnesses are psychological, when his daughter walked in. She must have been at least nine years old, but her walk mimicked a toddler. She crawled on Mr. B's lap and said in an affected voice "Daddy, time to paste tucky." Mr. B introduced us, and I realized that she had a mental disorder.

I had cheerfully dealt with children who had cancer, blind kids, children with brain tumors, autistic kids—but never had their disability moved me in the way that Mr. B's daughter did. I felt my own hypocrisies cave in on me. It wasn't his daughter's handicap that disturbed me nearly so much as the entire picture. I couldn't bear the fact that my mentor was a human being with a life of cares and troubles. He always seemed to have total control over the universe. Every day he was confronted by his daughter's "imperfection" at home, as he demanded the perfection of his students at school. I couldn't stand to see him respond to his wife in a manner that he didn't permit from his biology students. Mr. B looked at me with a sympathetic smile. Was I mirroring that expression?

Our silence was interrupted by the sound of his wife's shrill voice yelling: "EAN! You've gotta roast the bird!"

"Excuse me for a moment," he apologized as he got up.

"Listen, I don't want to interrupt your day any more. You've got a lot to do," I said, anxiously seeking a quick escape route.

"You're welcome to stay and watch me make the cranberry sauce."

"Thanks, but I have to help with my father's Thanksgiving—without the aid of a Bunsen burner." He smiled as we walked to the door. "It was great to see you, Mr. B. I'll keep in touch," I said as I hugged him.

"Don't you think it's time you call me 'Ean'?" All that conjured up was his wife's screeching of the name.

"Sure," I answered reluctantly. Mrs. B came to say goodbye to me, and her farewell seemed happier than her greeting had been. The door closed and, as I went down in the elevator, my stomach reached the ground before the rest of me.

I knew that it would be a while before I saw Mr. B. I needed time. Time to think, time to come to terms with something I didn't want to face. Mr. Biology was a man with a shrewish wife and a mentally handicapped daughter. After all the years of playing the great and powerful Oz, he was merely the man behind the curtain. I didn't want the curtain pulled, but when it was, I found that Mr. Biology was an ordinary man named Ean.

It wasn't until the end of April that I pieced together the shattered fragments of my broken image of my teacher. Somehow, with the passing of time, came the passing of my vision of Mr. B as a hen-pecked, victimized husband, as well as the tainted ideal of the omnipotent professor. But after all the images faded, what was left in me of Mr. B, was left in my heart. Whoever or whatever he was, he served as my mentor. I couldn't stop thinking about how much I loved him and what an impact he'd had on my life.

Although the semester was ending and I would be in New York soon enough, I felt the urge to write Mr. Biology a letter for the first time since I'd known him. I wrote that it was time for me to tell him what an important figure he'd been in my life and how much he'd influenced me. The letter turned into a kind of eulogy, summed up by my telling him that I really loved him and hoped I would know him for the rest of my life. I headed the letter "Dear Ean." I had finally come to terms with him as a whole person, rather than a holy persona. It was to that whole person I was eternally grateful, as I told him in so many words.

A few weeks passed, and I was a bit surprised that I hadn't heard from him. We had never corresponded, but this seemed different. At the end of May, just as my life at Tufts was concluding, I received a letter in the mail that had first been sent to our old New York address, then to California, and finally to Boston. I recognized my high-school insignia on the envelope.

When my eyes focused on the letter, my hands began to tremble. The black and white blurred into a mass of gray, as I read the announcement that Mr. Biology was dead. It seemed that he had an asthmatic seizure which led to a heart attack. The notice from school was a plea for funds to enlarge and improve the science lab with the facilities and equipment Mr. B had wanted for years. It figured, give the man what he wants—after he's dead.

I noticed that the date of death was the beginning of May. He must have gotten my letter only days before he died. I opened my high-school yearbook and looked at his picture. I wondered what he had done with his body. It must have been donated to science, but I couldn't help picturing him buried in a coffin with his lab coat and glasses. I read the message he had written in my yearbook: "Tammy, I'll leave it to your ESP to *really* understand my feelings about you. But anyway, I'm going to miss our tête à têtes. Mr. B.   P.S. I'll say write, but if you are as poor a correspondent as I, I shan't be disturbed. Anyway, again ESP will suffice. Ean." In high school, I thought he was teasing me about the ESP bit. But with the distance of time, I realized that he meant every word of it. I felt a little warm pang of delight as I realized that Mr. Biology, through the process of osmosis, had absorbed a little of me, as I'd absorbed so much of him. Although his heart failed him, it hadn't failed me. The last time I ever saw Mr. Biology— "Ean"—was on Thanksgiving. The last words I ever communicated to him were of thanksgiving.

Just as Thanksgiving shed light on the shadow of my professor, so did it lighten a weight in my father. I returned to my father's home for the celebration of the holiday. The day passed quickly, as did the spirit of the occasion. By nightfall, all that remained were leftovers in the refrigerator. But the following evening, after even the leftovers had been eaten, my father renewed the spirit of Thanksgiving.

Dad, Marge and I were watching a special holiday presentation of a movie called *I Never Sang for My Father.* The movie was about a tough old man who never showed appreciation to his children. He was too busy spouting his own moral precepts to take the time to understand the views of his offspring. I noticed that the person most touched by the film was my father. I couldn't remember ever having seen him cry before, especially not from something on television.

It isn't something I could prove, but I knew that, after that movie, my father had changed. The very next day he took me for a walk and asked me what I wanted to do with my life. I was used to this question from him, and I had always replied with a stock response: "Well, I guess I'll go to graduate school in psychology, and work with children." But I never had any intention of doing that since my freshman child-psychology course. I felt that everyone's theories of development cluttered my brain, and I found myself categorizing children when my main objective was to remove them from any predesignated expectations of development. Nonetheless, my plan for grad school was a conversation stopper which was very effective.

But on this specific occasion he seemed so open that I told

my father of my intention to spend a year in Nepal and India, studying Eastern religion. I admitted that I hadn't the vaguest idea what I'd do upon my return, but I welcomed him to cross that bridge with me when I came to it. My father's reaction was not the disdain I'd anticipated. I found myself immersed in a conversation contrasting my feelings of letting everything take its course, with his desire and struggle for security. He said that he respected my views and, although we were in disagreement, he would support any of the decisions I make for myself. He concluded our chat by saying that he didn't want me to feel alienated by our dissimilar views. No matter what I felt or did, he'd always love me and be there for me.

> *I'm finally coming to terms with the fact that my father is not the villain I'd made him out to be. I've moved most of my belongings into his house and I don't think I've ever seen him so pleased with me. He's been openly praising me, and telling me how glad he is that I'm making his home my own. He's even begun to display a funny, crazy side of his personality. On occasion he dresses up in his pajamas with a hat on his head and parades around the apartment singing wartime songs. I no longer feel inhibited about being myself around my father and stepmother. I can say whatever I feel to them and they'll either take it or leave it, but they always take me.*
>
> *I'm even finally opening up to Dad about intuitive sorts of things. And he's a lot more accepting than I'd ever imagined. Now, very often when I call him on the telephone, he'll insist that he was either just thinking of me or sending me a telepathic message to call him. I called during a party, and I heard him say to the guests: "What'd I tell you?" and then to me "Tam! We did it again! I was just sending you a message!"*
>
> *I can't figure out whether he's changing or whether I just never knew him. Maybe I didn't ever give him the chance to open up before. I guess I distanced Dad from me by placing him on a pedestal, just as I alienated myself from Ean, the real Mr. Biology.*
>
> *I watched Mom stomp on her pedestal, and it was then that I thought of her as saintly, in all the glory and totality of her devilishness. Mr. Biology tumbled off his pedestal and, after piecing him together again, I knew him to be a greater mentor than I'd ever imagined. When my father took my hand and stepped*

down from his pedestal, I saw him at eye level and finally recognized him as "Dear Ol' Dad." When all the molds shatter, all that's left is the love we share. To really know, is to love.

32

THE END IS INSIGHT

Js

Tammy had hurtled through high school and was now catapulting through college. She convinced me and her father she was eager to begin her life. From my still-new base in California the telephone bills to Tufts were assuming major proportions. She was considering spending the year following graduation in Nepal. "Think of all the money saved by finishing college in three years!" What would the phone bills be to Nepal, I wondered. "Don't worry, Mom, they haven't got telephones over there." No telephones! I shuddered. Just when I thought I'd done a good job of releasing.

I was feeling sentimental at the thought of my younger child unleashed upon the world. I found myself reminiscing at odd moments. I fantasized a career we both could share. She wanted no part of that, at all. Our styles were so different. We had learned to soften the edges of our often-quick criticism of each other's personality traits. Carleton College had been a good experience. I had surprised myself with the realization that I cared more for my children's approval than that of the rest of the world. I actually was embarrassed to speak on a platform with my daughter in the audience. I reasoned it was because that part of me that did the public speaking was not the me she knew. But it was more than that. I was shy of my fervor for the *Course,* and sensitive to jibes that I was trying too hard to be "spiritual." She really knew how to get me where it hurt. Yet on the rare times we shared a presentation, the interplay became a perfect balance of humor and sincerity. We sure knew how to play. Perhaps, I speculated, that was her function in my life. To remind me of the child that lived within. That child who didn't pontificate and who taught by gleeful demonstration. As in Tammy's quick response to my considered remark that I would have to consult the Higher Help to solve a certain problem. "Yes," she bounced back, "Highered help is so hard to get these days." A joke, a pun, a giggle, and I'm feeling joy again.

Joy is an emotion with which I'm becoming familiar. Not the everyday, garden variety joy but that deep, senseless extension of momentary bliss that catches me at unexpected moments. The holy instant. When vision is restored and takes the place of sight.

After napping late one afternoon, I awakened from a deep sleep and found I was unable to move or talk. I lay on my back in bed trying to get Bob's attention. He was reading the newspaper. I struggled to stretch a limb out to touch him, but could not overcome the leaden listlessness. I was filled with fear that I was slipping into oblivion.

The room faded out. I was swimming in a sea of fog. It was a long journey and I landed in the vastness of forever. There was clarity there and a huge yellow sun whose light was so bright I could scarcely gaze upon it. It held my total attention as if I were magnetized by it. I stood reverently in front of the enormous, shimmering globe and waited for something to begin. All at once the face of Jesus appeared in the center of the light and I fell on my knees weeping in ecstasy. The love emanating from the circle was almost too much to bear. With it came knowledge. "Now I know who you are," I whispered. When I looked up the Face of Love had disappeared and another had taken its place. It was my grandmother. I was astonished to notice that the intensity of the love extension was even stronger. Then, one by one, other faces flashed in its place. Slowly, and with purpose. The visages of the Hebrew patriarchs, my father, Tammy, Jonathan, my mother, strangers I'd never seen before. And still the love intensified. The faces kept changing. It seemed the whole world was going to be pictured in that light. Meaning burst into my mind. They were all One. I stepped into the circle myself in an implosion of light. I was part of that Love too! And then the miraculous. Every blade of grass, every tree, every flower, rock, animal, person, cell, was singing a crashing cantata of praise. Praise to God for the Creation. And God completed the chorus with the same hymn of thanksgiving to Life.

It *was* more than I could bear. "Wait for me, please wait," I cried as the sea of fog engulfed me again. "I'll be back, please wait." I was swimming furiously. I had to get home to tell Bob. I had to tell everyone. I had to bring the world there with me. I opened my eyes. I still could not move. I slipped out of my body to squirm across the room in a shapeless form and clutch at Bob. My formless fingers passed right through him. I forced my body's throat to convulse and choked out a scream. Bob looked up from his newspaper and walked across the room to stand over me questioningly. My eyes were blinking rapidly and I just had to communicate. I began to tremble all over. No, vibrate. I was vibrating so fast I could not catch my breath. Bob drew the bath and put me into warm water. I began to relax and melt back into this world. It took a few hours to relate the happening and even longer for the vibrating to cease. I *had* come back for my brothers and the Light *would* wait.

My father had taken ill and was in the hospital for an operation. I had traveled to New York to be with him and my mother for this ordeal. The operation was successful, but the anesthesia was not, and my father had unfortunate side effects. We brought him home for recovery. Tammy and Jonathan rallied round and eased my concern while I commuted between California and my parents' house in Brooklyn. Jonathan was now in medical school at the University of Pennsylvania, and I was relieved that he gave my dad's "case" so much attention. Helen had developed some physical ailments also and it was a trying time to keep one's philosophy intact. Often I turned to the beautiful final pages of the text of *A Course in Miracles* to remind myself that:

> Trials are but lessons that you failed to learn presented
> once again, so where you made a faulty choice before
> you now can make a better one, and thus escape all
> pain that what you chose before has brought to you.

I wanted to keep clear of guilt in both situations, as the temptation to feel so when loved ones are sick is strong indeed. I knew I could be helpful only if I stayed loving without judgment of the circumstances and the players. I appreciated my years of lessons and my training in vigilance. I certainly needed to monitor all my attack thoughts—of the hospital, of the medical staff, of myself. And of my father and Helen. They had both grown irritable with pain and, although I understood that I was not witnessing their "real selves" when I heard them complain, I was not always successful in looking past the illusion. I found I was walking the fine line between empathy and sympathy as if I needed to review the lesson yet again.

A special birthday of mine was approaching and I intended to celebrate in California with my extended "miracles family." I was planning the festivities when Jerry called to ask me to join him and some others in addressing a gathering in San Diego the day before my birthday. I declined at first, but Jerry urged me to "ask." The answer surprised me; I was to go. A few days before the conference my father was rushed back into the hospital for observation. He and my mother would not be able to come to California as I had hoped. I felt compelled to cancel the shindig, honor my commitment to share the platofrm with Jerry, and fly directly to New York. It was fitting to be with those who birthed me on my birthday. Jerry had to go to New York also, to attend his nephew's wedding. We arranged to take the same "Red Eye Special" and arrive early the next morning.

When we landed, Jerry rushed off to see friends before the wedding. I went to my parent's home, where my mother had prepared a mini-feast of my favorite breakfast snacks. Then we were off to visit my father at the hospital. I had asked both Tamara and Jonathan to join us there. After spending time with Dad, we would have our own dinner in a restaurant to honor the day. My mother and I gossiped in the car on the way to the hospital. We talked once more about my father's difficulty in accepting my connection with and commitment to *A Course in Miracles*. Phrasing it carefully, my father was articulately critical. I had not yet banished the familiar clutch of fear that gripped me when I anticipated my father's disapproval. I made progress, but had not arrived at completion. I was beginning to feel sorry for myself on my birthday, walking into perhaps another uncomfortable conversation with my male parent. And at my advanced age! Will it never stop?

I parked the car and we ventured upstairs. As we approached the room I heard happy laughter. Maybe it's the wrong room; maybe they moved him. It sounded like a party. We walked in. I was stunned to see my children's father perched on a chair, with my daughter sitting on his lap and my son nearby. "Oh hi, Mom," greeted Tammy. "Dad has a friend who's had an operation here and when I told him Gramps was in the same hospital he came by to say hello." I had not seen my former husband for more than a year. We were still stiff with each other. He nodded hello and rose to leave. "I must be getting along now." I followed him to the hall to thank him for coming. I knew it meant so much to my father, and told him so. He smiled, then gave me a hug. "Happy Birthday," he said and left. I returned to my father's room. He was beaming. "Darling, isn't that wonderful. Howard came to see me. And do you know what? Jerry stopped in just before on his way to a wedding. And when he was here, Bob called from California! I've had such a nice morning."

262

I reached for his hand as my eyes filled with tears. He held it tightly and wished me "Happy Birthday." I kissed him and started to cry. Instead of a party with my friends, made by me for myself, That Which Knows had given me the greatest gift of all. The celebration of limitless love. Love for my ex-husband. Love for Bob. Love for Jerry. Love for my father for appreciating all that love showered on him. Love for my children, my mother. And above all, love for myself for listening to that Voice telling me where my celebration was to be found.

In a hospital, by the bedside of my earthly father, who had been suffering, I saw a vision of a different world. It was new and clean and fresh and, as promised by the *Course,* I forgot that fear and pain existed at all. This single vision cleared my blurred double vision, and I took the gift and made it mine.

Let us be glad that we can walk the world, and find so
many chances to perceive another situation where
God's gift can once again be recognized as ours!

*Albert, Leesa,
Tammy and Tom
graduate!!*

33

A Familiar Interplay

Graduation from Tufts was the setting for a family reunion. Leesa and I had fulfilled our college requirements in three years so as to share commencement with Albert and Tom. The extra work was well worth the celebratory graduation get-together that followed the ceremony.

Our party was not only to be the meeting ground for all our parents, but it would also be the arena for the union of Bob, Mom, Dad and Marge. It occurred to me that on this one auspicious night all parts of my life would come together. I was prepared for complete chaos.

As the party got going at our rented college "home," it became evident that my life had been a three-ringed circus. In one ring sat the "grand" parents. While Albert's maternal grandmother and my grandfather discussed Jewish affairs (of a strictly political nature), my Grams and Albert's other grandmother talked about food. In a second circle were the mothers, whose voices competed with each other for the center of attention. Drowning out the women's chatter were the roars coming from the men in the third ring, reacting to the sports events on TV. Playing circus vendors, Leesa walked around pushing homemade lasagna, Tom served the drinks, while Albert passed around his salad creation. (He'd come a long way from burnt toast.) Our brothers and sisters had ringside seats that circled the forum throughout the night.

As I moved through the circles of conversation, I caught

enough to piece together one of the greatest shows on earth.

Albert and Tom were discussing the potential box-office draw of a Sumo mud-wrestling fight between Al's and my grandmothers. Grams began relating the events of the seance party we had for her dead mother's one hundredth birthday. Grandpa was playing "Jewish Geography" in name dropping all the rabbis he knew in Chicago. Bob was spokesman for his newest job of selling pieces of the Golden Gate Bridge. Dad did a home demonstration of how to remove stains on clothing as Marge stepped in as his assistant by helpfully spilling lasagna, very bloody mary, *and* salad on her silk blouse. Jon, Terry and John conspired on how to get recruits for Mendelson's Group Rate Funeral Plot and Service, which they'd discovered in the Yellow Pages. They thought they could sell Marge on the idea of "Buy now, die later." (The fact that Terry is going to be a psychologist and Jon a psychiatrist does not make me rest in peace!)

And last but not least, Mom was talking about how there was a set of *A Course in Miracles* in the White House. (Although Bob and Mom have moved to California, Mom has been frequenting Washington D.C., where she and one of the heads of the Library of Congress work with Senators and politicians, in an attempt to re-introduce spiritual values in political decision-making. She recently spoke to the Army War College on peace of mind and "defenselessness." With Mom let loose in the political arena, the country's never gonna be the same!)

The only person not performing in a side show was Hattie. (As she had a fear of flying, Greyhounding, and railroading, Hattie never moved with the clan to California. But she still "helped out" at Grammy's Jewish holiday extravaganzas. Hattie's absence was a trauma for poor Saki, who had to get used to meatball-like canned dog food. Only on the Jewish holidays was he blessed by his old trainer's treats.) With Hattie in mind, the circus was complete.

When our carnival began, I was aware of the building suspense over the congregation of Mom, Bob, Dad and Marge. My friends's families observed my parents, anxiously awaiting even the slightest show of dissension. Bob finally took it upon himself to draw the show to a finale. Mischievously cutting the suspense with a dagger, Bob impetuously bestowed a huge uncharacteristic hug on my unsuspecting father. The transfixed audience was completely taken aback! Whereas everyone was flabbergasted by my stepfather's "unconventional" behavior, I was in stitches over Dad's deadpan expression. I was later approached by at least one representative of each household with "Tammy, I knew your family was on good terms, but that was beyond belief!" And so it was. It was a grand finale brought about by the circus clown.

Although my family rarely joined together for one big three-ring circus, I realized that throughout my life, I had taken part in the development of each side show. And, inasmuch as I'd always considered myself the viewer in the stands, it became evident that it was up to me to conclude the show from the center stage.

Standing here now, "center ring," the spotlight harshly shines on me, illuminating the fact that all my life I was never on the sidelines after all. It seems that I have been the ringleader in my own life. As much as I claimed distance from my eccentric family, I was never immune to their effect on me. And as my eyes blur from the intensity of the spotlight, I see that the silhouettes of all my family members are in fact, me. So I'd better use my wits to caress my relations, or it is I who'll feel the lashes. In the blink of an eye, the show is over. Blink.

*Collage by
Tamara Cohen.*